Glimpses of Life

On the Fringe of Reality, Looking Out

Glimpses of Life

Stories of Family and friends, the kind like your own that you too may wish to write and share with others

JAMES STEPHEN FULBRIGHT, PH.D.

GLIMPSES OF LIFE
ON THE FRINGE OF REALITY, LOOKING OUT

Copyright © 2014 James Stephen Fulbright, Ph.D..

All rights reserved. No part of this book may be used or reproduced by any means, graphic, electronic, or mechanical, including photocopying, recording, taping or by any information storage retrieval system without the written permission of the publisher except in the case of brief quotations embodied in critical articles and reviews.

iUniverse books may be ordered through booksellers or by contacting:

iUniverse
1663 Liberty Drive
Bloomington, IN 47403
www.iuniverse.com
1-800-Authors (1-800-288-4677)

Because of the dynamic nature of the Internet, any web addresses or links contained in this book may have changed since publication and may no longer be valid. The views expressed in this work are solely those of the author and do not necessarily reflect the views of the publisher, and the publisher hereby disclaims any responsibility for them.

Certain stock imagery © Thinkstock.
Any people depicted in stock imagery provided by Thinkstock are models, and such images are being used for illustrative purposes only.

ISBN: 978-1-4917-4106-1 (e)
ISBN: 978-1-4917-4107-8 (sc)

Library of Congress Control Number: 2014915355

Printed in the United States of America.

iUniverse rev. date: 11/10/2014

Contents

Preface vii

Part I. Life's Beginnings and Uncertainties

PROLOGUE	The Book Club	3
GLIMPSES 1	Early Overview	13
GLIMPSES 2	Grandma and Boys Will Be Boys	17
GLIMPSES 3	Down Under	25
GLIMPSES 4	Susie and Young Ben Gone Away	35
GLIMPSES 5	Down in the Soil	43
GLIMPSES 6	Turning the soil	53
GLIMPSES 7	Enclose in Clay	63
GLIMPSES 8	The Darkest Closet	72
GLIMPSES 9	Firing Rifles	79
GLIMPSES 10	Aunt Jesse	90
GLIMPSES 11	Jessie and Lachrymose	101
GLIMPSES 12	A Widow's Suitors	112
GLIMPSES 13	Stevie Redeems Himself	122
GLIMPSES 14	War Time	132
GLIMPSES 15	War in Peace	141
GLIMPSES 16	Steve's Challenges	149

Part II. Life, With Hopes Mixed In

GLIMPSES 17	Ravenwood to Adele	161
GLIMPSES 18	"Horse Doctor"	174
GLIMPSES 19	"Suffer the Pets to Come Unto Me"	184
GLIMPSES 20	The Fire Stoker	193
GLIMPSES 21	"Friends, Romans, Countrymen!"	200
GLIMPSES 22	Jessie Fills in mythopoeically	210
GLIMPSES 23	Neel and Dave	223
GLIMPSES 24	Partners Amore, Memory	235
GLIMPSES 25	Richard Roden	244
GLIMPSES 26	Rosann: Soil and Water	260
GLIMPSES 27	Rosann, Romance and Reality	269
GLIMPSES 28	Gil Moore and the "I Can't Hear You!" metamorphosis	285
GLIMPSES 29	Steve—Towards Life's Work Vis-à-vis the Lost Generation	298
GLIMPSES 30	Life's Survival Boot Camp, Aberrating by Human Control	310
GLIMPSES 31	Survival of the Fittest	318
GLIMPSES 32	Survival of Another Kind	329

Epilogue [sic!] 343
Acknowledgements 349

Preface

So, you reader, have you started your life's saga (narratives)? I wrote this collection with you in mind. So, what's your answer? I pause for your answer.

You haven't thought of it? You never thought of it? You thought of it or something like it, but never got around to it? That's often the case, and then one day, suddenly it dawns on you, it's too late. I waited until it was almost too late. There are a few valid excuses or none at all.

Well, read on, and let's see what you come up with. Suggestion: As you read, keep a notebook handy. Things are going to pop into your mind. And when this happens, stop reading and write, write, write as long as the ideas flow. When the flow stops, return to reading. Until ideas come again. And write again. Later, you will be glad you did.

Keep it up and your manuscript will grow and grow and grow. And what will come of it? Your masterful saga? Who knows? Short stories? A novel? A play? A bio? But you and others—your loved ones, your kinsmen, your friends, your progeny—will emerge better for your having written and passed these on to them. Every person I have known, who has done this, has achieved great self-satisfaction or/and has been praised. When I have inherited these (too few, I'm sorry to say), when I have read these, I have enjoyed them tremendously. I thanked the writers, even if, and especially if, they have passed away, and even if, and especially if, long ago they have passed away.

Try this! And therewith, have your voice heard throughout the centuries. Why not? That's more than an invitation. That's a challenge!

For those interested in time-span, let me say that these my stories begin with the earliest about 1740 and with the latest stories, as such, concluding about 1965 and even as recent as 2014 if one counts the time during which one is looking back. It will be up to our progeny to render stories for the gaps, up to the present and, of course, beyond.

This work is mainly the result of the writer's observation, imagination and memory, the writer being me, James Stephen Fulbright, or Steve for short, and James, who is a part of me, who wants to see things outside of himself in an objective perspective. This work has been inspired by real persons and real events. The persons who inspired me were my relatives and close friends and an occasional stranger. I have nothing but praise for them and gratitude to them, for all of them, for bringing about my life and the lives of my kinsmen and friends, contributing to making life rich and full, and passing on to others the way of it and the knowledge of it

There is no conventional format that I have chosen to follow throughout this manuscript, but rather to follow my each inclination, as with Tennyson's *Ulysses*, "like a falling star beyond the realms of human thought," for telling an engaging story and presenting revealing, largely biographical, details. I can give no excuse for the occasional byways other than Sir Hillary's *because they are there*, so I hope the reader will find them, like the stories themselves informative, engaging and meaningful. I have reached that stage in life when I see history is everywhere, everywhere I cast my eyes, and what I see is sad, fascinating, exhilarating.

So basically, I am presenting stories, ones that can be read separately or read in relation to each other. At the end of the day, this work stands as a whole.

Because the stories can be read separately, I have them divided like chapters, and because I see them as less than whole entities, I wish to present them not as wholly comprehensible in and of themselves, but rather as, in view of the rich texture of real life, short glimpses—glimpses of life. To bring in other points of view with concern for meaning and understanding, I've created an audience of book-club readers who like to ask questions and delve into values, meanings and, in short, life's philosophy; hence, for each "glimpses" I invented a term "epiglimpselogue," which is an after-reading-each-story/narrative chat, one that I hope will stir the reader to not only follow the comments, questions, discussions, and arguments but also to carry them on in the reader's own mind as well as with others.

And speaking of words, words that epitomize and exalt an idea, I have deliberately brought in these word concepts: more commonly, stoker, redeemer, survivor, prevailer, and more or less commonly, mythopoeia, lachrymose, metamorphose, and aberrating (as a verb). Words are civilized. Words are fun. I hope you, the reader, will find them as brain-expanding as I do.

Maybe you will join in. Be a word-nut. Be a writer. Fire away! Read on, dear reader, and write on! Good luck, good writing!

Part I:

Life's Beginnings and Uncertainties

PROLOGUE

THE BOOK CLUB

Ring. James picks up the phone, "Hello. Ah, Charlene. There you are! Yes, we're meeting. Sure we want you here. We start with the previously-agreed-upon book, of course. You know, *The Mayor of Casterbridge*. Have you read it? Some of it? That's all right. We want you here anyway.

"Well, let me clue you in briefly. This guy Henchard is down on his luck. He feels he needs a libation, takes his wife and baby to a bar, drinks himself into a stupor, sells his wife and baby to a sailor. He wakes up the next morning, realizes he was over-libated, that is drunk, the night before. 'What have I done?' he says to himself. He is stricken with guilt. 'What a stupid thing!' He runs to try and rescue his wife and daughter from the sailor. He searches the town from end to end. He can't find them. He does not know if he will ever see them again, his own wife, his own baby girl!"

"You read that part? Well then, in repentance, Henchard mends his ways, becomes a success, the town's mayor in fact. Many years later his wife's grown-up daughter comes to town. Henchard greets her with great delight and with a sense of guilt. Thereafter, he becomes devoted to her. Later, climactically, he finds out that she is not his real daughter. It happened that his real daughter, that baby he had sold along with his wife to the sailor, had died, soon after the separation. Afterwards, his wife had another baby, this time with the sailor, and this young woman Henchard has become so attached to is she, the second baby girl, not his own child that he so carelessly sold off. Henchard is devastated."

"Sure," says Charlene, "but it serves him right."

"Well, our discussion will progress from this plot to other stories. About what? About family and friends. What … ? Oh, true stories, as we would have them. That is for the main part, based on memoirs, letters, interviews, word-of-mouth, documents, et cetera. Yes, we are caught up with narratives, stories. Recently, we have learned humankind is genetically prone to tell and hear narratives. The role of fiction? Fiction fills in the gaps, the details, catches up with a 'real' happening, makes connections and sets us on course, without which the whole thing might not be of much concern. Why Chaucer and Hardy? Chaucer sets us on journeys with stories as we've read and discussed in the past, that whole tradition. Hardy on realities, ironies and, of course, tragedies."

"So, are you coming?" asks James. "You're already on your way? Good. The others will be arriving shortly."

James adds, "Sure. They're all coming. All are welcomed. Bye."

James hangs up, makes some last minute preps. Ten minutes later, the doorbell sounds. "Ah, here they are. There's nothing like a book club of outspoken, highly opinionated people to get the ol' mental adrenalin flowing!"

James opens the door to numerous guests, arriving at the same time. "Hey everybody! Rupert, Sally, Ben and Lisa! Welcome all. Welcome to the light. The Tabard Inn."

They laugh. Especially Rupert. "You mean the Lion's Den."

"Ah—intellectually speaking! Otherwise, a humanistically friendly gathering."

"Humanistic—?" grimaces Rupert.

"Hooray for the humanities!" exclaims Ben.

"Sure. Come in Sally, Lisa, Ben, and Rupert. Charlene will be here shortly. I was just talking with her on the cell. Wait! Here she is now. Hey, Charlene!" From his doorway, James calls out to a car door opening across the street. Out pops Charlene's giving her everything's-right-with-the-world grin. Even from that distance, James can see Charlene grinning. She saunters over, walks up the steps and enters with James holding the door. Charlene holds out her hand for handshakes and hugs all around.

"Welcome all!" repeats James, bringing them in and closing the door behind them.

The usual casual atmosphere is enhanced this evening by the balmy weather, an early spring, surely a good sign, thinks James. Everyone enters in light-weight, loose attire, except Sally, who is bundled up as if she were prepared for the worst of winter.

James rushes to help her with her coat and then turns to address everyone. "Help yourselves to drinks at the bar. Have a seat …no, I started to say on the patio I'm so taken by this unseasonably warm weather—but sit here by the patio doors, which I've opened a tad, symbolically… wherever you like … Make yourselves comfortable." Six dining room chairs with small folding side tables had been arranged in a semi-circle.

"So," says Charlene, pouring herself a glass of Chardonnay, "You're the Tabard Inn guy ready to assist us with our pilgrimage, so-called."

"Yes, so-called. A journey of the mind, no less real than that over land and sea., an Odyssean feat."

"Yeah," voices several, among whom Ben's rings out, "And you are going to set us on the narrative this time. Right?"

"Yeah," joins in Charlene. "James is our Homer, our narrator this time. He is you and I. Right?" They nod assent.

"We'll buy that this time," says Rupert, raising his glass.

"I'll do my best. But first let me point out that there are two Steves we're dealing with here: Steve who early on is a boy referred to as "Stevie," and then there is Steve the same person, but older in the tales, an older boy and then an adult but the same person."

"I'm neither one." He winks. "I'm James the narrator, the

masterful eaves-dropper. At your service, ol' chaps." He bows. They click glasses.

"James, ol' chap, I like it," says Lisa, "an English gentleman."

"Yes, let's get on with it," says Sally who always seems a tad impatient.

"Everyone has a drink? Help yourselves to the veggies at the sideboard, crackers and dip. Good. So here we go."

"Where is here?" asks Ben.

"Oh no!" Sally screeches, "not that."

"Yeh!" echoes Ben. "Not that existential stuff."

"Don't tell me," says Rupert, "we're going to start with that Planet Earth malarkey!"

"Speaking of the Planet Earth, we only just started on that last time."

Lisa's eyes sweep the room. "That's when we turned to literature—Thomas Hardy's *The Mayor of Casterbridge*."

"Exactly," jumps in James, "and we've all read it. Right?"

"Whoops!" says Charlene, grinning. "I didn't finish it. So I'll keep quiet."

"No you don't," James states emphatically. "We understand. When you-re working two jobs and taking care of a whole batch of people/children ... anyway, we need your perspective."

"The rest of us have read it at least once," says Sally, the librarian, the only one who voted against reading the work for this month's discussion starter. "As you know, I'm not one of Hardy's most ardent admirers."

"Sorry about that, Sally. So let's use this as our starting point."

"Oh, that's alright. It's just that Hardy is so damned gloomy."

"Agreed," nods Lisa, "So what is Hardy's point?"

"Touché," said James. "We'll come to that."

After the group's brief discussion of the novel's plot, James hands out copies of Hardy's poem "Hap."

"We need to get a clear understanding of where Hardy is coming from, so let's read the poem out loud and discuss it as we go. Would you start us, Sally?"

"Sure. Will this get us into the point of Michael Henshard's pathetic state of mind?"

"I believe so. Fire away."

Rupert jumps in. "The question is, what kind of a universe does this poor shmuck Henchard inhabit?"

"Precisely," responds James. "And it's up to us to decide if it is the same universe that we ourselves inhabit. Carry forward, Sally."

'If but some vengeful god would call to me
From up the sky, and laugh: "Thou suffering thing,
Know that thy sorrow is my ecstasy,
That thy love's loss is my hate's profiting! ...'

Sally looks up and around at the others. Silence. "Then the second stanza reads:

'Then would I bear it, clinch myself and die,
Steeled by the sense of ire unmerited;
Half-eased in that a Powerfuller than I
Had willed and meted me the tears I shed.'"

"Note," said James interrupting the ensuing silence, "This much was conditioned by the word *if*. And moving on to the first phrase of the third stanza, it reads clearly, 'But not so.' In other words, as bad as such a world would be, that is for us poor humans to be subject to the tortures of a sadistic god, things are not really that way."

"Thank goodness for that," says Lisa. "You wouldn't know it by reading Hardy's novels." Several laugh.

"Ah, but," says James, "things are actually worse."

"Of course!" says Sally, laughing ironically. "Wouldn't you know."

"Yes. Depending on how we look at things," says James, pointing up in the air. "The second stanza says that in the first hypothetical instance, I would know that I didn't deserve what the sadistic god deals out to me, a bad hand, but I would know that I didn't deserve it. I'd have to lump it. That's just the way things are. But in the last stanza, Hardy says, essentially, things are actually worse. Reality is heart-breakingly worse. Read on, please, Sally."

> "*How arrives it joy lies slain,*
> *And why unblooms the best hope ever sown?*
> *Crass Casualty obstructs the sun and rain,*
> *And dicing Time for gladness casts a moan ...*
> *Those purblind Doomsters had as readily strown*
> *Blisses about my pilgrimage as pain.*"

Ben throws up his hands. "What do you make of that!"

James nods. "'Crass casualty'" and 'dicing time' say to me that there does not exist a loving nor a sadistic god. Instead there is nothing, nothing sitting out there that cares about us one way or the other. At least not an interceder that jumps in to torment us or rescue us. Instead, we humans are subject to sheer accident—natural occurrence. In other words, vis-à-vis the entire universe. Nothing cares for us; therefore, we must care for ourselves. Ladies and gentlemen, we are on our own!"

Lisa shakes her head. "How could a Victorian take such a position? Was he not raised, educated, nourished by a Christian nation?"

"Ah, but Hardy composed, wrote, most likely in the intellectual atmosphere of Charles Darwin. Not that he was a thorough Darwinian. We are not instructed in evolution in Hardy's novels although a case could be made out for such. I am not sure that Hardy's universe is endowed with observable, predictable natural laws. But it makes sense that often humans, like his characters, have been and are ignorant of natural laws. Knowledge is indeed limited. Our ability to grasp natural laws may be highly limited. The natural laws that we have been able to work out have served us well eventually and not always but generally. We work at it. But the histories of our lives attest to little knowledge of how to cope with what concerns us most as human beings: how to cope with illness, old age, dissension, disappointment, untimely death of our loved ones, anticipation of our own death, and time itself."

"Well aren't we cheerful this evening," says Sally. "How about reading *Winnie the Pooh* for next time?"

The others laugh but Rupert grimaces. "So in other words, our sufferings are due largely to our lack of knowledge and understanding of the laws of nature."

"Quite so, and by such, we are blessed or cursed, depending on what we know, genuinely know, and what we do with and about what we know."

Lisa, a tad sneeringly, says, "In other words, we must all believe in scientism."

"Not at all!" James is prepared for this one. "It means we must not be committed to so-called time-honored cherished beliefs, or should I say, superstition, which contends to have answers to so much in life that we really don't know at all. Real science does not hold such presumptions. It operates steadily, bit by bit. Science, not an ism, is distinctly different from religion. It deals only with the provable and disprovable. Most of our concerns operate in the unknown."

"Then should we all become modest petite scientists?" offers Ben, smiling. Suddenly becoming more serious, he adds, "Sorry. I mean, should we all become astute scientists?"

"This is a matter for the individual to decide. It is a matter of whether he/she wants to be able to cope with reality as well as possible or wants to envelop the self in superstition which can be more comforting. One thing we have going for us: It seems that a trait of human kind is its propensity for stories. Stories can alert us to accident. And everybody loves a story. Start telling a story and watch people lean forward in their seats. Like the Oedipus story itself. Is it possible that from our stories about ourselves and others we learn most about ourselves and life's dilemmas?"

"Whoa," calls out Rupert with his flattened hand up like a traffic cop. "Consider this: Hardy has a god, his own god, and this god is—contrary to what he says in 'Hap'—a gleeful God of Irony, a god that delights in watching people's bitterness over their disappointed hopes. Hardy—read Hardy's god—contrives this unhappiness. This is the basis of Hardian tragedy."

"But ..." counters James, his face set like a debater's, "but ironies do happen, uncontrived. They occur strictly by accident. And yet we humans are so naïve, so unaware, we are the real enhancers of our tragic lives."

"Regarding the natural world," James continues. "I choose the word 'uncontrived.' With Hardy, these ironies may very well be manipulated by the writer-poet, himself, to show us how we deepen our own sorrow. Perhaps this is the basic flaw—Sally here might agree—in Hardy's work. They might appear to be accidents, but when the plot is taken apart, there is the neat contrivance of the author behind it all."

"Yes, and looking at the broad spectrum of classical literature," says Sally, "we are being told to become aware, to wake up to reality before it is too late. It turns out that the tragedy occurs, in that sense, largely because of our own doing."

"People do often screw up," interjects Ben.

"Sure," continues James. "People look at things the way they want to, heavy into their own egos as the ancient Greeks alerted us to, their hubris. The strongest message we get from Sophocles tells us, for example, to look out for the hubris of Oedipus. He was sure he knew what there was to know. One's supposed knowledge. The ultimate hubris. In ignorance, he kills his father and marries his mother. What could be worse!"

"Yuk!" cringes Rupert. "Yet how are we to know such things— as I recall the myth—that we cannot know or are most unlikely to know? We would have to go through life questioning everything."

"But, Rupert, if we have reasonable values and a wide experience with life's occurrences—stories if you like—seeing, listening and telling, we become better at knowing what to question and possibly what does not need to be questioned. Even with misjudgments, sometimes these things work out all right, or for the best, in the long run. At least knowledge-wise, that is, in enhancing our own capabilities, we are the better for the experience, albeit tragic, heartbreaking."

"Let's look into it," says Lisa. "So we humans are winging it. We're out here on a limb, or should I say, on our own. And the more life-stories we know, the better we may be at making judgments and handling our lives, avoiding disappointed hopes."

"Absolutely." says Charlene. "I think of this even as I read little stories to the children.

"I hope not with drawn-out, useless complexities," says Rupert, "all deep into tragedy."

"No. I suggest they be glimpses of real life," responds Ben, "as much into light-heartedness, humor, and comedy as into tragedy."

"Hear, hear," quietly agrees Charlene.

"You are right there, Ben. A reflection of all sides of life," says their host, glancing around at the approving guests. "All right then, are we on our way?"

"Voila," mumbles Sally. "We're on our way."

"Lead on, Chaucer!" exclaims Lisa.

The Book Club: James as Narrator, Larry Sokol as Rupert, Rebecca Winter as Charlene, Shamin Ansari as Lisa, Deborah Burns as Sally, and Trevin Jones as Ben.

GLIMPSES ONE

EARLY OVERVIEW

The decade of the 1920s was wrought with change. This part of our story sets the stage for the coming together of the Garrisons and the Fulbrights, which by marriage took place in the middle of the roaring twenties decade, 1925. With the early popularizing of radios, love songs, jazz music, dance numbers, speak-easies, cinemas—it was a lively time, indeed. And Harry Wilks Fulbright married Gladys Jewell Garrison. Harry was an aspiring lawyer, and Gladys was an aspiring pianist. She learned early to play both classics and the popular music of the day. Harry and Gladys grew up roughly one hundred and fifty miles from each other. He was from a country farm near Marionville, Missouri, and she from the country town of Russellville, Arkansas. Each had four siblings: he, being the youngest by far, had three older ones, sisters, and Harry had had a brother who had passed away very young; and Gladys, being in the middle, had two older sisters, one younger sister and one younger brother. Their families were different in many ways.

Like so many of their times and like so many of their recent predecessors, especially the younger ones, they left the traditional country life and went for the opportunities and excitement of the city. Harry, intelligent, interested in law, like his cousin (the late Senator) J. William Fulbright of Fayetteville, Arkansas, one day might very well have been, like J. William, elected to the United States Senate or to the House of Representatives or to the state legislature, or like his uncle James Fulbright, might eventually have been appointed to a judgeship. But fortune would not have it so. He and his young bride had to contend with the, perhaps, subtler realities of life. It is not that we play no part in bringing about our own misfortunes. Yet Harry's major life intentions were noble. Harry, the young idealist, headed into law because he "wanted to see justice done." And how might justice be achieved if not by hard work, determination, and wise choices? With Harry, morality in law as in life was a major factor. He was brought up to it. How did this play out? And what went wrong?

Harry was the fifth borne to William and Jennie. After three girls and a boy, who passed away before Harry came along, a strong lad like Harry was much appreciated. A time to rejoice. Harry was brought up a useful farm hand. By the time he was eleven, he was handling the reigns of horses for traveling, plowing, and harvesting, much to make a father proud. Harry was as good, or better than, a hired hand. Without a tractor or modern farm equipment, running a one-hundred-and-forty-acre farm was no easy task, yet even though Harry's father set a precedence for his son Harry by studying law at Christian College, he preferred farming to a legal career. William was a successful farmer, working with and promoting the Missouri State Agriculture Department program to spread successful farming methods to others throughout the state.

When he wasn't baling hay, slopping the pigs, cleaning out the barn or hen house, the latter chore he sorely abhorred, handling the horses for plowing, cultivating or harvesting, or some dozens of other jobs about the homestead, Harry was to be found fishing down at the river, now and again, on a hot summer day jumping in the water to cool down, or throwing stones to watch them plop into the water right where a fish gulped. He especially enjoyed finding flat stones to skim across the water's surface—what young boy wouldn't? One game he invented was "heave the spear." Often his father grumbled about the persistence of weeds that would spring up in his finely cultivated fields. "If only we could sell those weeds!" Harry took to pulling the big weeds in the woods that grew tall and straight; they had roots that came to a point, so when he pulled them out of the ground, five or so feet tall, and trimmed the branches and leaves off, he had a fine lance or spear that he could throw at rabbits, squirrels or whatever might pose a threat to their crops. (His father would not yet allow him to walk unescorted out into the fields with a rifle.)

Harry was a whiz at finding bait, worms, insects, baiting a hook, locating the right spot and coming home with a decent catch. There was one big fellow he toyed with but never quite succeeded in landing. The rare bass. Others had tried to catch it too—they called it "Moby" after Moby Dick—but without luck. It was typical of Harry to come home with a catch but complain, "I saw ol' Moby again, Dad, and nearly snagged him, but the big fellow got off the line. I'll get him yet!" But Harry never did.

By this time, two of his sisters had married, moved away and had children of their own. Harry's third sister was Jesse. She was a headstrong young lady ready to spread her wings. Although she had taken care of Harry often when Harry was a baby and a young child, Jesse was not greatly fond of him, seeing him as a competitor for attention, and if there was anything that Jesse liked, it was attention. She was married at eighteen and moved to St. Louis, becoming the wife of a wealthy man. So later, when Harry reached his twenties, his responsibility was to look after their aging parents.

Earlier, when he graduated from high school, Harry went to Drury College in Springfield. Upon graduating, he went to Harvard for a law degree. But trouble was brewing in Europe, and soon his country was drawn into war. In 1917, Harry left Harvard to join the army and serve his country. When he returned from the army, he helped his dad on the farm but soon left the farm to attend Washington University Law School in St. Louis. He became alarmed about his father who, suffering from dementia (or Alzheimer's), was trying to manage the farm, which although previously profitable, was always challenging. Harry took a position of instructor of physical education at his alma mater Drury College and moved back in with his parents to help manage the farm.

Meanwhile, Gladys Garrison, born in 1905, nearly 12 years younger than Harry, graduated from high school in Russellville, became quite the pianist, playing for a local band and went north to Drury College to continue her career in music. It was there that Harry met Gladys, a student in his class.

Epiglimpselogue One

Sally: "So this sets the early background and frame work for the stories to come?"

James: "Several stories, exactly. We'll see that this relationship grew out of a conflict here. We shall see how the unexpected changed everything. And then how a tragedy shaped the family's lives thereafter."

"Sounds heavy. Any humor in here?" asked Ben.

"This very next story is amusing—yet real," James replied.

GLIMPSES TWO

GRANDMA AND BOYS WILL BE BOYS

Through Steve's eyes, this story is about his grandmother, his mother's mother, in other words, the Garrison side, the dominant factor in Steve's early life. After the tragedy of the death of the boys' father—cancer at the age of forty-three—(which gets ahead of some stories) this misfortune, among numerous other effects, lessened the Fulbright factor in the boys' lives. Their mother, thereafter having the sole responsibility of provider, handled two jobs, taking on more students as a piano teacher, and working a forty-hour, nine-to-five office job, with the A & P in the regional office located all the way down town, St. Louis.

At seven and nine, Dave and Neel were public-school boys. Stevie was four years old, about a year from starting school. Occasionally, Grandma Susie looked after him. From that time, he remembers her well—a country woman with a funny country way of talking and always highly careful about her charge, little Stevie—he gained his sense of caution from her and maybe (in part), ultimately, his longevity! But, of course, the next September, like his big brothers, for the most part, he looked after himself.

That next September, all three were in school during the daytime, but there were evenings when their mother would be teaching piano at someone's home. Occasionally, their 'Granma' would come over to fix dinner for them. Of course they would have rather fixed their own, probably peanut butter-jelly sandwiches and a divided-up brick of Neapolitan ice cream, all three flavors shared. So as free little spirits, when their grandma came over, they could be little demons.

Poor unsuspecting Grandma—or so she seemed to be—would come in high spirits. She would pop in through the front door and say, "I have a special dish for you boys tonight—a mess of cookin' greens!" Then she would raise a bulging old grocery sack up to the kitchen counter and dump out what they saw as a bunch of weeds and roots with clinging clods of dirt. They pictured Grandma going about the old city's vacant lots finding and pulling up the nastiest plants by the roots. Despite the fact that greens were probably healthy, the boys (in any case) had no appreciation of her native expertise in identifying, picking, and cooking up this scaly-looking treasure in the way of old Arkansas. Mother's words were always "Mama can cook up the best mess o' greens, better than anybody from miles around Russellville!"

Even during the cooking, the sizzling-dung odor that penetrated everything inside, it seemed, would nearly drive the boys out of the house. But there was no escape. They could swear that the doors had been locked from the outside.

"It's ready. You boys come to the table now!" Then from a large darkened pot, she scooped out a pile of gooky stuff for each of their plates. Then she heaped some on her own plate and plunked down with a look of delight on her face. Needless to say, she dug right in.

Stevie's first thought was the Fido trick. Man's best friend. In this case, boy's best friend his dog—good ol' Curley. An outside slam attracted Granma's attention long enough for Stevie to make a fist-full sweep and offer down low to his little friend. Curley had taken his usual place at dinner time under the table, lying beside Stevie's feet, handy enough, but one could see that Curley's quick wrenched nose told him not to bother this time. Curley was Stevie's best friend in boyhood. He would have defended Stevie against a pack of ravenous wolves. But eat Granma's greens for Stevie—no way! Stevie was reminded of his big brother's favorite saying, "good for neither man nor beast!"

It wouldn't have been half so bad if it weren't for a green ooze that threatened to contaminate everything else on their plates. Stevie watched big brother Neel. He had likely been through this multiple times before. Stevie often had thought during their growing-up years that Neel would have made a marvelous engineer. He set right away to constructing a mash potato barricade to stop the green ooze. Of course Stevie hadn't thought enough ahead to load up on mashed potatoes. But soon Stevie had the dam constructed although he regretted the cost in hopelessly contaminated mashed potatoes.

'Don't play with your food, Stevie!"

Oops. Granma's on guard, thought Stevie.

Dave had a decided advantage. His and Neel's chairs were nearest the open screenless window. The screen had popped out earlier that day when one of their friends, playing inside tag, had found the window the easiest escape route.

Oh-oh. Davey was nearly caught red-handed, or should we say green-handed, pitching a handful of green slime out the window.

"What-er you doin', Davey?" She frowned, looking at his near-empty plate, Granma declared, "Turn 'round here and eat up. Laudy, you need some more greens"

Stevie noticed, pitching catches Grandma's eye. Then he winds up with more –yuk! Not the answer. Then Stevie noticed that Neel's nasty mound has all but disappeared. Admiration. *How ... ?* Suddenly Neel's hands felt his shoulders.

"Dang, if it isn't getting cold in here." He got up, reached for the window and slammed it shut with a simultaneous, distant "Smush!" Amazingly this time Granma didn't catch it, and later, probably no one was going to tell her.

Their come-uppance comes on Sunday when mother is doing the family laundry. She reaches into Davey's bulging pant pocket. "What's this!" She pulls out a handful of dark brown muck!

Had Granma caught any of them in some kind of deception, she could get angry. She could blow sky high in an instant. They remember on more than one occasion when the two brothers would get into one of their characteristic scuffles, starting with a push and a shove, then a "trip 'im," and "throw 'im down," pounce on him, and sometimes even with a few wild punches. Dave and Neel were close enough in size, muscularity and temperament to pose a good battle between them. Such impasses were not rare. What Stevie remembers most about this was Dave and Neel reaching a point of wild duking it out. Stevie was too little to jump into the fray—or he knew if he tried, he'd get the stuffing knocked out of him. After a few frustrating warnings, usually a low-key, "Now you boys behave," words too civil to have any real effect, Granma would suddenly explode. Her voice would raise an octave or two with a screech, reaching an incredible volume for her small size:

"Get the butcher knives! Get the butcher knives!"

Stevie's head would swing around, looking toward the kitchen, picturing the drawer where the knives were kept, and then back at his brothers and again toward the kitchen, swiveling back and forth. Fortunately, and considering the dire emotions, amazingly, his brothers never went for the butcher knives, so one would think this horrific outbreak of Granma's might have had her intended effect. After all, this was such a shock—her voice at such a high pitch— Stevie never knew about his brothers, but such incidents had a lasting effect on him. For the rest of his life, whenever a quarrel of anyone within earshot seemed to be getting out of hand, sometimes even in a modern, hot political debate, in his head he could still hear his Granma's screeching rage, "Get the butcher knives! Get the butcher knives!"

Their lack of appreciation of Granma carried over to holidays, to their family get-togethers at their Aunt Dot Dugger's. With her two sons, Robert nine and Benny six, Neel, Dave, and Stevie, were a formidable team, they had great times exaggeratingly mocking their poor Granma's country ways.

There the five would be, in the upstairs' attic room away from the grown-ups. Years later, Steve could still picture Robert looking out the front window and seeing guess-who coming up the walk.

"Y' lookie here who's a-comin," said Robert in his finest falsetto. "Lookie here out this here windeer." The boys thought 'windeer' the funniest word they 'd ever heard.

"Laudy!" says Neel in his phoney granma voice. "If it isn't ol' Gran'ma Garrison! I declare, you'd wonder how her aches an' pains are a-comin' along."

And, not to be outdone, Dave limps about. "Lands sakes, It's my lumbago actin' up again. Come to think of it, how's your rhumy-tism, Neel?"

Neel could rise to the occasion. "Why you know, it's a actin' up somepin' awful." Then they would all peel with laugher. Of course, their Granma didn't deserve such bantering. She had her own sorrows and tragedies to contend with. Nevertheless, the boys would howl with laughter.

Suddenly it seemed from out of nowhere, a man's gruff voice would bellow, "What in blazes is going on up here!"

"Ye-ow!" The boys would scramble to the closet and under the beds. Uncle Art was known for throwing the boys into the heebie-jeebies. His favorite trick was coming up after dark, flipping off the light switch, and in the dark he would appear, his dark straggly hair down over his eyes, two match stick fangs from his mouth to his nose, a flash light shining up his face from below, and screeching like a banshee. "Aaa-eee-ya!"

After the tumbling racket, Aunt Dot from downstairs would call up, "Art, what are you doing to those boys?"

"Nothing, Dot. Just the usual!"

Epiglimpselogue Two

"You grandsons should be ashamed of yourselves!" said Sally.

"Oh, those guys were just having some fun," said Rupert. "You should have heard us make fun of our second-grade teacher, ol' Mouse-shoot."

"I'll have to admit that these country folk from earlier generations had something to teach us about life and longevity," said James. "Some of these greens of various kinds have come back for health benefits. His mother picked up on that old fashion buttermilk not only from her own childhood downhome life but also from a nutritionist expert of the times, who praised the benefits of that old cultured butter milk. And she decided one of her children was going to benefit from it. So she raised little baby Stevie on the stuff that most kids and adults found was downright disgusting. Today that old downhome disgusting stuff is mixed with flavors and has come out as healthy Kefir. Then there was their father's farm wisdom—he grew up on the farm—who, according to his mother, often said the best stuff they grew they fed to the cattle—soy beans. And look at today's wisdom and practices—heart-healthy soy milk!"

"Sally is right," said Lisa. "In their treatment of their grandmother, the Fulbright-Dugger boys were disgusting."

"Did these kids have any feelings of remorse?" asked Ben

"Then? Of course not. But later, yes. As the years passed, Steve came to appreciate his grandma more and more—she and her quaint country ways. Besides, yes, she was country and amusing, but she was also charming, and she was the only grandparent Steve would ever know. As he grew older, he came to appreciate her life, including that part she survived long before he was born, long before their boyish mockery, going back some 13 years, back to 1919."

Glimpses Three

DOWN UNDER

Gladys' parents were in their early to mid-40s with seven mouths to feed. It was Monday morning, February 17th of 1919, a morning like so many mornings in this small town of Russellville, Arkansas, a country town with a population of some 6,000 people. Quiet, peaceful. Many breathed sighs of relief; the war was recently over, and the doughboys were coming home. By 8:00 a. m. this morning, Papa Benjamin, or popularly "Benny," had dressed, drunk his coffee, kissed his wife of eighteen years and said goodbye to several of his five children and was about to open the door to leave for work.

"Daddy?" He looked back and there was his youngest, the image of his father, his father's pride and joy, little Benjamin, the fifth-born child now nearly eight years old and the only boy who, of course, was given his father's name. He had on his baseball cap, his ball and glove in his hands. "Can we play ball?"

"Not now, son. Daddy has to go to work. But we'll play when I get home."

"I swear," said his mother, "the little guy wants to play baseball all the time, but the girls are not into it. Hurry home, dear, so you can play with little Benjamin before dinner."

"I will," said Benny as he opened the door and departed. Playing ball with his little son before dinner had become practically a ritual, but one the father looked forward to as much as his son.

The second oldest daughter Violet, only just fifteen, was already off to work; she worked as a stenographer in the Southern Anthracite Coal office of the mining operation, an office a mile or more distance from the mine that was being reactivated just where her father was to direct preparations on this particular morning. The owners were in a hurry to get this defunct mine into operation.

Times were not always pleasant for this loving family. The oldest daughter Grace, an exceptionally pretty girl, of whom, in later years, Gladys would say, "Grace was the prettiest of us Garrison girls," was especially boy-crazy. At seventeen she had already gotten herself pregnant, which made her father furious. So with not a little pressure, the town twenty-two-year-old aimless oaf named Al Kemp—"not only a womanizer but also a free-loader"—nevertheless performed the decent, albeit pressured, thing and married Grace. He then proceeded to move in with the Garrisons at the corner house, which Benny had expanded upon their return from Oklahoma—but hardly expanded enough. The neighbors easily enough in small town Russellville got wind of the truth and engaged in a little quiet gossip, but the marriage and move-in helped to absolve things. Violet and Gladys were old enough to feel the vibrations of their mother's and father's anger toward Grace and the proximity of "useless Al," but had no choice, of course, but to flow with it.

Unfortunately, Al couldn't change his ways. Soon Bennie reached the end of his patience with Al coming in late at night from God-knows what and upsetting his daughter and the family. After just a few months, despite Grace's mixed emotions, Benny had had enough and kicked the non-contributing Al out of the house. Al had three hours to get his belongings and find another place to live. He removed himself, fortunately, and with the word of the end of the marriage having gotten around town sufficiently, Grace, with her father's assistance, went for a divorce which was quickly finalized. All the Garrisons breathed a sigh of relief.

After the birth, Violet, and especially Gladys, became quite fond of little baby Marie. As little Marie grew, Aunt Gladys and Aunt Dorothy provided care after school and between chores. Many years later when Marie grew into a fine young lady, Gladys and Marie became the best of friends always in contact with each other, each regarding the other not as aunt and niece, but as sisters.

Tranquility restored by February of 1919, music reigned supreme in the Garrison's Russellville home. Regardless, or because of, sibling competition for the piano, Gladys became the most persistent of the children at practicing and genuinely learning the piano, the prized and obvious home diversion, but not the only instrument in the Garrison home. Susie Garrison ordered several instruments, including a guitar and a violin for the family because she and Benny wanted their own family orchestra. This was a dream of Benny's, that one day they would be known far and wide for their family Garrison orchestra.

During those growing up years, the family's home-played music, classical, folk, country, popular, had been the form of entertainment that out-shined all others. They played for themselves of course but also for visiting friends and relatives. Her parents discovered that Gladys in her ability to read notes, to improvise with chords, and to apply amazing finger dexterity, was exceptionally talented. As the family became known for their musicality, Susie and especially Benny praised and encouraged Gladys. It seemed she could play straight off any song put before her. There seemed to be little doubt but that Gladys would become a professional musician. Interest in music and not a little musical talent became a tradition that would be carried on by future generations.

By this day, on Benny's modest income the family was getting by adequately. Indeed, modest was their house by the railroad tracks. Five and one-half rooms were only just room for the six family members, consisting of four girls and their parents. But then a fifth child, a boy, came into the world. Little Ben, named after his father, early grew to love to play ball with his father. After the wife of Susie's father died, Grandpa Fielding Guthrie, a former gristmill owner/operator, a fine country gentleman, now all alone in the world, moved in with the cramped Russellville Garrisons.

And wouldn't you know, he had to have his own room. So after they returned from their brief move to Oklahoma and Benny had added another room to the house, there was still more doubling up and the full use of the porch was required. They could not afford to move into a larger house so this modest, white wood frame, six-room bungalow near the railroad tracks had to suffice. Rather than doubling up, some children preferred sleeping on the porch, especially on warmer nights. Shortly, Grace with baby Marie in tow, went off to look after ailing Aunt Belle in Van Buren to help with the housekeeping.

This arrangement lasted for less than a year, long enough for Grace to meet another beau. When she returned to Russellville, indeed, things had changed. Susie Garrison was a good mother, attentive to the usual household chores of which she was not fond. She had a useful talent. She was a first-rate, small-scale farmer-gardener. All over town she was known as "the green-thumb," which made Benny especially proud of her. No one could grow garden vegetables like she and in so little space. When husband Bennie had time, he would help with the hoeing and cultivating. Her crops included tomatoes, cabbage, spinach, radishes, carrots, and of course, several varieties greens. There was hardly a spot in her back yard that wasn't an Eden of vegetables and flowers. Susie was known too for her expertise in picking out the ripest wild greens in the fields nearby and bringing them home, and with a few strips of bacon, she could cook up a delicious batch of greens (later so unappreciated by the boys, her grandchildren).

And further, how else could the Garrisons raise five children through from infancy if they hadn't owned a cow. Bessie was kept in a small shed and pastured just out past the edge of town. It was the duty of the two youngest girls, Gladys and Dorothy, to take lumbering Bessie to pasture in the mornings before school and to bring her back again after school. It was Bessie that brought Gladys and Dorothy notice by neighbors down the road. The neighbors knew the girls by their regularity and promptness.

"Must be 7:30 in the mornin'," the neighbors would say. "Hello there!" they'd say. "What're your names, young Garrison girls?"

"Hello-o-o!" Gladys would say. "I'm Gladys."

"Hi!" Dorothy would say, sharply.

And what's your name, little miss? Are you Dorothy?"

"No," she replies. "I not Dorphy. I Dot."

In this way, the two little darling Garrison girls became known throughout the little town of Russellville as "HelloooooGladys" and her little sister "I-Dot"!

Time passed. They grew. Then along came another Garrison. And on this particular morning, 17 February, 1919, Gladys was fourteen, Dot twelve, Ben seven when the totally unexpected occurred that would change their lives forever. Benny had been re-hired (after their return from Oklahoma) to oversee the preparation for re-opening the coal mine, which had been invested in by two brothers named Puterbaugh and two brothers of another family named White. Working in the mines, although sporadic, was the place a person could make a decent wage, decent enough to support a family with five children. The Puterbaugh brothers had mauled over the question of opening the old mine. Coal was fetching a good price at that time—with factories on the increase. The two Puterbaugh brothers conferred:

"Plenty of ore down there, if'n we could jes' get at it."

"Benny Garrison may be just the man who can do it."

That morning Bennie came to work and joined by two others, struggled down into the old defunct mine. The mine was never in ideal shape. With jagged outcrops, the entrance was ragged and narrow. Being close to the river and subject to the changing river banks, the mine had fallen into disuse and was going to take considerable labor to bring around to operating conditions. The experienced Benjamin Garrison was the man to see that this was accomplished, this earthy task.

Ben had years of experience as a miner and an ancestral past that made him a part of the soil, rocks, the very earth. It could not have been easy surveying the earth's narrow, rugged hollows. At one point a huge rock suspended from the wall and ceiling was an acute obstacle to reaching the main mineable seam. Benny took his time and looked all around, in and out of the bends and crevasses. Finally, he turned to his two men who were awaiting their foreman's decision.

He had reached it. "Look right here. Seems little doubt about it. There's a rich lobe here if'n we can jis' get at it. But this here rock has to come out."

So here it was. Deep underground, in Puterbaugh's coal mine, foreman Benjamin Garrison, Bennie, raised his hammer and tapped the giant rock that seemed hard-wedged just in front and above him and the two other miners. Such a rock anyone would think would take several sticks of dynamite to dislodge. But at this place on this day, it took only the indicator tap to spring it. Suddenly, without time for anyone to think, let alone act, there came an instant shifting, a mighty rumble—Oh my God!—a great crashing down!

Before such weight, such hardness, and such falling power, what chance is there for the fragile human body—sinews, heart, bones! Crushed! Gone forever. A bag of bones, tissue, sinew to be lowered into the ground. What mighty cost to human lives!

Word spread miles away. A siren pealed. Shortly, the Russellville Christian Church bells rang out! The sounds and the words carried.

"A cave in?"

"Who's down there?"

"Which miners?"

"The injured? The dead!"

In the mining operations office, springing up from her desk, Violet Garrison was one of the first to reach the window overlooking the sloping away hill that allowed a view in the direction of the mine. Quickly, several office workers joined her.

"My father! What's happening?" That mine planned for

reactivating was located a mile and a half from the operations office, which was several more miles from the heart of town. After the siren went off, how long would it take for anyone to know exactly what had happened?

The dreaded sounds, the siren and ringing, continued. By now, all had risen and were in the dreaded state.

In the mining office, everything seemed frozen in place. Minutes passed. Nothing. Several moved toward the door. The view looked down a hill and off toward the river. More minutes passed. Then suddenly, in blackened-smudged coveralls, a miner swung open the office door.

"In mine three ... no warning. A bolder crashed down! Send for medical help!"

"They're on their way. May already be there," exclaimed the assistant supervisor. "Violet. Your father ..."

All looked at Violet and the supervisor. Violet stared at the assistant and waited, mouth open, eyes wide. Minutes later, another miner rushed in through the office door.

Violet turned to him. "My father ... ?"

He turned toward Violet. He had deep hurt in his eyes. "Benny ... very bad! Square down on top of him. He never had a chance."

The event, this was the very moment so many feared, especially miners' families. It was unreal. Or was it too real, too real to bear? Violet, like others experiencing such horror at these moments, would be haunted by this for the rest of her life. Her own dear father. Her tears welled up. Some went to her. Others questioned the miners further. More came to the doorway.

"Who's down there?"

"The rescue team are up. The medics are at the entrance."

"And Will Bently is ...," gasped the miner, "badly injured. Some are just now coming up the hill." He turned and raced out the door.

"Not all?" shouted Violet after him.

Another miner appeared in the doorway, panting.

"Is it true?" asked several.

"Who's killed?" asked several, almost disbelievingly.

"So far as we know," said the newcomer, another miner who had not been in the vicinity of the disaster, "Ben Garrison. I'm told it was an enormous rock. It was quick. Ben had no chance. He was directly under it. Will Bentley has been taken to the hospital."

The head supervisor came in. "Violet, you must go at once to comfort your mother. Peter will take you. Tell her when we know more, we'll come … " He turned to a foreman. "Bring him up. It'll take several strong men."

The teary Violet followed the driver. They drove to town. When they reached main street, shopkeepers and customers were pouring out, coatless, hatless. The schoolhouse was emptied, and children stood looking out over the playground gates. On the road in front of their house, Susie Garrison was already standing aghast with neighbors looking toward the sounds. She held young Ben's hand.

Amid the siren, she had heard several voices saying, "There's been a terrible accident at the mine!"

"Oh God," she thought. "Not my Benny. Please, God, not my Benny!" She spotted her daughter rushing toward her. "Violet?"

"Oh mother!" Violet cried out, sobbing and out of breath. "Oh mother! Mother, Daddy's killed!"

"No, no, child. No!"

"Mr. Nielson said it. Daddy's dead. Under a great rock." Violet became hysterical. She cried out loud.

"It can't be," her mother responded. "Just can't be."

Sobbing into her hands, Violet, a small woman, leaned against her mother's shoulder.

Neighbors gathered around them. "What happened?"

"Who's killed?"

"Who's down there?"

Susie Garrison looked to the sky. "Oh Lord! Oh Lord!"

"Mr. Nielson said he's coming," sobbed Violet.

"Poor Benny. My dear Benny." Susie Garrison gasped, struggling to regain her breath. Little Ben, dropping his baseball, began to cry.

Looking down at him, Susie shook her head. "My God, the children!"

Epiglimpselogue Three

"Always the absolute unexpected," Sally muttered. "An experienced miner. A mere tapping …"

After several minutes of silence, Rupert spoke up. "Okay. Ben Garrison is dead. What do you intend to prove by this? As we learned from Arthur Miller, every man's death is a tragedy. Is there something more, James, Mr. Narrator?"

"I don't know that any one has told this story to posterity. After such youthful hope …"

"And?" Rupert said, folding his arms.

"Well, I, the narrator, can be looked upon in two ways: I am a survivor buff. Bully for me! Or, rather, the truth be known, I am basically a coward. That is, I don't want to die. At least, not until I absolutely must. So I take to, and have always taken to, ways of hanging on. I just read in this morning's news that two young ladies were crushed to death by a train hitting their car at a railroad crossing near Hillsboro, Missouri. The accident and deaths were clearly preventable. So often this happens. Doesn't anybody realize the crushing power of bulky, inanimate objects against the fragile human frame? And it seems as if it passes to me to tell about their maternal grandfather, Steve's own kinsman, whom Steve always wished he had had the opportunity to know, who was such a fine provider for his family, who wanted a family orchestra, who was coaching his little boy in baseball. And then, what tragedy! How many lives are adversely effected by ..."

"I know what you mean," said Sally. "We crash into each other on the highway all over the country, hundreds of thousands of times a year, and do people really think about this—great heavy stone-like metal smashing a light human frame? What makes us so nonchalant about such calamities?"

"Well, what account do we have next?" asked Ben.

"Is there more to Susie Garrison's tragedy?" asked Sally?

"Certainly, and that's next. You would think that she had suffered enough."

GLIMPSES FOUR

SUSIE AND YOUNG BEN GONE AWAY

Russellville's last mining accident had occurred nearly two years before Benjamin Garrison's tragedy. In a cave-in six miners were trapped below, and the eventual rescue brought them up—with two fatalities and several injuries. In the mining business, even today, mining accidents are not rare. In the past as in Ben Garrison's time, there had been really no great improvements in mining safety.

In February, 1919, occurrence there was only one fatality and one injury. It was unfortunate for poor Susie and her children that the one fatality was their dear husband and father. Of course, he was the family breadwinner in a time when there was but a small mining company compensation. Will Bently was rushed to the hospital and survived. One other miner had his foot crushed, but this passed nearly unmentioned in the local news. No one else was harmed.

Three days later at the Methodist Episcopal Church, a simple funeral for Benjamin Satterfield Garrison was attended by his wife, children, kinsmen, friends and townsfolk. And afterwards Benjamin was laid to rest in Russellville's Oakland Cemetery. Little if anything was said about mining industries' responsibilities, pro or con, the need for more safety measures, or even anything about the forthcoming unions. After all, no one told Benjamin that he had to work in the mines. He did so at his own volition because he could make a decent income to support his growing family. Who would have thought it would cost him his life and so soon? And his grave would have no tombstone?

This was not known to the family until some thirty years later, and that not until Susie Garrison herself would pass away; Violet, the second oldest daughter would travel from her home in Denver, Colorado, where she had a husband and two daughters of her own, to accompany her mother's body to the Oakland Cemetery, Russellville, and would discover that her father's grave had no tombstone. Very likely, an inscribed tombstone even at the modest prices of the times when Susie first suffered widowhood was a difficult expense to handle. But Violet found the lack of a stone monument most inappropriate and, at her own expense, ordered a tombstone set in place with "Susie Garrison" inscribed along with "Benjamin Garrison" sharing the same tombstone as well as the same grave.

Modern day perks, like accident compensation and pensions and even social security did not exist in 1919, although labor unions were beginning to be spoken of, and in a few years, these mines would be shut down, pending the outcome of union negotiations, at which time young Violet would lose her job, a tragedy of its own. Because Violet was helping Gladys pay for her college education at the time, the early 1920s, this brought a close to Gladys's promising future. But misfortunes don't end.

This is not about unions and compensation. Back in 1919, after the mining disaster, during these dire circumstances, all the family had to pitch in and help. Young Ben and Dorothy were yet too young to help, but not too young to feel the pinch. Violet, for the time being, was still working for the mining company, as painful as its location was, and Gladys with her musical/piano talent had already shown her performing ability—she and older sister Violet took turns playing the organ at church. Gladys, who could manage whatever had a keyboard and pedals, branched out. She earned money playing the piano at the local cinema in the accompaniment to the silent movies and, too, she played with a local band. But Grandpa Guthrey put his foot down. Gladys could not go to such places as dance halls unchaperoned. Uncle Bud volunteered, so Gladys was family chaperoned on those occasions. The dance band hired her at age fifteen. Thereafter, Gladys spent a lifetime as a professional musician. Playing with the band brought in $5.00 per week and playing for the movies another couple of dollars. Every bit helped. Indeed, the widow's pension of Susie Garrison's was minimal. So the Garrisons of Russellville struggled on.

Grace's amorous affairs were not to end with Al Kemp's being booted out of the house. While living at Aunt Belle's in Van Buren, Arkansas, Grace met and fell in love with a man far more worthy of her than Al Kemp, one Harry Guiney. They married, had a new baby and soon moved themselves and little Marie hundreds of miles northward, eventually to Chicago, Illinois. Time passed. Gladys finished high school at the head of her class, received a modest scholarship for music and with the help of Violet (while she had her job at the Coal Company office), went off to attend Drury College in Springfield, Missouri. Meanwhile, Susie Garrison continued to raise the now teenager Dorothy and the little boy Benjamin, seven, who had been his father's pride and joy for most of those years. How sad it was now that little Benjamin, who loved baseball, would not have his father's loving hand in raising him.

As the house became empty and competition for the family piano diminished, young Benjamin took up piano playing, following in his mother's and big sister Gladys' footsteps and in the family tradition, a decision that few would believe could turn out tragic. By the 1930s, Benjamin became quite accomplished playing the current music, mainly jazz, which was all the rage. Of course, he could play the melodious songs such as those of Rogers and Berlin, but more so the real grabbers, the rhythmic music of Fats Waller and Louis Armstrong. Soon, he would be on his way out into the world. He would play with bands but more often, play singly in bars and honky-tonks. His interest in jazz would take him southeast to New Orleans, Atlanta, and Tallahassee.

Meanwhile, World War I having ended, Dorothy met a young man, Art Dugger, who had been recently discharged from the navy where he had learned to be a first-rate painter; as a civilian, he turned his skill into house painting. He and Dorothy fell in love, married, and moved to St. Louis, where he joined another painter, Fred, and together they formed a successful house painting company.

Meanwhile, Gladys met Harry Fulbright, her P.E. teacher, at Drury College in Springfield, Missouri. With the closing of the mines and Violet no longer able to send her money, Gladys eventually went to St. Louis to look for work and possibly to become a piano student of a favorite piano teacher who had left Springfield to join the teaching staff at McKendree College in Illinois, across the river from St. Louis. Gladys' minister back in Russellville wrote to the YMCA downtown St. Louis to provide her a safe place to live until she could establish herself. Shortly, she acquired a receptionist's job to provide for her basic needs. On streetcar rides, not entirely coincidentally, Gladys bumped into her former teacher Harry Fulbright on her way to work and his way to Washington University where he was finishing a law degree. They began to date in St. Louis and soon fell in love. When the year was out, Harry completed his degree and went to work for Stanley Sidman's law firm in suburban Wellston, an up and coming community. It was 1925 and Harry, now thirty-two, was ready to propose marriage. But, coincidentally, his father in Marionville, Missouri, fell seriously ill. Harry went home to look after his parents and the farm. Then shortly, in June, his father passed away, a crushing blow to his mother and son.

All gone from Marionville, there was nothing for Harry but to continue his life. In a letter to Gladys he proposed marriage. Gladys accepted and took the bus to Springfield, where she was met by Harry and driven to Marionville. Here they were married. In the fall, less than six months after his father died, Harry's mother passed away. Gladys soon was pregnant with their first child. A younger family was taking the place of an older family. Neely Fulbright was born in a log cabin near Marionville. Many years later, Neel would be kidded about how he should, with his log-cabin background, go into politics. Soon after their new baby arrived, Harry sold the farm, and he moved his family to St. Louis, taking up residence in Normandy, north St. Louis Country, about ten miles from his law office. The Fulbright's new house was a two-storey brick in a new, pleasant suburban neighborhood.

With her children now gone from Russellville, Susie Garrison sold out and moved to St. Louis as well. There she took a flat in a rooming house on Sarah Street in north downtown St. Louis. Now she was close to two of her children, Gladys and Dorothy—Grace and Harry Guiney having already left St. Louis and moved to Chicago—"Go where the Jobs are!"—Susie Garrison's remaining two daughters now had children of their own. Ah grandchildren, mostly sons, to enjoy. Now that her only son Benjamin had left to pursue his career as a popular-music pianist, perhaps she could enjoy these very young grandsons. If only her dear son Benny could be here with her—with Gladys' three boys and Dorothy's two boys. And what did these five growing little boys do but make fun of her. Her

craving for attention and sympathy did not help but only fed her unhappiness. Never mind. Sometimes, there seemed to be a touch of stoicism about her. Perhaps one could hear her say, "What will be will be," a phrase close to her stoicism.

That morning, when her son Ben left his mother in his model T, the last words Susie spoke to him were, "Keep in touch, Ben!" One would wonder if she told herself, "Don't be stupid, to think that the morning you say goodbye to Ben, it may be the last time you will ever see him. Never mind there was nothing that could be done about it. Therewith, Susie sent him on his way to perform, to shape his own fame and make his own way.

Ben did keep in touch, but nowhere nearly as often as his mother wanted. She was always concerned about him, his finances and his well-being. In St. Louis no one seemed to want the burden of a mother-in-law, especially one that had never gotten over the early demise of her beloved husband. So she lived alone in a far-from-elegant set of rooms in the city, barely enough space for one person, alone and more and more alone as her grandchildren grew.

In 1939, she received a call sounding desperate from her son Ben in Florida. He told her he wanted to come home to her, which she had hoped and prayed for, but he was short of funds for gas and lodgings. If she could send some money, he would shortly be on his way. How did this happen? Had he run himself so short, this was his only answer? Was there some kind of pressure on him? His location in Florida seemed thousands of miles away from Susie, and might as well have been. But he could come to her. Ninety dollars was a lot of money, but she could send it. Immediately, she wired him the money via Western Union to the rented apartment to which she had previously sent him letters. Now she was greatly excited to see him, in four or five days maybe.

But more days passed. A week passed. He did not come. She received no message from him. She wired him a short note. "Please let me know, Ben, that you received the money and when you will be here." Two weeks passed. No message. Susie was beside herself with worry. She wrote again—out of desperation. No word. Three weeks passed. Still nothing. Now she went nearly out of her mind with fear for his safety. "Please, Ben, please!" Now she tried contacting his landlord, places where he played, but to no avail. Finally the police department. These were difficult times. War fears were growing in Europe. Fears and dangers. Finally, the Florida police responded. The news was devastating.

They found his model-T in a solitary, wooded area, with a dead man inside. There was an I.D. in his billfold and no money. The I.D. indicated the body to be that of missing Benjamin Satterfield Garrison, Susie Garrison's only son. The car with the body inside had been in an isolated spot for some weeks. The body inside was black so at first, the police thought the deceased man was a black man. Hearing that Ben's car had been found, Susie hoped to God that the body was not that of her dear son. She made many calls and inquiries. But the lack of any contact and the details of the car and the presumed person of Ben appeared to leave little doubt that this was the missing man. According to conclusions from the police report, Ben had been robbed and murdered.

It was up to a member of the family to go to Florida and to thoroughly investigate the findings. Yet, no member of the family had the qualifications or finances to travel there at this time and conduct the kind of investigation that was needed. It was talked about. Several ideas were suggested, but when it came down to actually doing it, there was no one willing to make that kind of sacrifice. Harry Fulbright, lawyer, probably the best qualified to do the investigation had passed away in 1936, nearly three years earlier, and the Fulbright family, widow and three young boys, were still reeling from the loss. Charley Chafin, policeman in Colorado, may have been the most logical member of the family to send, but he had very modest means, a wife and three little girls to support. When it came down to it, there was no one to make the journey and to check out the whole horrible occurrence. For Susie Garrison, this was a devastating, incomprehensible tragedy.

Epiglimselogue Four

"Terrible," said Lisa, "but that was some seventy years ago. That kind of thing now could be investigated to a much greater extent right from home. Was nothing else ever done about it?"

"Actually, no. Nothing. A man's life was taken from him in the ugliest manner and that's it, like he never mattered at all. Like he never existed at all."

"Did they ever talk about it afterwards?" asked Sally.

"No. What was the use? They probably didn't want to upset Grandma. But this sort of thing happens today. Even worse. A person lives a meaningful life for sixty or so years and bang, bang, the person dies, and that's it." James shook his head in disgust. "But that suggests a later story."

Glimpses Five

DOWN IN THE SOIL

They had a fine name. The Fulbrights went all the way back to the founding of Springfield, Missouri. There were one or two other families that claimed this distinction, but most evidence indicates the Fulbights were THE originals who purchased the land in that proximity, owning the water spring for which the town was named and the spring that to this day, along with probably the oldest road passing through the city, bears the family name.

To be sure, when the brothers Wilhelm and Jacob came to Philadelphia in December of 1740, they came, whether they realized it or not, to establish a lineage, ultimately a distinguished family. One can only imagine how the name came about from its original Volprecht. Perhaps upon disembarking, the brothers were asked by the dock (government) officials to state their surname. And perhaps in their German accent the second syllable sounded like "prite."

"How's that?" the Anglicized clerk inquired of the brothers.

The German V of course is anglicized to F and thus "Foleprite." One further short step would bring about "Fulbright," a nice name suggesting full of brightness, light, associated with intelligence, hence a precursor to promise of what's to come. Shall we ask with Shakespeare, "What's in a Name?" Is it sound, anticipation, association, and manifestation into reality?

This would manifest in time, down the family lineage, in such distinguished servers as Senator J. William Fulbright of Arkansas, one of the outstanding senators in American history, responsible for the Fulbright scholarships abroad and the Fulbright-Hays teacher-scholar Exchange and Grant programs. Of course, along the way there would be also judges, teachers, successful, noteworthy farmers, and distinguished scholars and citizens. One, also, must acknowledge the contribution through their wisdom in their selection of spouses coming into proximity in the amazing environment of the New World. But these maiden names need researching. Nevertheless, tribute can be paid to Wilhelm and Jacob in appreciation of their momentous and adventuresome voyage and their laying the foundation of this American family that so many today can take pride in.

Of course we needn't go into the deliberate distortion of the namesake that wags have put the Fulbrights through along the way to advancement. Five-year-old Stevie became aware of such name distortion when he heard one of his big brother Dave's friends call to him, "Hey, emptybright, what's up?" He had heard many times before, "Hey Full, throw the ball!" but "emptybright" was a bit much. When he told his mother, she replied, "Oh yes, people love to distort our name. We're called all sorts of things: empty-dull, dull-wit, brightless, faulsprite."

Blurting into this conversation, brother Dave added, "Yea, how about 'Hey full-of-it!'"

"Now David, we don't need that!"

Like most mothers, Stevie's mother was not to be side-tracked or offended by any outsider's taunt. "Stevie, don't listen to those things." She often mentioned "those kind of people." Dave escaped being "those kind" by being a family member, but as we shall see, Dave had the inclination to take up with the riff-raff of the neighborhood, and his humor reflected their waggish distain. Then their mother would follow her rebuff with her favorite, "Sticks and stones may break my bones, but names can never hurt me."

As young as Dave was, he was not to be put down. "I don't know about that," said Dave. "You should hear the guys."

"We don't have to hear that," says their mother.

So, not knowing the riff-raff vocabulary, Stevie nevertheless comes up for Dave with what he knew his brother disliked. As he is running away to another room, Stevie blurts, "Yea, Davy Gravy!" He had better run, for he knew that if Davy Gravy caught him, he could very well make gravy out of Stevie. Now "Davy Gravy" does not sound that insulting, but it goes with the main Stevie-Davy taunt, "Dear little Davy loves chicken gravy," which, when Stevie sing-songs it, could send Dave into a furor.

Speaking of the family name, many years later, when Steve found his father's grave in Jefferson Barracks National Cemetery, he was stunned to discover the tombstone had his father's name misspelled: "Harry W. Fullbright." Oh my! Disgusting! He learned that mistakes of this kind were not infrequent among tomb-stone engravers. Looking up to the sky of puffy white clouds against the rich blue, he uttered, "Mother, you were such a spelling buff, why hadn't you corrected it?" (More about his mother's spelling expertise later.) Nevertheless, looking back over the two hundred and seventy-two years of Fulbright history in America, heirs can see that the luster of the Fulbright name has prevailed.

From Northern Europe, the Fulbrights settled originally near the East Coast in Philadelphia and in North Carolina, but eventually branches moved west across the Appalachians, Kentucky and Tennessee into Missouri and Arkansas. They were prosperous farmers, building up estates and educating their children. One branch went to Fayetteville, Arkansas, and established a newspaper. Others settled around Fulbright Springs (above), eventually Springfield, Missouri.

Late in the nineteenth century, it was not surprising that William Neely Halstead Fulbright II, well into the second century after their American beginnings, would be looking forward to having a son to one day take over the farm. He often felt his name was too heavy for a down-to-earth farmer, so why burden his son with the father-son formal tradition. He loved the land and loved to render the land productive. For passing the farm on, his wife Jane Wilks was obliging in becoming pregnant soon after their marriage, but the blessed event borne a girl. Yes, girls were beloved too. They named the girl Edna.

Never mind, "a girl this time, a boy next time" said the apprehensive Anne Bolyn to the much irritated King Henry VIII. But for these Fulbrights, the next time brought another girl whom the parents loved too and named Carrie, but a girl nevertheless. Then there was a third girl, whom they named Jesse. Now this was getting to be a bit much. "Where's this farm boy I'm looking for?" He might well have asked, what about the law of averages! And as she grew, the strong-willed, overly sensitive Jesse felt the disappointment. What was to happen to William Neely Halstead's distinguished name? Finally, over a half a decade later, on 8 June, 1893, a boy was borne to William Neely and Jane Wilks, a fine boy in keeping with his German heritage, healthy, strong, blond and blue-eyed.

And William surprised his co-genitors and named his son Harry Wilks Fulbright. As he looked at the baby boy's large hands, according to William Neely, Harry Wilks was destined to become a farmer and, as the boy grew up, he was exposed to the hardest and the most active of farm life, including digging, hoeing, cultivating, raising cattle and hunting in the woods. Wilks, of course, was the mother's maiden name, and Harry (an admired form of the royal Henry) was a favored name nevertheless. If William and Jane were to have no more boys, then it would be up to their one son Harry to advance the family name—if he so desired. William Neely gave the tradition a shrug.

With the approach of the twentieth century and modernism, more and more people were packing up and moving into multiple bee-hive dwellings. William Neely felt the city was rank with sewage and disease. Perhaps he felt that farming was the favored skill and trade, that city life was not all that it was cracked up to be. Growing up in light of his father's advanced agricultural techniques, Harry grew knowledgeable, confident and free spirited. He loved to help his father with the chores of the increasingly prosperous farm, one of the best farms around, one that became an exemplar of successful farms around the state, so much so that it came to the attention of the State's Department of Agriculture, which made use of the Fulbright farm to instruct other farmers of its successful methods. So young Harry had much to be proud of. Then, too, Harry loved to hunt and fish.

Nevertheless, young Harry began to have his own, perhaps more serious, thoughts about his future. He would go to college, of course, Drury College, near home. He would set out upon a career from there. Finishing at Drury, Harry had an opportunity to go to Harvard, and off to Harvard he went to pursue an education, ultimately in law, an important field still in those days of claim and land settling. Additionally, his fine athletic build stood him well in Olympic challenges. He won a position on the Olympic team for one season as a javelin thrower. But then the World War interrupted his schooling and athletic program, and off he went, a dough-boy from the Middle West.

When the War was over and he was released from the army, he decided that for his career, he wanted to stay closer to home.

His parents were getting older, and there was much to help with now and again on the farm. Further, there were prospects at home.

Harry became interested in a young local woman named Mildred Kastendick. It is not clear if Mildred was solely interested in Harry or if she had as much or more interest in a local farmer named Joy Brown. Nor is it clear if Joy Brown was already married to one Mariam. In any case, she chose to marry Harry, the tall, handsome, blue-eyed blond and to settle with him into a house near Harry's family at Marionville, some twenty miles west of Springfield, close enough to have the advantages of the larger town and the advantages of being related to one of Springfield's more prestigious families. Mildred was just finishing up college (and one day would become a school teacher). Harry took a teaching position at his alma mater, thinking eventually he would complete a law degree at Washington University in St. Louis. Between 1920 and 1923, he and Mildred had two children, first a girl they named Mary Jane and soon after a boy they named Harry Wilks after his dad.

Harry the father had a keen interest in history and writing. At Drury College, he taught academic courses, but when the administration heard that he had participated in the World Olympics as a javelin thrower, they bade him double as an athletics instructor.

When their son came along, Harry and Mildred couldn't see burdening the little fellow with the heavy family name, so they named him after the boy's father, Harry Wilks. Besides, being young and most likely to have more children, the family traditional name could come later. They had made friends with a couple on the next farm over, Joy—Mildred's earlier beau—and Miriam Brown and they settled in for what seemed like would be for years to come. Unlike his father, Harry knew that they eventually should move into a city, at least into nearby Springfield, if not St. Louis or Kansas City where he could most likely more profitably practice law, assuming of course that he would have an opportunity to finish that one more year of law school. To a lesser extent, he managed to get attached to a local law office in Springfield. But career successes take time, and meanwhile, Harry was enjoying his nearness to what he had known most of his life, his family, friends and farming.

The family tradition was with him. His Uncle James Fulbright was a State judge, and his cousins in Fayetteville, Arkansas, were gaining prominence that would soon put one of the family Fulbrights, the family who started the local newspaper, into the U. S. Senate. Harry made several trips to Fayetteville to firm up the family contact.

So Harry's bucolic and local favored-son life might have been wonderfully sustained if it had not been for a twist of fate. One morning Harry had his breakfast and coffee, kissed his wife and two small children goodbye and set out in his model T Ford toward town to his teaching and legal work. A short distance down the road, it dawned on him that he had forgotten something, and everything that he needed to advise a case was back home in his briefcase; there was nothing that could be done but to swing around, go back and get the "damn thing!" Never mind, there was time enough to make his nine o'clock class.

His house in the field at the end of a gravel road was rather solitary; other farm houses visible at some half a mile or more distance. But he had a funny feeling that there was something not quite in sync at his place. There was the barn, but there was something remote added to the barn—to the side, around behind?

No time to even ponder what that was. He swung his car around in the gravel barnyard driveway, shifted into neutral, pulled on the emergency, and jumped out. He remembered he had left the briefcase on a kitchen chair while he was having his coffee. He popped into the side door. There it was. He grabbed it and started back.

Wait! What was that? Sounds from the adjoining room, the bedroom. He moved silently to the door. Spring noise. He turned the knob. Locked. Abruptly the spring noise ceased. He pushed the door. It held fast. Latched? Why latched? They rarely ever latched the door, allowing the children to come to them if in need. He lunged at the door with his shoulder. The latch broke, the door sprung open. What he saw was not a total shock. Sitting up in bed over bare-breasted Mildred was Joy Brown, Mildred raising up from below him. He knew they had had relations before. He was not the insanely jealous type. He was aware of human weaknesses. And he couldn't deny some pangs of jealousy.

Now Mildred. What about Mildred? He was studying legal defenses. Sure, well enough, wouldn't she demand loyalty from him? And still, wasn't he a man? He demanded loyalty, too. What is there without loyalty? He had previously confronted her about Joy Brown. On that occasion, she had been quite pitiful, wept desperately and assured him the affair was over. But now this. It was the last straw.

"Damn you!"

He slammed the door. Two little faces atop pink and blue pajamas looked out from down the hallway, their bedroom doorway. But Harry saw them and hesitated.

"Harry!" Mildred called out. "Wait, Harry! Please!"

"What. More promises!" Her shrill—he felt—shallow voice interrupted his sympathy for the children. He stormed out of the house, drove away.

When he returned that next day, he demanded a divorce. He had already looked into filing.

What had happened the rest of that day and evening? He had gone to work. After work, he drove to his parents' house to talk with them. What would they advise?

"I'm telling Mildred I want a divorce."

So now when he told Mildred, she screamed, "You don't care about the children. I know you love the children." She was weeping, crying. "You don't care what happens to them."

"The problem is I do care about the children, he replied. "That's what makes this so difficult. I have to finish Law school or I won't be worth a damn. He felt his resolve more now than ever. "You will have to take care of the children. Last night at Mom and Dad's, I thought it over. You can get the divorce. We'll keep yesterday's debacle to ourselves. That'll keep you clear from scorn, a bad reputation, even though that is probably what you deserve.

"No. I'll let you get the divorce. You're going to have to take care of yourself and the children. I'll help all I can though you don't deserve it. It's your doing. So let's get this thing over with. You apply for a divorce. If you don't, I will and that will make it all the harder on you and the children." His eyes too, now were tearing. He breathed deeply. His voice softened. "You and the children will be all right here. I'm going to St. Louis."

Mildred knew Harry. He often took time to think things over before making a final choice. But once decided, there was no changing his mind. He's right about the divorce, she concluded when she collected herself. I should file for it—to protect the children from any scandal. This could go hard for Harry, but he means to have it this way. I have no choice.

Epiglimpselogue Five

"And so it was," commented James, stoically.

"How do you know ...", said Rupert, with little hesitation, "that it wasn't the other way around, that Harry was the one fooling around and that Mildred found out and demanded a divorce—as it is in the legal document—was her demand, not his?" This brought the attention of the others, especially Ben who scooted to the edge of his seat.

"I don't know ... for sure, but years after Steve's father's death his mother told him the story. Further, in 1995, Susie Fulbright, the granddaughter of the deceased Harry Fulbright, working on family history, made several long distant calls to her father's half-brother Harry Wilks (Jr.), whom none of those of the second marriage have ever met, leaving messages each time, but she never had any response. Recently, years later, Steve tried as well with the same nonresponsive results."

"So," Rupert says, "you conclude ... ?"

"I conclude that if there were no scandalous secrets on their side, why wouldn't Harry Jr.'s family be willing to respond? I know this is not conclusive evidence, but it seems strange this many years after the concerned parties are deceased that there should be no response from the Harry Wilks' progenny."

Rupert shook his head. "Maybe they were trying to spare Neel and Dave and Steve and their family the truth."

"Well, this can be an ongoing inquiry. We'll keep this in the active file with other sought out mysteries. Nevertheless, Steve and company owe their existence to the tiff whatever its substance."

CHAPTER SIX

TURNING THE SOIL

Going back to the night before: "But what about your children?" his mother said tragically when Harry had told his parents that particular night the disappointing news about his demanding that his wife Mildred file for a divorce.

"What about whose children?"

"Your … " She turned slightly red with embarrassment. "Harry, you don't think that Mildred …"

"No, I don't think so. But when you come right down to it, how would I know? You don't know this, but what I've told you I saw was just the latest episode, the final straw." Harry walked over to the window and looked out far away. "I can't take any more of it. She and this creep have been at it for some time. When I've confronted her with it, she promises it's over. But it never is. What's over is our marriage. She's made the choice."

"But the children, Harry. Regardless, I can't help but feel sad for those two little ones."

"I'll tell her I'll leave it to her: she can file for divorce. Mildred has money enough to get by on. Then she can teach. With the house and land, financially, she's in better shape than I am. I have to finish another year of law school. For me, this makes finishing law school obligatory. Mildred can marry again. Maybe that creep will get a divorce and marry her. Better, maybe she'll pick a man who will make a decent father and, for her sake, husband."

"But no one can take care of the children like their real mother and father," said his mother.

"Why didn't Mildred think of that? But you know, in other ways, she is a capable woman. She's prepared to teach, you know. She's already qualified. She'll manage the children well. Yes, I could have helped. I would have gone to the ends of the earth for those children. But I've played it fair. I've been true. And I am entitled to better. Maybe I can find a real wife. There're bound to be some intelligent women who are capable of loyalty, a woman I can begin a real family with." Harry turned and looked at his Dad. "You're always talking about having a real Fulbright family tradition." He looked deep into his father's eyes. His parents both looked greatly saddened. "My first son—this time I'll name him for you, Dad. The distinguished old family name."

"I was hoping that Mildred would work out." His father spoke meditatively. "Yes, she's quite a capable woman. He sighed heavily and after a pause said, "Are you sure you want to end things this way? Maybe another …"

"She had her chance. I've demanded this time. Maybe she'll marry that creep. She's agreed to a divorce—bitterly. But after a scene, she will agree. She's going to get the divorce—for the sake of the children. I've got to finish law school this time. The children are so young they greatly depend on her."

"How are you going to handle the settlement?"

"As I've said, I'm turning the house and acres over to Mildred. Let her run the farm with that good-for-nothing Brown, that whoremonger. When the time comes for me to return to Springfield, I'll take over that cabin Grandfather built. You said I could have it. That is where I will start my family, one based on decency and loyalty."

"I don't know, son …," his mother said in a nervous state of confusion. "Are you sure you want to do this?"

"You won't have much land to farm," rejoined his father.

"I'm a lawyer and a farmer, in that order, Dad. I'm desperate to get my last year in at Washington U. in St. Louis, and to get on with my law career. If I hang on here with Mildred, I might never make it. I'll be a weakling. I'd never make it." With a look of hope, he turned and looked out the window again up at the sky "Now I can make plans to get moving. Anyway, the cabin will be it until I can get my feet on the ground."

Within the next six months, Harry had his divorce and was legally and emotionally ready to move his career forward and to look around for a new wife. This was a bit of a problem because Harry was already about to have his thirtieth birthday, and at the college where he taught, most of the available women were too young, eighteen or nineteen, just out of high school. He would have to keep his head about him. Not jump into anything too soon, and yet time was passing, and it seemed very strange to start family building all over again. Several months passed. Already it was November, nearing the end of the semester, his final semester of teaching.

Just thinking about the wrap-up perhaps made him more personable in his surroundings than he had ever been before. It was mid-April while he was walking along, thinking about his life changes, that he spotted one of his students, a young lady from his physical education class, a little on the short side but very pretty with very alert brown eyes. She seemed to pay attention to him—especially. He thought that he would like to know something about her. But he knew such motivation among faculty members would not exactly be approved by the college.

The next day while walking the same way, he overtook the young lady with the alert brown eyes—Garrison was her name, he knew from the class roster—and spoke with her briefly. Now, out of her gym attire, she wore a cute white dress with a wide blue navy collar and was walking across the campus with ease, probably to her next class.

"Hello, Miss Garrison."

"Oh, hello," she said a little startled, having a hello somewhat drawn out and rather sophisticated sounding. "... Mr. Fulbright."

"What is your major, Miss Garrison?" Harry was not much into small talk, but the early green, spring leaves of maples along this path were in themselves mesmerizing.

"Music. I'm on my way to piano now." She glanced in the direction of the Music Hall. How appropriate, he thought, on this lovely spring day.

"Do you like music, Mr. Fulbright?"

"Very much. What kind of music do you play?"

"Oh, several kinds. Classical and popular and ragtime. Folk, too. What's your favorite?"

"Classical, but I like a variety. Some popular. What are some of the classical songs you play?"

"Of the composers, I like Chopin, Beethoven, Tziakowsky, a number of the operatic composers like Verde, Puccini, Mozart, Biset ..."

"Sounds like you have quite a repertoire."

"Not really. I'm working on it." She looked up at the gray-stone building. "Here I am. Thank you for asking."

And she was off, up the steps and, quickly, the large entrance doors swallowed her up.

He wanted to follow her and listen to her play, but maybe she was not very good, just a starter and an accidental confrontation might be embarrassing. Harry was always impressed by outstanding performers and such a young student, just beyond a girl really, might by comparison be a disaster. He would feel compelled to compliment her on her playing and convincing insincerity was not his forte. Another time, another day.

Several weeks passed, and the end of the semester was nearly upon them. He saw no one else that perked his interest like this little, pretty lady, and who knew, if he decided to act, with his being away to law school, he would see very little, if any, of her when she was enrolled in the fall semester. Rarely would he be able to get back to Springfield. Once he was determined to make a move, there wouldn't come an opportunity to meet her casually and to walk her to the performance hall.

A few days later, he walked down the halls at the performance building when he knew she would be there on the chance that he would run into her again. Such, perhaps destiny, prevailed, but not as he expected. Rachmaninoff came dramatically to him from the concert chamber. That's wonderful, he proclaimed to himself. Such feeling, such expression! I wonder if some day Miss Garrison could play like that. I'll keep walking, he decided. He soon passed several piano practice rooms, but none of them, evidently, were occupied. He returned the way he came, passed the Concert Hall, where now Chopin's Polonaise embellished the building. He stopped to listen. At the crescendo, he began to move off. The piece ended, and he heard a few people applauding.

Wonder of wonders, he heard her voice: "Thank you. Thank you." No question: the voice belonged to Miss Garrison. To himself, he said, "And I thought the pianist couldn't possibly be that young Garrison lady!" He hurried to the entranceway of the concert chamber and looked in. Sure enough, there she was standing on the stage next to the college's recent purchase, a magnificent concert Steinway. She looked so young, so minuscule beside it. Heavens, was she the one playing the grandiose "Prelude in C-sharp Minor' on that magnificent instrument?

"What are you doing here, Harry? Aren't you afraid you'll catch some culture?" Behind him, the familiar voice of a long-time friend and colleague. Harry turned and there he stood, with a wry smirk on his face, harkening him back to his early college days at Drury when the two used to argue legality versus humanity; Harry remembered these sessions well. Now John was a humanities instructor, yet as Harry had heard, very much into administration politics.

"Culture?' Harry rose to the remark. "Of course. That lady who just played, she's quite an accomplished pianist. And so young."

"Sure. She's one of our fine students. Her name is Gladys. Gladys Garrison. Small town girl from Arkansas. Unspoiled. She's here on a music scholarship. She has the potential of being a concert pianist. If she sticks with it and doesn't run off, get married and have babies." They both laughed. What do you think of our new college president? Come around to my office and we'll discuss ... oh, here comes Gladys." She had left the stage and come up the aisle to the entranceway toward the two men. John faced her and smiled.

"Miss Garrison, this is a friend of mine who was just admiring your playing, Harry Fulbright ..."

"We've met," Harry said. "Miss Garrison is in my P.E. class. Yes, I enjoyed hearing you play."

Gladys smiled. "Thank you."

"Gladys is playing in a recital that's coming up. You may want to come, Harry."

"Yes, I would."

That was the start of a closer acquaintance with Gladys, a small-town girl, as John had said, from Arkansas, an unspoiled young lady. Harry attended several open practice sessions and also the student recital performance before the public at the end of the semester. But Harry was off, or very soon to be, and his thoughts were dominated by the professional change he was making. Unlikely was he ever to see this attractive, talented young lady again.

"I enjoy your playing very much, Miss Garrison. I hope I will have a chance to hear you again."

"Sounds like you're leaving the campus."

"Yes, I am going to St. Louis to finish my law degree."

"Really, I'm leaving this semester too. I have to go back to Russellville to decide what path to follow next."

"Your music … ?" began Harry

"Yes, I'm thinking of going to St. Louis myself, to study piano."

"Perhaps we'll bump into each other there."

"I don't know. It's a large place, and I'm not sure when and even if I am going. McKendree College near there I hear has a good music department. I'm looking into it."

She's young, he thought, probably ten or so years younger than me, but unspoiled, I can see clearly enough. "Word has it around the college that you have it in you to become a concert pianist."

"Well, I don't know about that, but I'd like to try." He admired her ambition.

Harry invited Gladys out to several non-college social functions. Gladys was very much up on the popular music of the day. On several occasions, he watched and listened to her play in a music hall practice room. Harry soon learned that if she had the music in front of her, she could play straight off. If not, with her skill at chords and quickness at picking up tunes and melodies, she could improvise to her listeners' delight. She was professional too. For part-time wages, she played with dance bands both here and back home in Russellville. She knew fox trots, jazz music and ragtime. He soon learned that she was composing her own music.

When she began seeing Harry, some of her college friends teased her about a song she played, a song recently composed and popularized, "I'm Just Wild about Harry."

When they dated, they occasionally went dancing. They both enjoyed socializing, drinking beer and smoking cigarettes. This was the time of prohibition. They found themselves surrounded by the naughtiness of an era. Folks back home in Russellville would have been shocked to witness such degradation, albeit up-to-date, behavior. Word spread, of course, and back home tongues wagged about Gladys and her much older, divorcee gentleman friend, and Gladys received occasional word of their disdain from her sisters and friends. This separated Gladys for the rest of her life from "moss-backed hypocrites," as she called them, mainly "church-people." Like so many of their era, Harry and Gladys were not about to give up their new- found enjoyments—the latest songs, dancing, smoking, drinking beer and their being together with each other.

Harry took Gladys to his parents' farm to meet his father and mother. Before the summer was over, the relationship grew into a romance. In St. Louis, they met on the streetcar rides across the city, Gladys to her attendant office position, Harry to the Law School at the University.

Just about the time Harry finished law school, his father was ailing, and he hurried home to help with the farm. Shortly after his arrival, his father grew gravely ill and before the end of June, he died. By mail, Harry proposed to Gladys. She accepted by mail and went to Marionville to join him. Before the end of the year 1925, they were married, and moved into the historic Fulbright family's, timely restored log cabin. Less than six months after his father died, his mother died. Gladys was pregnant, and in January of the following year, 1927, a boy was born, whom they named William Neely Halstead Fulbright III. It was sad that William, the child's grandfather, did not live quite long enough to see what he, and especially his father. so much wanted, a namesake.

His parents gone, the Fulbright farm was sold and the inheritance divided among the four grown offspring. By this time, all three of Harry's sisters were married, had moved away and had families of their own.

Jesse, the youngest girl but half a dozen years older than Harry, was not happy with the inheritance settlement. She blamed Harry for what she felt were the inequities of their rather modest inheritance. She had married well but was always jealous of Harry, who had taken her place as the youngest and favored one. Had it happened that William's one belated, surviving son took too much attention and fuss away from Jesse in the early days of the family nest? Would Jesse ever forgive her young brother? Jesse would see to it that the settlement would haunt Harry for years.

Still, moving into the professional world and settling into his new home in the up-and-coming St. Louis community with his new young bride and young son, Harry could well identify with Ray Henderson's latest song of 1925:

> *I'm sittin' on top of the world, just rolling along, just rolling along, I'm quitting the blues of the world, just singing a song, just singing a song.*

Right away, Harry saw to it that his musically talented young wife had a piano to play, so this expensive instrument was one of their first purchases.

Epiglimpselogue Six

"So William Neely, Harry's father, was really into the family name?" asked Ben.

"William Neely thought that he was responsible for carrying on the family name tradition. This, he himself had not done. He had three daughters and one farm-boy son surviving him."

"I can see it: for posterity's sake," said Lisa.

Rupert frowned. "For whatever that's worth."

Would others after William Neely Halstead Fulbright III carry out the tradition?"

"Not so far."

"So as we have seen, Harry chucked one family and started another," said Rupert.

"Doesn't sound like a very good idea," said Sally.

"True," responded James. "But he had his own career to be concerned about. He had to respect himself. All around him, change was rampant—automobiles, tractors, airplanes, radios. He wanted to finish that law degree so he could practice law and play a more personal role in bringing about justice. That, too, was a family tradition. That had been a priority with the family for some time although his mother and father did not like the idea of Harry divorcing Mildred or the other way around with Mildred divorcing Harry at Harry's instigation. Somehow, it wasn't as bad that way. After all, it was her doing that brought it on."

"But can you blame him when he walks in on his wife's affair," said Rupert. "In this day and age, Harry could have had a DNA test on the children and himself to see if the children were actually his."

"True," said Sally. "But would this have changed Harry's mind about their getting a divorce?"

"Have there been more sons in the direct family line?" asked Ben.

"Yes. Three. One was named Neal Blaine Fulbright, but that is as close as they come. Anyway, you will shortly hear about William Neely Halstead Fulbright III. Coming up."

GLIMPSES SEVEN

ENCLOSE IN CLAY

When the Fulbrights first moved to St. Louis, the city was prosperous and growing and full of promise. Life was full of promise. Times were good again. There was much to look forward to. After all, Harry had been a bright young man with college behind him (Drury College and Harvard and Washington University). His legal writing skills had come to the attention of Stanley Sidman whose offices were in Wellston, a promising community on the rise (not the deteriorating one it was later to become).

A little history produces the greatest ironies. Now Fulbright's St. Louis was not the joyous St. Louis of "Meet Me In St. Louie, Louie." The Fulbight's home was a two-story house in a middle-class, up-and-coming neighborhood in the suburbs. Like so many other cities of the Depression, St. Louis was economically frozen in its tracks; it would remain so for another nearly half decade, that is, until government contracts for war—airplanes, munitions—would flood in and restore its economy. But for now, the World's Fair-days and Forest Park Forever and the winning baseball-Cardinals city was on hold. But then Harry and Gladys were not native St. Louisans; they were country types, who had fled the country to establish through their own efforts and talents a better life.

It didn't look like a bleak winter coming on. It was November of 1936 and fall weather, the Indian summer, was holding. The Fulbrights of Oakridge had seen better days. And then again, so had most of their neighbors and most Americans. The Depression had caused many to struggle. Gladys Fulbright's husband Harry, now husband of eleven years, the father of their three children, had been a highly promising lawyer with a brilliant future. Nevertheless, he had not had enough time in his law partner position to accumulate a financial buffer.

If the times were not bad enough, Harry became ill, a severe swelling of the lymph nodes. It was soon identified—Hodgkin's disease, cancer, most commonly the death knell—nevertheless, after two years of illness, a new still experimental surgical procedure, brought the hope that removal of the cancerous tissue would stop it from spreading. He was hoping for a quick recovery and a return to full time work so they could pay the mounting bills.

The three young boys—Neely the oldest at nine, Dave next at seven and Steve the youngest at four—were alone a full-time job, and Gladys had no wage-paying job, so there was no other source of income, and steadily bills continued to come in. The cancer cure appeared to be failing. Her sister Dorothy and her mother came around to offer Gladys moral support, but they were in no position to give financial support.

Weekends were the days for their visits. Gladys' mother Susie Guthrie Garrison, "granma" to the children, was herself a widow who lived entirely on a small coal-miner's pension, and Gladys' sister Dorothy, "Dot," with a painter husband, had three children of their own to raise. And these were not entirely pleasurable occasions. Usually, the sick man was sleeping in the first floor dining room, recently made over into something like a hospital ward room to keep the sick man from having to climb stairs, and so Gladys could give Harry close attention. The door, which usually remained open, was now kept shut most of the time so Harry could rest and recuperate rather than have noisy children running in and out. Occasionally, when he rallied, he would venture out to shop with his wife for the family provisions. He still drove the Model T Ford. Gladys had never learned to drive. Earlier, back in Russellville she had barely reached driving age when her father was killed.

In later years, one of Steve's few memories of his father ("Stevie," barely four at the time) was of his parents returning from the grocery store. His child's focus:

Mother and Daddy come home from store. Daddy wears his straw hat. Groceries out. Daddy's still sick. Big brothers make hat for Stevie out of grocery bag. Put on Stevie's head. Bag is tall like cook's hat. They laugh; Stevie doesn't like cook's hat. Pushes it off to floor. Neely picks it up and puts it back on Stevie's head. He laughs. They laugh. Stevie pushes it off again. Neely puts it back on Stevie's head again.

"Keep it on," Neely says.

They laugh. Davey-gravey says, "Daddy, look at big cook's hat on Stevie."

Neely and Davey laugh. Stevie laughs too. Daddy takes off his straw hat. Neely says daddy is so strong he saw him tear a straw hat in two. Daddy is very strong, Neely says. But now Daddy sets his hat on the table and wipes his face with his handkerchief. He says something too quiet to Mother.

"Why don't you lie down, Harry," she says. "I'll call you when dinner is ready." *Daddy goes, closes door.*

Neely and Dave go out the back screen door. Stevie finds Uddie. Stevie hugs Uddie. Uddie is "rag dog, old, dirty, and ugly," says Neely. Stevie sometimes sees Uddie in the garbage. He takes Uddie out of the garbage. Stevie sleeps with Uddie. Swishes him off a bit.

Stevie is four. His birthday was in September. Now it is November. Next September, big brothers won't leave Stevie at home any more. Stevie will be big like big brothers and will go to school.

Cold air comes in the hall window upstairs. Curtain shakes. Mother says soon snow will come and lie on the ground. Daddy coughs. He is in his room lying down. Aunt Dot's come. She is with Mother. They scrub clothes in sink. Oh-oh, Stevie does it again. Stevie is "underfoot."

"Run outside and play," says his Mother, sad but not mean this time.

Just then, Neely and Dave pop their heads inside back door. "Mother, can we play on Soapstone Hill?"

Usually, mother says no 'cause she doesn't like how dirty we boys get on Soapstone Hill. "Land's sake!" she'd say. "You boys beat all!" But instead she says, "Oh, I guess so." Then she says, "Watch Stevie."

Brothers don't make ugly faces and grumpy sounds like they always do when mother says "watch Stevie" 'cause brothers want bad to play on Soapstone Hill. Wasn't that why! "Come on!" says Davey-gravy. Quick, they're out the screen when Mother says, "Don't let the—" and the door slams. Stevie runs after them. Door slams again. "I wish those boys would learn not to—" but Stevie can't hear the rest. He is running fast as he can to catch brothers.

Stevie doesn't catch up until they almost reach the end of the street and over the hill to the big drop off that all boys in the neighborhood know as Soapstone Hill.

"Look at the rainy creek down there," says Neely. The creek, at the bottom of the nearly fifty feet cliff, was swollen because of the steady rain the night before. The boys intuitively knew at the glance what that meant. That meant if you fell and rolled to the bottom, you would get soaked. The trick was not only to hold or reclaim a spot at the ridge, but also to keep dry, the status symbol of superiority in strength, balance and courage. For Stevie it meant he'd get soaked and muddy and go home the scruff that mother didn't want to see.

Nevertheless, for Stevie, size or little size, strength or little strength, it was always better to face the punishment than to be left out. His boldness that was apparent by his stance and folded arms meant that no one could yell at him, "Sissy, sissy, doesn't want to play!"

Besides, Stevie likes the smell of the earth and the thrill of falling. Stevie would come here sometimes by himself, when everybody was sad, and he'd smell the dirt, dirt like it was way down in the earth dirt, and he would watch the creek way down below. The water usually trickles among the rocks, but now it gushes through them. Dave said that what Stevie smelt was clay, and clay when it was pressed for thousands of years becomes soapstone that the hill was made of. It has layers and layers of soapstone that went all the way down to the creek. Could he wash with it? One time he took some home and tried it out in the bathtub.

"What is that stuff in your bath!" said Neely looking in and quickly holding his nose. "Hey mom, Stevie pooped in the bathtub!"

"Not poop. Soapstone," trying to emphasize "soap." Still, he jumped out of the tub like it was poop.

His mother looked in. "Clean that stuff up this minute!"

But now Stevie knew better. He never asked his brothers why it was called soap-stone. But he liked soapstone and Soapstone Hill.. Other boys liked Soapstone Hill too. Lots of boys played there. "Girls don't play here. Neely says mothers and girls don't like dirty."

The creek is not a big creek like a river, except when it rains and rains hard like it had the night before. In a heavy downpour, the creek could be like a river and wash you away to the big river. Mother wouldn't let Stevie come here when it was raining hard. When she was home, that is. But now the creek is knee-deep when usually it was ankle deep.

Stevie looks out at the tree tops across the creek. It is forested. Beneath him are the outcroppings of soapstone. It is somehow exotic. It is slippery after the rain. "Neely, if I started slipping, I'd fall down cliff, way down, wouldn't I?"

Neely ignores him. Stevie is accustomed to being ignored by his big brother. It is probably a stupid question. He knew that he'd have a long slide down with soapstone and gravel, leaves and sticks, and he'd go all the way to the bottom and into the fast-running creek. He'd have bruises and scratches and the water would be cold. He'd get all wet and dirty, and his brothers would laugh. Stevie liked them to laugh. When they laughed, they wouldn't be pushing each other or pushing Stevie or beating each other up. If they beat on each other, Stevie didn't like it.

Stevie picked up a piece of soapstone. Some boys would take pieces of soapstone home and carve things out of it. They carved rings out of it. Once, Stevie went to make a ring out of soapstone. He would make one for his daddy to wear. He would make it nice and shiny. But after the third try and it was almost finished, it broke. He looked around and found, next to a sign, a piece of soapstone the size of his fist. When they would leave, he would take it home and try again. Wouldn't Daddy like a nice shiny ring?

Neely read a sign: *The dead with charity enclosed in clay.* Neely shook his head and took a stance.

"Look at me!" shouted Neely at the ridge. "I'm King of Soapstone Mountain!" He pounded his chest with his fists. He stood at the topmost part of the hill overlooking the North Woods. He looked down the cliff. He raised his arms and made muscles like he was the strongest man in the whole world.

"Me too," said Stevie. "I King of the Mountain." Stevie tried to nudge Neely away from the topmost part of the ridge.

"No!" shouted Neely. "Only one King of the Mountain." Neely pushed Stevie, and Stevie slipped and fell, but he caught a branch of shrub and dangled there with rocks and dirt slipping and falling around and under him. "See, I'm King of the Hill!" repeated Neely, masterfully.

"No, you aren't!" said Davey Gravy. "I am!" From behind, he shoved Neely, but Neely held his balance, turned and shoved back. Dave grabbed Neely and pulled and twisted toward the edge. Neely, the bigger, stronger, took Dave in an arm-lock around his head and tried to swing him over the cliff. Stevie climbed back up on the ridge, righted himself, and entered the fray by butting Neely in the side. Neely swung his knee into Stevie's buttock and sent him over the edge. Stevie slid and tumbled, trying to grab anything he could to stop his fall, but his momentum was too great, and he tumbled down and down. Near the creek's edge, with dirt and gravel and rocks splashing into the water, he was able to grind away with his feet and prevent himself from plunging into the creek.

Silence ensued. Back at the top, Neely and Dave had stopped their fighting to watch Stevie's tumble and outcome. When Stevie rose, half stood, shook himself off and looked up at them, they instantly continued their fighting, with Neely shouting, "I'm king of the mountain!"

Dave, almost losing his footing, shouted, "You're King of the Horses' Asses!" smirking his teasing-est smirk which matched the mud and dirt browns of the fall season.

"Oh yeh?" said Neely. He went for Davey to give him the final shove off the ridge, but Davey grabbed his arms and held on for dear life. While they are grappling, Stevie began climbing back up the cliff. Roots and branches and outcropped stones layers being his handles as he made his way two-thirds of the way back up. Quickly he clung close to the soapstone wall when his two brothers, locked in combat, came hurtling by in a mass nearly carrying Stevie with them. Except for Stevie's genuinely cowardly act of reflexively flattening himself against the jagged wall. The two brothers came apart and separately plunged to the bottom and into the creek.

Stevie now struggled to the very top. Once there, he was exuberant. He righted himself and looked out imperiously upon his new domain.

"I King of the Mountain!" he shouted. He jumped up and down. "I King of the Mountain! I King of the Mountain!"

It took very little time for him to feel a tight grip on his ankle. "What'd you say, squirt!" Hair dripping, face smeared with mud, eyes glistening, Neely had Stevie's ankle in a vice-like grip. "You're king of the mud creek!" shouted Neely. He jerked Stevie hard and sent him flying head-first off the ridge.

"Hey, easy on him!" shouted Dave who was only half way up when Stevie came slipping, sliding and tumbling past him. Dave tried to grab Stevie to slow his fall, but he missed, Stevie's momentum being too great. Stevie tumbled passed Dave with such speed that this time, he fell out into the middle of the creek and with an impressive splash. When Stevie stood, he was dripping with water and muddy gook.

"You boys come home!" thundered a man's voice from up above.

A sturdy, rough-looking man stood at the top of the hill behind Neely. He wore a suit and a tie. He held a child in his arms. This was Uncle Art, the boys' normally funny uncle. But now he was not funny. He was deadly serious. "You boys come home now. Your mother wants you." The child he held was Benny. Stevie's cousin who was a year and a half younger than he. Stevie felt big; he could play with his brothers. Benny was too small to match in play his older brother Robert.

Dave and Stevie struggled up to the top, and once there with Neely, they all headed for home. Just now Uncle Art seemed quiet. He was quiet, solemn. Why was he so quiet? When they arrived at the house and just before they entered, Uncle Art said, "Now you boys stay quiet and close to your mother. We'll be back tomorrow right after church."

Epiglimselogue Seven

"The boys really liked that Soapstone Hill. Right? " said Sally.
"You bet."
"But tragedy is approaching," said Rupert.
"It was ironic that their easy-going, funny Uncle Art would be the symbol of the approach of tragedy," averred James.

"What's the point of this Soapstone Hill stuff and the approach of tragedy?" asked Lisa.

"I can answer that," said Rupert. "Even with a dying man in the house, boys still must be boys. They have to get out and rough and tumble in King of the Mountain to be themselves."

"Certainly," confirmed James. "For two years, their father had been mortally sick, and for that last year he grew steadily worse. This was a happy, growing family, full of hope with a bright future ahead of them. And now what?"

GLIMPSES EIGHT

THE DARKEST CLOSET

Sunday afternoon and Daddy's in bed and very sick. He is sick in bed all the time now. When your neck is all big on one side and you're all sick-white, Dave says you're goin' to die. What's die? No more. Where's Uddie? Cousin Charlotte was asleep and all sick-white and mother said she died. She went into the ground, and Aunt Violet and Uncle Charley, Charlotte's mother and daddy, had to go back to Colorado without Charlotte because Charlotte was dead and in a box and in the ground at the graveyard. Aunt Violet cried and cried; and Uncle Charley, Neel says, was a piece of stone. That's why Aunt Violet always says never tell anybody good-bye.

Stevie doesn't want dead. What is dead? You get sick. Sometimes you touch somebody dead, and you get sick and die. You touch their clothes and you get sick and die. Charlotte's in Arkansas dead and in the ground. She was little like Stevie. Stevie didn't know Charlotte. But Stevie knew Raymond from up the street. Stevie saw Raymond think in funny ways. And Raymond died. Stevie couldn't say it right, but he had gulliver-marbles. Stevie felt funny saying that word. When he said the word to a lady, the lady knew at once and looked like she tasted a sour lemon. It made her sick. Stevie didn't like to say the word. It was a mess-word. It could make you sick and dead. One day Raymond was on his porch and called to Dave. Dave went over and he and Raymond talked. That night they rushed Raymond to the hospital and he died. Dave says, no more Raymond.

Not only that but Stevie makes people look in funny ways and they die. Stevie made Raymond look in a funny way. Raymond got sick and died.

"Where's Uddie?" Stevie asked mother.

"You boys—find Uddie for Stevie."

Dave says it. He says when you die, they put you in the ground. Lots of Garrisons are in the ground in Arkansas, Dave says. Granpas and granmas, aunts, uncles and long-off cousins, says Dave. Stevie's never been to Arkansas. There's lots of dead people in the ground there. Gran'ma goes to Arkansas to see dead people. Granpa is dead in Arkansas. Stevie never saw Granpa. He died in a coal mine before Stevie was born. Dave says he was kilt by a big rock in the coal mine. Now he's dead and in the clay like at Soapstone Hill. Granma came here to see us. She talks funny. She says 'win-deer.' She says "somebody close the win-deer." Granma says, 'Oh, my lump-bago is actin' up agin.' She limps when she says, 'My limpbago is actin' up.'

Aunt Dot and Granma and Ev-lyn are here. Mother talks with them a lot. Doctor Kerrerin'ton is here too. Stevie can smell his pipe. He is in with Daddy and the door is closed. Daddy is in bed. And the doctor's there and Daddy is very sick. Everybody says so.

"You sure have had bad luck, Gladys," said Granma.

Aunt Dot gets angry with Granma and says, "Mama, I swear." *Aunt Dot says 'I swear' a lot. Mother goes in to see Daddy.*

"Honestly, Mama," said Aunt Dot, "Don't know what you are thinking of to say such a thing." *The clock in the hall chimed. The tick-tocks seemed to lead up to a sad bong.*

Stevie heard the doctor come out his Daddy's door. He called. Aunt Dot went in. The door closed. Then the door opened and Granma went in. The door closed. Stevie could hear them talk far away. Stevie was afraid. He wanted to hide. The doctor's big coat hung long in the closet. The door closed and it was dark. Light comes under the door. Stevie could barely hear voices from daddy's room. The voices were different. Not like voices. Stevie twisted. The doctor's big coat fell down on Stevie. It made him warm. He closed his eyes. He smelled the Doctor's pipe. The voices drifted away.

Suddenly from far, far away Granma said "Oh Lord!" *Suddenly he heard daddy's door open.*

"Oh Lord!" Now it was closed and loud. "Oh Lord!"

And there was crying, like Stevie never heard before. Mother is crying. Granma is crying. Aunt Dot is talking high and different. It was somethin' awful. It went on and on. Then mother wants her boys to come to her. Neely goes first and then Dave.

"Your daddy is dead," she told them in tears. Stevie could just see them. Neely blinked and set his jaw, a man's jaw for a boy of eight. Dave frowns; it is a stone-frown for a boy of seven.

"Where's Stevie?" asked their mother.

What were they thinking? In these dire times, with this intense feeling for the father, Stevie was gone! "Mama, where is Stevie?" she calls out through the house.

"Lord, I don't know," she called back. "He was in the kitchen just a minute ago." The voices were all different.

"Look upstairs, you boys," said mother.

"Maybe he's outback," said Aunt Dot. "Art, go see if he's out there."

The boys came scrambling down the stairs. "He's not up there."

"Did you check all the rooms?"

"We'll look again, mother," said Neely. Up the stairs they trampled.

In a few minutes they came back. No Stevie.

Dr. Ketterington stood by with papers for Gladys to look at. Everyone was confused. Mother's face turned from sorrow to fear.

"Oh Lord!" said Granma.

"Now, Mama," said Aunt Dot. "Stevie's here-abouts somewhere. We'll find him."

"Stevie!" Dot called loudly. "Come here this minute!"

After a brief wait, Granma groaned, "Oh Lord, he's not here."

"Well," said the Doctor. I'm sure you'll find him. "Can you get my coat, young man." He said to Neely and followed him to the closet.

Light from the opening door fell across the closet revealing the Doctor's large black coat hunched up on the floor like some big beast hibernating. Suddenly the beast moved.

Looking passed Neely, the doctor, the man of science, said, "What have we here?" He picked up the coat uncovering what looks like a sleeping child. "I believe we solved the mystery," he said with as much of a smile as one could muster under the circumstances.

"Stevie!" cried Dot,

"Land's sake!" said Granma. "You gave us such a fright!"

Dot stood with her hands on her hips. "Have you been in that closet all this time?"

"Stevie," said his mother, "why did you scare us so?" She lifted Stevie, hugged him, put him down and went back into his Daddy's room.

Daddy died today. Can't tell mother that I cause people to die. I make people think in funny ways from their faces. Mother comes back from dead-Daddy's room. Can't look at Mother's face.

"Does Stevie want to see his Daddy one more time?" said Mother with her eyes watering.

"It's the last time," said Granma.

"Gladys ... Mama ... Stevie's so young. Maybe not," said Aunt Dot.

"Do you, Stevie?"

Stevie looked puzzled. He looked around. "Where's Uddie?" He wanted Uddie. His Mother and Granma looked at each other.

"Here's Uddie, Stevie," said Ev'lyn who picked up the rag dog off the closet floor and handed it to Stevie.

"Stevie, one last time to see Daddy?" said Granma.

After while some came. Two men Stevie had never seen before. Two men came to take Daddy away. Stevie went to the kitchen. Stevie stayed in the kitchen. He stayed in the kitchen with Uddy.

Epiglimselogue Eight

Sally spoke up: "I can see what was going on here. The mother had just seen her husband pass away and turned to have her children close by her. There's Neel and Dave, 'but where's my little Stevie? Dear God!'"

"And of course, here around, just taking refuge from what he senses is painful," adds Lisa. "So there he stays away from that which he cannot understand. In the closet's darkness, he can hug his little stuffed animal Uddy and wait for happier times to come."

"That's true," said James. "What do you think about that bit when Stevie is looking in certain ways, bringing on death?"

"Certainly," said Rupert. "A child's myth. I had a few of those myself when I was a kid. I thought that if I went down the neighbor's back alley, I would bring sorrow unto my family. There was something about that back alley that threw fear into me. Perhaps I was told never to go down there. I did once, and when I got home, all hell broke loose. Things were bad and, of course, they had nothing to do with my venture down that alleyway."

"Childhood myth," said Sally. "This gives us an insight into primitive myths."

"True," said Anne. "A little anthropology?" She looked over at James. "So what was this myth about?"

"I don't know, really. If that someone Stevie was looking at had a funny expression on his face, Stevie would think of what it was that person was all about. He felt he shouldn't do this, that this might make them or somebody die. Weird, eh?"

"Oh my," said Sally. "What a burden to carry around! So Stevie thought he had something to do with his father's death?"

"True," said James.

"We want to think we have more influence over events than we really do," said Ben. "For years while I was growing up, I thought that I caused my mother and father's divorce. I thought so from nine to eighteen, and then It took a shrink to get that out of my head."

'I can assure you, Ben,' he said, 'you had nothing to do with your mother and father's divorce. Ask your father,' he said, 'since he's the one that went for the divorce,' he said. So I did, and my father said, 'Ben, if it hadn't been for you and your brother and sisters, we would have divorced years sooner than we did.'"

"So much for childhood myth," concluded James.

David, Neely and Stevie Lose Their Daddy

GLIMPSES NINE

FIRING RIFLES

It was a ceremonial funeral, one fit for a war hero. Harry had joined the army during the First World War and now, some eighteen years later, was being buried at the Jefferson Barracks National Cemetery. Their mother had seen to it that the boys were all dressed in their best. Harry had been prepared for rest at White's Funeral Home on Natural Bridge Road in Normandy. Gladys, Harry's widow and their three children along with Aunt Dot and Uncle Art and their oldest cousin Pat, who was eleven, two years older than Neely, attended the funeral. Stevie stayed in the back of the funeral home room with his grandmother. The other boys walked with their mother to the front to see Harry for the last time. Now it was the next afternoon. All was ready. A dozen soldiers with rifles on their shoulders were marching into position. Rows and rows of tombstones stood on both sides, and a fresh mound of earth beneath a young sapling lay in the middle.

On the moderate November day, with their rifles on their shoulders, the soldiers marched up and came to a halt at the near side of the grave. Next, a hearse appeared, moving slowly and into position on the gravel road; it pulled to a stop on the far side of the open grave. Four soldiers came up from behind, unloaded the long box Stevie learned was a casket and moved it into position by the great hole in the ground.

It was sunny but a little chilly that day. Stevie wore a white sailor suit with short pants while his big brothers wore white shirts with ties and dark-blue long pants, and they all looked "very nice," said their Aunt Dot. Stevie's white sailor suit had a blue collar, and his hair was "greased down" so that the breeze couldn't ruffle it. The four soldiers lifted the casket up and topped the gaping hole in the ground with their Daddy's coffin; it was placed on planks with ropes so that it could be lowered down into the hole. A man spoke sad words. Then the soldiers aimed their rifles into the sky and fired. The loud bangs echoed across the fields. Beyond the ridge, Neely said, was the river. Could the bangs be heard at the river, the river that Stevie could not see but could imagine? The soldiers fired again and the echoes floated far away. This field was Jefferson Barracks. Barracks were where soldiers stayed. But Stevie did not see barracks. The soldiers fired again. If Stevie were over the ridge there and was wading at the river's edge, could he hear the loud bangs and see the water ripple? The soldiers lowered their rifles.

"Why did the soldiers fire the guns, Mother?"

"Because your daddy served in the army. Sh-h-h."

"Daddy was a soldier," whispered Dave. Neely said nothing. His lips were tightly drawn. Neel is a soldier too, thought Stevie. That was the look so typical of him.

Two soldiers folded the flag into a triangle. With clicking of heels, a soldier handed the triangle to their mother. Then the four men slid out the planks, took hold of the ropes, and lowered the coffin. Their Mother cried. Mother cried because daddy was in the coffin, and she would never see him again. Then a red and white bouquet of flowers was laid on the mound of dirt that was to be shoveled on top of their Daddy's coffin. The flowers had large blossoms. These were red and white with blue ribbon around them. A dog barked in the distance. The wind picked up. Goose bumps rose on Stevie's bare legs and arms.

On Monday, Gladys began four weeks of training on a comptometer business machine. This would qualify her for a job which had not yet opened up, but her math skills put her high on the list.

It was Christmas Eve and snowing when Gladys finished her first week of training. She had very little money to get them through until she could start earning a salary. Their life insurance agent had overlooked the fact that premiums had not been paid for nearly a year, and the company paid $700, which bought a little time for Gladys to become a qualified employee of A & P. The drawn-out death, nearly two years, meant numerous debts that the $700 could not settle. The worst was the rent. The rent money was three months in arrears, and the landlord was giving Gladys until Monday to come up with at least one month's rent or move out. "I have bills too, you know!" the landlord told her in disgust. Through the graces of Pevely Dairy, milk continued to be delivered even though the bill had not been paid for nearly six months. Growing boys need milk, Gladys kept reminding herself. Could she go on for a few more months with paying very little on the bills?

The temperature dropped below freezing during the day while she was at training; she scolded herself for not preparing for the cold. It was, after all, December. And then there were these six weeks since Harry's death; so much was needed doing that Gladys hardly knew if she was coming or going. But soon she would have a job, and now the insurance money was delayed in coming and deducting a month's rent from what was left of what little savings they had left her with only a little over twelve dollars for food and bus fare for the next week. Other bills, of course, had to wait. And now, Christmas Eve, and she had not a single present for the children. What was she to do? Disappoint them? Could she stand to see yet another disappointment in their faces tomorrow morning, that most important morning in a child's eyes? There would still be an hour or so left to buy something after she got home. She must do what she could.

Finally, after what seemed like forever, she arrived home to find Granma in the kitchen and no sign of the boys.

"They went to the basement a while ago, Neel and Dave—"

Gladys spoke quickly, quietly, "With all that's been going on ... and tomorrow being Christmas ... I haven't gotten those boys a single ..."

Granma practically in hysterics, "Well, I declare! You haven't bought those kids anything? What have you been thinking of?"

"I haven't had a pay check yet. Mama."

"Well, land's sakes, what are you going to do now?"

"If you'll give the boys some dinner and watch things for a while, I'll run to the stores and see if I can get them a few presents. Some stores are still open, with the last-minute sales ... maybe they'll be wanting to get rid of some things super cheap."

"Well, you don't want to be spending a lot on those boys. You don't have it to spend. And don't be too long. This cold house gives me such chilblains, and those boys just don't care how much pain I'm in."

Gladys called down the basement stairs. "You boys get that furnace going. We need some heat up here, for heaven sakes!"

Not seeing Stevie behind the large box, mother rummaged through the clothes to find her winter coat. "Whew! Moth balls. Seems to be my perfume these days." She donned the coat, checked her purse, and went out into the snowy evening. Seeing that the streets and walks were already becoming slippery, she cursed herself for not grabbing her galoshes as well while she was at the winter box, already feeling dampness through her stockings and her feet growing cold. It was normally not a long walk to the stores, but in the winter storm, it took longer, what seemed like hours.

She spotted the decorative lights at the corner. "Thank heaven one store at least is still open," she said, and shortly she entered the Five-and-Ten. There was not another person in the store.

"We're closing in ten minutes, Mam."

"So soon," she said, almost in tears.

"Yes, Mam. Christmas Eve, you know."

Did he have to tell her that? Was she herself not painfully aware herself of the time, the day, the hour? She scoured the counters, looking for toys and games. Nothing looked appealing. "How can I find toys for three boys in ten minutes?" She could feel a tear rolling down her cheek. She spotted a flashy little tin police car. "I bet Stevie would like to play with that, but the price was one dollar and twenty-nine cents. Way too much. It was her turn for reminders. She called out to the clerk who was rattling his fingers on the counter, "Isn't this car on sale? It's Christmas Eve, for heaven's sakes."

"That IS the mark down, Ma'am. That's already 50 percent off."

She found three pairs of gloves that looked as if they would fit her sons and "God knows they'll need them," she thought as she wiggled her wet, cold toes. "How much are these children's gloves?"

"Good sale there, mam. A dollar ten a pair."

Altogether nearly three-fifty. Too much. I'll never make it. "And this? Your best price on this?" It was a football. Neel and Dave loved football. It wouldn't hurt for this store to drop the price a little for children who'd lost their daddy. How could she express it without welling up? But the clerk said nothing. A wave of despair came over her. She was at his mercy.

He now seemed to take notice. "That football? The price is on the ticket, Ma'am. Dollar forty-nine."

No break on the price. Still, that could be a combined gift for Dave and Neel. Of course, they would fight over it; still, that was one of the advantages of having two boys close in age. And half her time was gone. Now another little something for Stevie. Neel and Dave at least had a little understanding of death and their family's circumstances. But Stevie was too young. He needed Christmas. A glittering object caught her eye. "This top is twenty-nine cents?"

"That's a yo-yo, mam, Ma'am. Twenty-nine cents, as marked."

Yo-yo of course. Did he have to keep saying "as marked," for God's sake! "Oh, those marbles over there—Stevie likes marbles." She picked up the little bag and turned it over. "Now I know there's no price on these."

"Those are thirty-nine cents for the set, mam." Growing irritation was evident in his voice. It seemed to say, "Lady, don't you know it's Christmas Eve, and we have our own families to go to?"

She shook it off. Why couldn't he throw those in gratis? Just little balls of glass. Sand really. She continued to look around.

The clerk shrugged. "I'm sorry, Ma'am, but I have to close now."

Hastily, she brought the items to the counter, including the three pairs of gloves. The clerk began adding them up. "Let's see, dollar and twenty-nine cents for the car, three and thirty for the gloves—"

"I better eliminate the gloves," she said, but suddenly she caught sight of the falling snow out the large window, "No, wait—what am I thinking!—they need the gloves. Include the gloves."

"Three and thirty for the gloves—that is, let's make that three-even for the gloves," he said magnanimously. "Then, a dollar-forty-nine for the football, twenty-nine cents for the yo-yo and thirty-nine cents for the set of marbles—let's see, that comes to six dollars and sixty cents with tax."

She frowned. What can I do? That leaves me less that $5.00 for all of next week—bus fare, lunches, everything.

"Say, why don't we round this off to six dollars even."

Her eyes filled with tears. "Thank you, Mr.—?"

"Groker."

"Mr. Groker. I really appreciate it." Anybody else wouldn't cut the price in half, she thought.

"Merry Christmas, Ma'am."

"Merry Christmas. Thank you again."

"That's all right, Ma'am."

The snow was heavier now, and with her feet slipping with every step, Gladys felt she would be happy just to get home in one piece and to warm up in bed. She had to be careful. All she needed was to be laid up with a broken leg. She'd lose the opportunity for the job and add a doctor's bill to her pile of debts. What she had gotten for the boys' Christmas wasn't much, but at least they had something to open tomorrow morning. So it was worth it. The walk home was tedious, and finally when she did arrive home, it was past nine o'clock, and the house was still cold. She could smell the burnt wood and feel a little heat coming up the ducts, but it would take time before the house would warm up. She lit the gas burners on the stove, sat at the table and removed her shoes. She rubbed her numb toes. Where were the boys?

"Mama, are the boys in bed?"

"I tried, Gladys, but they won't mind me. They're out in back, running around in the snow—they don't care about my aching corns. They don't care what pain I'm in."

"Outside?"

She looked out the back-door window. The boys were running back and forth between the house faucet and a small slope the backyard consisted of, taking bowls of water and dumping the water to make a sheet of ice on the ground. What was it for? When they stopped and went for the sled, she realized their purpose. A sled runway. She watched for a minute to see each child take his turn, running and flopping down on the sled to slide on the new ice some fifty feet or so to the back steps.

"My turn, next!" she heard Stevie shout.

She allowed them a number of turns before intruding. She opened the door a crack. "If you boys want Christmas tomorrow, you better get in here-- now!" She no sooner used the word "Christmas," then she regretted having to say it, but it was the magic word. The boys came in at once, puffing and pulling off their jackets.

"Mother," said Neely, "can we slide again tomorrow?"

"No," said Stevie, "Tomorrow we open presents."

"Stop that! There aren't any presents!" snapped Neely. "Daddy's dead and we don't get any presents."

"But Santy Claus will come," said Stevie, his eyes watering.

"Well," said Mother, "we'll just have to wait and see," her voice half-way sinking, thinking was it enough?

When the boys had gone to bed, Neely slipped into his mother's room. "It's okay, mother. I mean that we're not getting any presents, Mother"

"Don't expect much. You know how hard things are."

"I know, Mother." He went to the door. "It's okay, Mother. Really."

She had already turned away from him. And he left. Looking in the mirror, she could see herself dry her eyes. Suddenly, Neely popped back into the room. "Mother, that thing that I told you about … You know, Wally's … tomorrow. Is it okay?"

"We'll see tomorrow."

"I mean, Stevie would .,, with Santa and all …"

"I know, Neely, now off to bed."

Neely stopped Dave before they entered the bedroom where Stevie was already getting ready for bed. Neely said quietly to Dave, "We got to tell him. It's only right."

In their bedroom, Dave said to Stevie, "I got something to tell you, but don't tell anybody."

"Is it a secret?" asked Stevie, his eyes lighting up.

Yeh. A big secret. It's only for us guys. I'll tell you real slow and see if you can get it. And if you don't get it—well, anyway. Now repeat after me. Ready?"

"Uh-huh."

"There—are you listening?"

"'There.'"

"Isn't. Got it?"

"Yeh. 'Isn't.' Is this a Christmas game, Dave?"

"Just repeat after me. Any. Got that? Any."

"Yeh. 'Any.'" This is fun, thought Stevie.

"San."

"'San.'"

"ta."

"'ta.'"

"Claus."

"Santa Claus!" shouted Stevie, proud of himself.

"Now put it all, all of it, together."

"There—oh I forgot."

"Isn't."

"Oh yeh. '"There isn't"'

"There isn't what?"

"'There isn't any?'"

"There isn't any what?"

"Santa Claus. There isn't any Santa Claus!" He was proud of himself, even more so because it seemed that his brother was glad he'd said it.

"Sh-h-h. Don't say it so loud. It's a secret. Don't tell anybody. Don't tell anybody I told you. Okay?"

"Okay." He said in a sing-song manner. "There isn't any Santa Claus."

"Now you know," said Dave. His eyebrows knitted. "So don't tell anybody."

Neel looked in. "Did you tell him?"

"Yeh. It's okay."

"Yeh," said Stevie, sounding just like Dave. "It's okay."

Those words took on a cadence in Stevie's mind: There isn't any Santa Claus, there isn't any Santa Clause, there isn't any Santa Clause. Funny. He could hear shots echoing out over the river.

That is, for the main part, what happened. The next morning was Christmas, nevertheless. The boys liked what they received in the few, small make-shift gift packages, and they made their own Christmas, this one a winter slide in the backyard. And later that day, they went to Aunt Dot's and Uncle Art's for their traditional family Christmas dinner (send up a thanks and prayer for dear Aunt Dot) and got to play with their cousins and their cousins' toys.

But something else happened that Christmas morning that was quite unexpected. About mid-morning when it seemed that Christmas was entirely over, the front door popped open, and Neely, who had disappeared twenty minutes before, stood there at the open door. In his arms was a small brown and white puppy. There was nothing distinctive about the puppy. "Just an ordinary cur," some would say. It certainly was no pedigree. It would never win any canine show prizes. It was a plain brown and white mutt, actually, with a tail that curled up over its back, and hence, the boys quickly named it" Curley." But that little ball of fur, with the licking-est tongue in existence, was, on that Christmas Day—seventy-six years ago now, a beginning; clearly, it was love at first sight. For the next seven years of its life, the little pup became a prize to all the Fulbrights and to Stevie most of all, who had another eight months before he could start to school, that little four-legged mutt, the little ball of fur, became his most loyal and affectionate companion.

When they saw Stevie play with the little fellow, they all agreed, Grandma, Aunt Dot, Uncle Art and their mother: "It was certainly God's gift to a little boy," on an otherwise bleak Christmas day of 1936.

Epiglimselogue Nine

"I see. His real live dog Curley takes the place of Stevie's make-believe dog Uddie," said Sally. "Life went from life to death with make-believe and back to life again."

"I can see …," said Lisa, "this is where most likely Steve became a lover of pets."

"True. Most all animals, actually, to this day. And all the life around us."

"We can see, too, that Gladys has been left with her hands full," said Ben.

"Indeed," replied James. "Had she some other means to sustain them, she could have followed her career as a pianist. This was her natural gift, her talent, but a few more years were needed to cast her as a concert pianist."

"But she made her choice when she decided to have you kids," said Lisa. "She made herself vulnerable. She placed herself at the mercy of chance."

"Sure," said Sally. "We have to maintain our focus, make careful choices. Perhaps she could have sustained her musical career by sheer determination."

"How could she?" said Rupert. "She had to take a nine-to-five job to put food on the table. No getting away from it. Sure, she and Harry wanted children, and it might have worked out if he hadn't died."

"Was it her fault or his fault that he had to die?" asked Ben.

"Maybe," replied Rupert. "If you're going to have a batch of kids, you have to be ready for serious sacrifices. How did he contract Hodgkins? You said, James, that he and Gladys joined the in-set, drinking beer and smoking."

"True. That all happened before Steve was around or capable of witnessing it. But he remembered many years later that his brother Neel said, when he himself was dying from lung cancer, 'The damn things should be illegal.' Of course such knowledge came too late for both father and son. Not for us, the younger ones. We had the benefit of medical science."

Rupert shrugged. "Science or no science, people should know their bodies and eliminate dangerous exposure, dangerous habits."

"But, Rupert, you understand how they would be duped by their times? Moving to the city, swinging with that jazz music, defying prohibition, enjoying naughtiness!"

Rupert guffawed. "No excuses. Nature doesn't honor excuses."

"Consequences are consequences!" added Sally.

GLIMPSES TEN

AUNT JESSE

Saturday morning found Dot rushing over to learn the news first hand.

"I've got a job!" exclaimed Gladys. "A & P downtown. Another woman is quitting, and I start—two weeks from Monday."

"Wonderful! How far away?"

"With A & P's main office downtown, a thirty-minute bus ride."

"The last six weeks' training paid off quick. But how about the boys?" asked Dot.

"When the fall comes, they'll be in school most of the day. Stevie turns five on the second of September, and he starts to kindergarten at Garfield Elementary, where Dave is. Dave'll be in second grade."

"So you're going to keep the boys with you."

"Well, I don't know what else to do. I can't turn them over to an orphanage, just like that."

"But no one would blame you, Gladys, if you did. What's happened is downright tragic! Unbearable. Harry's long-suffering illness and his terrible death."

This was a dash of cold water. Dot was right. It was like bringing Gladys back to reality. Gladys became pensive, rose up, and checked the coffee.

Finally she blurted, "I've thought about it until I'm sick. I haven't been able to cry. Not since the funeral. You know, Harry'd lived only half a life. And we'd just started our family and had so much to look forward to.."

"It certainly isn't fair," averred Dot.

She poured them cups of coffee. A child was heard calling out in the back yard. Suddenly Gladys perked up, "I just can't wallow in self-pity. I have children to raise. I have to go on."

"Well, Gladys, I hate to bring it up, but what about money? Is there anything left of the life insurance money?"

"If it weren't for our insurance man Mr. Wilson paying the last few months of our premiums himself, I wouldn't have received anything. We'd have been a charity case, for sure. Anyway, I've made a start with it. $800 sure doesn't go very far in this day and age. Out of it, I paid the funeral expenses—thank God, the burial and plot were taken care of by the Veterans—and I paid our bills for the two months while we moved twice and got my training while Mama looked after Stevie and the older boys when they got home from school."

"I'm glad you got out of the city."

"No more glad than I am. When Stevie got hit with a brick—"

"What's this?"

"Oh? Didn't Mama tell you? The boys hit a ball over the fence into the next-door neighbor's backyard, and Stevie went to get it. A boy came around the garage and threw a brick at Stevie for no reason at all. Just like that! It hit Stevie right in his face. Stevie screamed and bled something awful. He came in covered with blood. Fortunately, the brick missed his eyes—just by an inch. That's when I knew I had to get the boys out of that awful neighborhood."

"I heard him in the backyard just now. Is Stevie okay?"

"Yes, but we had to take him to the hospital for stitches—seven of them. Just below the eye."

Silence ensued. Dot shook her head with disdain and pity. "Land's sake." She sipped her coffee. "So I guess your savings are all gone."

"Most of what little we had went for bills on necessities while

Harry was still alive. Look." Gladys took dollars out of her purse and spread them out on the table. She counted them. "I have seventy-six dollars left." She dumped coins out and separated them. "And ninety-seven cents. But the rent for this month is paid, thank heaven! And I've got a job." Children's laughter from the backyard wafted on the breeze through the window. She looked around at the opposite walls and ceiling of the kitchen as if she could see the house, yard and whole neighborhood in one sweeping view. "We've got a decent place to live now, I think. We're out of that hellhole of the city. And with the last of the money, I want the boys and me to get away."

"What do you mean, Gladys?"

"Take the boys somewhere. For a week. Away from St. Louis. Away from memories ... and tragedies."

"Where to?"

"Helen McCord, my old college friend, has often invited us down to Marionville to stay with her family for a few days. That's where the boy's father grew up, you know. I'm taking her up on her offer. I got enough money for the bus fare to take me and the boys down there and back. And we're going first to spend a few days with the boy's Aunt Jesse, then on to Springfield, where Helen will pick us up and take us on to Marionville." She laughed ironically. "I'll have almost nothing to spend on the trip, but I'll pack a picnic basket, and we can buy a few things at the grocery stores along the way."

"Gladys, a trip is a wonderful idea. I can let you have a few dollars." She reached for her purse.

"No, no, Dorothy, you've three of your own. You need the money yourself. No, we'll manage."

"Well, do you think Harry's relatives will offer to help you out?"

"It would be nice, but I can't plan on it."

"Isn't this Aunt Jesse you're going to see the wealthy sister?"

"She was wealthy at one time when she was with her first husband. She and her most recent husband have left their posh home on Lindell near Forest Park and taken up a country life near Camdenton at the Lake of the Ozarks. She's married to a Dr. Schultz, ENT. He's opened a practice in Camdenton. Living there is really different for a society lady like Jesse."

"Say, wasn't Jesse the sister that said she would never speak to Harry again?"

"Yes, she's the one."

"The one you said was kind of off in the head?"

"Acts strange, yes. She went about suing everybody under the sun. She's one tough lady. And getting divorces and remarrying multiple times. The latest one, this husband is number four, I believe."

"Good Heavens! And you're going to visit her—with the boys?" Gladys was silent. "Still, she must be a woman of some wealth."

"Harry said not. She went through a fortune paying legal fees. As I said, she's always suing somebody over something or rather. But seldom if ever wins her case. Harry said Jesse was trying to show she knew the law as well as he. 'Always feeling competitive with me,' Harry said, 'she tries to outdo me in legalities.' Jesse's the one that has always said, 'I can lick my weight in wildcat!' Back in Marionville, even in her youthful days, she was known as Jesse I-can-lick-my-weight-in-wildcat Fulbright."

"Well, I don't know about you and the boys going to see this woman, staying in her house, eating at her table."

"I know, but her letters have been decent if she is a bit strange."

"Well, good luck."

"Thanks. I hope we won't be needing it." They laughed.

On a nice sunny day, Wednesday morning of May the 22nd, on Market Street, Gladys and the three boys boarded a Greyhound bus bound for the Ozarks. With the last of the passengers aboard, the bus's low rumble revved up, and the large silver coach pulled away. Inside the crowded bus, about ten rows back, Stevie sat next to the window. Beside him was his mother, and in the seat in front of them, the two older boys sat. While the engine droned away, Stevie cupped his hands about his face, and with the tip of his nose flattened against the window, he watched the buildings, houses, streets and people floating by, leaving Gladys alone with her own thoughts.

It had been a long time since she had come this way before—nearly eleven years. That was when she left the small log cabin that she and Harry had moved into right after they married. She brought their first child, Neely, when he was a baby, to start their new life in St. Louis. Harry had preceded her to take up a position in the law firm of Stanley Sidmond.

Now, it wasn't long before their bus broke out of the stopping and starting of the stoplights and city streets and cruised out into the open country. She thought of herself on the bus on this same road, Highway 66, speeding her northeast in the opposite direction. Life was full of hope and promise in those days, those days before the Depression and Harry's prolonged illness and death. She remembered when they picked out that nice two-story house in the suburbs, out on Oakridge Road, put money down on the house and moved in. What sheer luxury after primitive living in a log cabin, and now, too, they were within a fifteen-minute drive to Wellston, where Harry's law firm was located. Harry drove his Model T Ford to work every day. It wasn't long after they moved in that they were expecting their second child, David. Less than three years after his birth, they were expecting a third, and two years after that, they learned that Harry had Hodgkin's, and two years later, came his death.

At one time, she thought she would never want to leave Oakridge, but since Harry's death, she was desperate to get away. And at last, they were getting away. But it was not just getting away, she admitted to herself. Dot had put her finger on it—as iffy as it might be. She had to think of the boys. Maybe Jesse would help her, or maybe put her in touch with other members of Harry's family who would help her. And while she was in the southwestern part of the State, maybe she could contact and see some of Harry's other relatives.

She felt it would be sad for the boys to be cut off from the Fulbright side of the family altogether. The Fulbrights had such a fine tradition, such fine connections. Of course, she would not ask them for any kind of help or expect it; after all, what kind of a family would ignore a brother's death and his widow left with three young children to raise? The chances of help were slim. Although she had taken great pains to notify all of Harry's relatives about his illness, death and funeral, so far no one had come forward with any kind of attention. Maybe that was because contact had been lost because of his previous marriage and subsequent divorce, and maybe because of Harry's prolonged illness. No one responded except one, that is, Harry's sister Jesse, nearly ten years older than Harry. Gladys exchanged letters with Jesse, who invited her and the boys to visit her and her husband "the doctor"—it sounded good to Gladys—William Schultz, M. D., for a few days in the Ozarks on their way to Springfield.

In the seat in front, Neel and Dave started getting antsy, scooting around a lot and then punching each other.

Gladys called out, sticking her head around the seat, "You boys play a game or something!" They stopped their roughhouse for a moment, and she leaned back.

She was learning every day that raising three boys on her own, considering what she had already been through, was not going to be any picnic. "Turn those boys over to an orphanage, Gladys. You can't do that on your own," she had been told by several well-meaning friends. "You're still young and have a life of your own to live." And there was Dot's persistent advice: "Get some of Harry's relatives to help out. They've done nothing to help during his illness!" And her friends persistently advised her to marry again, "while you're still young and have your looks," Perhaps they were right. But who would want a thirty-two year-old widow with three young boys to raise? At the first inkling, a man would take to his heals. She chastised herself: with Harry so recently in his grave, one couldn't even begin to think about taking a new husband.

What about an orphanage? If she turned them over to an orphanage, she could meet some one and remarry. Yet how could she turn her very own children over to someone else to raise? Then again, if she could bring herself to turn them over to an orphanage, if she were to remarry, perhaps she could get the boys back again, one at a time—

"Look, mother, see the horses!" Stevie pointed out the window.

"Yes, and you'll see horses at Aunt Helen's too."

No, she thought. They had no money, but she would keep her family together as long as she possibly could. Now she had a job. There was some good luck at last.

The boys' voices ahead of her were loud. They were arguing, probably over something senseless, she surmised. They frequently argued over something senseless. Soon they would be in school most of the day. She had to get someone to see to them after school until she got home. I'll think about that later, she decided. Take each problem in turn, she told herself. Something will work out.

As she dozed, an image of Jesse Schultz came before her eyes. Jesse looked as she had in a painting, one done in the manner of society women, the one where she appears in her Parisian gown. In Gladys' doze, Jesse's haughty manner turned to a sneer. "I'll sue you!" she shouted. "I'll sue for every cent you have!" It jarred Gladys to consciousness.

Yes, and what about the insane Jesse Schultz whom they were soon to see? Was Gladys really wise to accept Jesse's invitation? It was Jesse that Harry had had a falling out with over their inheritance. Harry's mother and father died within six months of each other. The farm and all its contents were sold and divided among the four children, but Jesse insisted some of the family heirlooms had been promised to her and her alone by their mother. Harry objected. Such was not spelled out in the will. In the end almost everything was sold and the money divided among them. "It was all Harry's doing!" Jesse swore that she'd never speak to Harry again.

In the early stages of Harry's illness, Gladys had gone to Jesse's former, elegant home on Lindell Avenue, St. Louis, near Forest Park, and rang the doorbell. For an instant, she espied someone looking out the upstairs window. After her persistent knock, she heard Jesse's voice screaming out from inside. "Don't let that hussy in here!" Gladys went away without receiving a single how-do-you-do. Regarding Harry, Jesse had kept her word; she never saw him again alive, but Gladys was surprised that Jesse came to the funeral and expressed her condolences, brief though they were, and that had paved the way for the coming visit. Perhaps Jesse with her own divorces had come to a better understanding of Gladys.

Then, too, there came to Gladys the image of Jesse, this older sister, as quite the St. Louis socialite. How well she dressed. Very upper class. And how emotional she was. Her loud attention-getting laugh and, too, her sudden break into sadness and even crying. She was her flamboyant self with her dear friends, the famous Bartlett's, Mr. Bartlett who founded the Dye and Shine Company, which he had sold off at great profit, and his wife whom Jesse called "Tootsie."

Before the trip, Gladys had warned the boys not to be surprised if their Aunt Jesse should swing from intense delight and hilarity to sudden weeping. Gladys began to doubt the wisdom of this side trip.

Suddenly, she opened her eyes and glanced out the window. The bus was slowing.

"Next stop Camdenton!"

Could that be true? It couldn't have been three hours since they left the station. Already to Camdenton? Somehow, she wasn't ready to see Jesse. Where had those hours gone? The terrain became quite hilly, and now they saw the lake in all its richness below in the distance, winding its way around the hills. It was a beautiful lake, glistening in the afternoon sun, with a few white clouds drifting at peace. A few cabins and cottages dotted the way.

Soon, "Camdenton!" called out the bus driver.

It was a small town indeed, but charming. A drugstore, grocery store, a gas station and a half dozen modest shops and houses. They pulled up just before a bus stop sign. The bus doors swung open, and the driver spun round in his seat. The chirpings of birds marked the pleasant silence.

Suddenly, seemingly from nowhere, came the roar of a powerful car engine. A large black sedan, a Pierce Arrow, swerved around the bus and skidded to a halt in front, dust and gravel flying. All eyes and attention focused on the dissipating cloud in front of them, the bus driver no less astonished as his passengers. Before the dust had fully settled, a figure popped out of the large black sedan and briskly strode to the doors of the bus. It was a woman! And although she was not exceptionally tall or husky she seemed to command everything in view. She took the bus steps in stride, ignored the astounded bus driver, and stood tall as a general at the head of the troops. The passengers sat in awe.

Then the woman's centurion voice brought them to full attention. "Is my sister-in-law, Mrs. Harry Wilks Fulbright, on this conveyance?!" Without waiting for a answer, she informed them, "Mrs. Harry Wilks Fulbright and her three sons are my late brother's family, the eldest William Neely Halstead Fulbright III carrying the distinguished family name." Although this greeting was seemingly cause for a spontaneous round of applause, no one made a sound. But Aunt Jesse was in no way diminished. "Harry Wilks, my distinguished brother, was of the same family as J. William Fulbright, outstanding law professor at George Washington University in our nation's capital, Washington D. C. [as if people didn't know what the nation's capital was] the cousin of Judge James Fulbright of Springfield, distinguished judge of thirty years, all descendants of John Fulbright who founded Springfield in 1846."

"Who are they, Mother?" asked Stevie.

"She means us. Grab Uddy and your bag there."

All eyes swung around to directly focus on the Fulbrights, Gladys and her boys, who were stirring out of their seats, eyes that seemed to say, "Really? Are these the famous personages?"

But Jesse wasn't finished yet. Her demeanor and voice exceeded that of an evangelistic tour guide. "The Fulbrights originate from Johann Wilhelm, who came to this country in 1740 at Philadelphia port of entry. We have documents!" Jesse exuded knowledge and energy with every syllable and every breath. "Yes, documents!" She asserted as if someone had challenged her, which no one on the bus in their furthest imagination was about to do.

"We better hurry off," whispered Gladys to the boys, "before we get enshrined."

Stevie looked wide-eyed at his mother. "What's 'enshrined,' Mother?"

"Never mind. Just move!"

Epiglimselogue Ten

"Aunt Jesse was a case!" Lisa said, shaking her head. "Was she really that overbearing?"

"Yes," replied James. "I'm not exaggerating. But she had her own cross to bear. It is hard for us to understand. You will hear. Would we somehow be all the better for having known her?"

"Her own tragedy could explain a lot," rejoined Lisa.

"Yes," said James, "she was a genuine eccentric. A Dickensian type. The Gladys Fulbrights had never known anyone like her. You should have seen the fuss she made over the Bartlett's, the retired Shoe Shine magnate. Mrs. Bartlett she called " my dear Tootsie!" And she and this woman, when they met, were always so dolled up, you wouldn't believe it. Have you ever seen the fashion ads from the 1920s? Sights to behold! You'd be amazed."

"I quite like her already," said Lisa.

"Wait til you hear," said James.

GLIMPSES ELEVEN

JESSIE AND LACHRYMOSE

"All aboard! Hold on to your seats!" Aunt Jessie peeled with laughter. She gunned the Pierce Arrow and off they flew. With the windows wide open, down the narrow road they flew at eighty miles an hour so it seemed. Gladys in the front passenger seat held on for dear life. Eyes wide, mouths agape, the boys, Neel, Dave and Stevie in the back, clung to their seats in sheer wonder and delight! In a few minutes, the black sedan skidded around onto an unpaved, even narrower country road and spun off with gravel, dirt and dust flying like there was no tomorrow. Gladys began to wonder if Jessie had invited them there to do away with herself and her brother's family all in one grand Wagnerian swoop.

Yet Jesse, grey hair flying, blue eyes intense, steered with the finesse and skill of a race car driver in the Indy 500.

"Down to Aunt Jessie's lair!" she screamed with laughter.

"Yeh!" exclaimed Dave.

"Yeh!" Stevie didn't know what lair meant, but figured that it must be something neat if Dave liked it.

The Arrow slowed around a bend. Then Jessie shouted, "Little ducks, you better skee-daddle!" She gunned the Arrow nearly fricasseeing a whole family of mallards.

Neel whispered, "Mother, is this a society lady?"

"Sh-h-h."

When they jerked around and in through a narrow opening in a barbed wire fence, slamming on the brakes and sliding to a halt amid a cabin, a chicken house, a small barn and a well, while a half dozen chickens barely made it to safety, Gladys was already trying to figure out how to make the return trip to the Greyhound bus stop without the services of Aunt Jessie's Pierce Arrow.

"This is it, folks, country estate of Jessie and the Doctor!"

"Wow!" exclaimed Dave after Jessie bounced out of the car and was on her way around to open their doors. "Can we do that again?"

"Sh-h-h-h!" said their mother, as reprimandingly as she could without raising her voice.

Jessie swung open their doors. "Shultz's terminal! All out!" She pealed with laughter.

"You've a neat car, Aunt Jessie," said Dave, scooting out from his seat with genuine admiration.

"You like cars, little man? You should have seen my '28 roadster. What a doozie! Drove 'er in forty-two states. Couldn't get parts in West Texas. Had to come back to St. Louis and never made it to New Mexico. Of course, I took 'er to Maine, Florida, Washington and California. I hold the record for cross-country safe driving!" On the last words, she nearly choked. Tears began to well up in her eyes. "When you boys grow up and start driving, you'll always drive safely to please your Aunt Jesse, won't you?"

She brightened suddenly. "Who wants some of Jesse's down-home lemonade. The Doctor says it's the finest lemonade in the whole county."

"That'd be nice," said Gladys, anxious to get out of the hot sun and away from the metal demon.

"Come along for Jessie's famous lemonade!" She pealed with laughter. She swung the screen door wide. "Come in! Come in! Now where is the Doctor? Doctor Schultz! I always call him 'the Doctor' out of respect. Doctor Schultz!"

Inside, the little cottage looked more like a storage house than a domicile, it was so packed with furniture, pictures, mirrors and other household belongings. "Come along—right through here." In her floral gown ill-suited for housework, Jesse glided the way down a narrow path through the furniture. The adjoining room, the dining room, was similarly packed with furniture except that a twelve-place dining table dominated. A pitcher of lemonade sat in the middle. Alongside it was a bowl of oatmeal cookies. The table was set with six blue glasses with gold rims and six party napkins.

"The Doctor is out back," said Jessie. "I'll go 'fetch him in." Those are the words of great Aunt Carie. 'Go fetch 'im in', she'd say. 'fetch 'im in!' " Jessie stepped through the small kitchen and opened the back screen door. "Doctor Schultz! Your Sugar Plum is back with Gladys and Harry's sons! Doctor Schultz!" She turned back. "He always calls me his sugar plum!" She laughed and a tear rolled down her cheek. She turned back. "Ah, here's the Doctor now."

Doctor Schultz entered, tall, elderly, with white hair, small white mustache, looking every bit a gentleman. He smiled a gold-tooth smile.

"This is the Doctor. That is, Doctor Schultz, and this is Gladys, my dear departed brother's wife and widow, and these are his three young, handsome sons."

"Yes?" He smiled.

"The Doctor is a little hard of hearing, you know. A wonderful man, a fine doctor. A little hard of hearing." Now she shouted in his ear, "Sister-in-law Gladys and sons!"

"Yes, yes." His front gold tooth glittered. His face changed to taut and then a smile. "Did you have a nice ride?"

Gladys replied, "Yes, Doctor, the boys enjoyed it immensely."

Dr. Schultz looked puzzled.

Jessie leaned to his ear. "She said the boys liked it!"

"Yes, yes. Good." He smiled again.

"We're all sitting down to some lemonade, Doctor. Will you join us?"

"Yes, yes." He moved into the dining room and sat in the large chair at the head of the table.

When they were all seated, Jessie poured the lemonade.

"Doctor Schultz, shall I tell them how we met?" She blushed like a sixteen-year-old virgin. "Shall I, Doctor?"

Despite his solemn look, he seemed to nod in agreement.

"Well, I was in the hospital with a terrible illness. This was before I knew Doctor Schultz. You see I had this terrible illness and was in the hospital—at death's door—when a Doctor William Schultz took charge of my case and pulled me through. It was a miracle. Other doctors had given me up for dead. The Doctor is a brilliant doctor, you know. Well, he pulled me through this terrible illness, and while I was recovering, he came into my room to inquire about me, his star patient. And I said, 'Oh Doctor, I'm so worried about my bill. How much is my bill?' And he said, 'Oh, my dear, it is a big Bill!' You see, his name is William Schultz. He goes by Bill, you see. And he said, 'Oh, it's a big Bill!'" She pealed with laughter. She shouted into the Doctor's ear. "I told them about your marriage proposal. 'Oh, it's a big Bill!' you said." Jesse's laughter rang out so that one would think the cottage would collapse around them.

The Doctor smiled, his gold tooth glittering. "Yes, yes."

The boys smiled broadly. Gladys managed to break into a smile. Jesse settled into drinking her lemonade.

Dave glanced around the rooms and said, "Aunt Jesse, you have lots of furniture," to which Gladys quickly added, "Very nice furniture it is, too."

"Oh, my dear, it is such a shame we had to sell so much. Priceless furniture. No room for it all, you know. I kept our most valuable pieces. The bedroom set, this dining set, the old clock that belonged to the boys' great-grandfather. Priceless pieces. The pride of St. Louis our house was on Lindell, you know. A lovely home." Here her eyes welled up with tears. "It was so sad to have to leave there, the good old times, the teas, balls, garden parties. Grandfather Fulbright would turn over in his grave if he knew how we had to change our lives."

"Still you have lovely pieces remaining, Jessie," observed Gladys.

Jesse became meditative. Suddenly she said, "Harry left you money?" The question seemed to come out of the blue. "You have an income?"

Gladys' reply was prompt. "No. But I'm starting a job when we return. And I have my piano teaching."

"Oh my dear, you are so talented."

"Well, I think we'll manage."

"You're a young, pretty woman; you will marry again."

Gladys smiled. "No prospects, I'm afraid."

"Now Gladys, you really should apply for an Indian pension. The boys have Indian blood on both sides of their family. One quarter Indian. The pension would be a great help to you for bringing up the boys.

"I don't think they'd quali—" said Gladys, looking around as if for an escape route.

Not the least dislodged, Jessie pressed on. "You must apply. The boys are direct descendants of Pocahontas and Captain John Smith. Mark my word. The boys are descendants of Indian royalty on both sides of their family tree. I've been a DAR all my life and I've checked into these matters thoroughly. Yes, the government owes you an American Indian pension for separating your family from their lands. And on your side, my brother told me, you are descendants of Francis Polly Poole, the daughter of a Cherokee Indian chief."

"Are we Indians, Mother!" Stevie was ready for a whumpums.

"Sit down, silly!" said Dave. "Neely's the Indian. "He's got brown eyes and dark skin."

Stevie looked at his big brother, at first wide-eyed and then with eyes of envy.

"All you boys have the same amount of Indian blood," said Jesse gulping down another draft of lemonade. "See to it when you get back, Gladys. An American Indian pension for giving up your ancestral land."

"Did we have some land, Aunt Jessie?" asked Dave. Stevie thought of the vacant lot near their house back on Ravenwood. Lots of trees and tall, spear-like weeds

"You certainly did," insisted Jessie. "And it's time to stand up for yourselves."

When the boys ran out to play, they never felt so perfectly justified acting like Indians. They pulled tall weeds out of the ground and used them to spear imaginary animals and enemies. Soon Jessie came out to fetch them fishing poles, lines and hooks so they could go fishing in the lake. Never had they seen such a giant lake. Was it an ocean? They had never seen an ocean. The boys were excited and followed their Aunt Jessie about the rustic lakeside barnyard like three ducklings.

"Now for some bait," Jessie said, looking around for a can of worms she had dug up in preparation for the boys' arrival. She found them on a ledge in the tool shed and gave the can to Stevie, who put his finger into the can and stirred the dirt to bring up some worms. Sure enough, there were a half dozen or so.

"Aunt Jessie," said Stevie, "My friend at home puts old worn out coffee grounds in the garden ... an' ol' worms come like crazy!"

"Oh, really. I must do that. We have old coffee grounds I throw out every day. And it'll bring the worms?"

"Yes Ma'am, by the hundreds an' thousands."

She smiled. "My goodness! I better start my worm garden right away."

Eventually the boys were all equipped and set on their way to the lake shore. Gladys and Jessie followed a watchful distance behind to keep check and yet to keep out of the way. The four o'clock sun sparkled across the broad branch of the Lake of the Ozarks. The boys stood on the waters' edge and cast their lines out into the water. Three round, white and red cork floats bobbled in the water.

"The boys are certainly enjoying themselves," said Gladys.

"All boys seem to like fishing. I remember when I took ... " Tears came to her eyes.

Gladys knew Jesse's tragedy and looking around thought it best to say, "It's a beautiful spot you have here, Jesse."

Jessie brightened up. "It's peaceful, but goodness ... a bit dull except with boys ..." She looked out and pointed, "Little farther, boys! Good catching up there!" It was up the coast line, she indicated.

The next morning the boys were out fishing as soon as they could. By midday Jesse, with Gladys's solicited help, brought the boys sandwiches and drinks. After lunch, the boys continued their fishing for most of the day. Late afternoon, the boys brought back to their aunt and uncle's cabin a string of fish, and Jesse accommodated the boys by having an evening fish fry.

After dinner, Jesse and Gladys conferred about old times, when Harry was a boy and his three sisters were nearly adults. Then, years later, there were Jessie and the Doctor, as she called him, living in St. Louis and following an active social calendar.

"Haven't you found it nice to get away from the busy city life?" inquired Gladys.

"Yes, and the Doctor has set up a practice here where he takes patients three days a week. But you know, I'm used to an active life. Weren't you and Harry anxious to get away from the small-town life of Marianville?"

"Yes, I was. Small town people nosey into your life."

"Well, they were shocked at Harry's abrupt leaving Mildred with two children to rear. And I'll have to say mother and father were not too pleased either. It nearly broke their hearts. They died not long—"

"But surely they didn't blame Harry for the breakup."

"He left her."

"Yes, but not until ... after she 'left him,' in a manner of speaking."

"Left him?"

"Yes, by having an affair with that neighbor—what was his name? Joy Brown?"

"Oh? Who? If small town people spread rumors, I'm disappointed that he would pay attention to them."

"It wasn't rumors." She stopped abruptly and faced Jessie in disbelief. "You mean you don't know what happened? Didn't he tell you? No, of course you don't know. Nobody did, then. But now I thought maybe everyone would know the truth."

"The truth?"

"That Harry caught the two in bed together."

"What!"

"Harry left one morning for work but came back for some papers he had forgotten. The children were playing in their room. Mildred and this man were in bed together. Harry left and never went back, except for his things."

"Why didn't he tell us?"

"He didn't want worse consequences than there already were. There were the children to think about. He didn't want to take the children away from their mother. He told me this. Whatever Mildred was, she loved the children. Harry felt that children should stay with their mother. And they should not grow up thinking the very worst about their mother. About this, he was adamant. 'Let whoever will, think bad of me,' Harry said, 'but not of their mother.' And he loved his children so."

Tears welled up in Jesse's eyes. "I never knew … and this is true? Oh my poor, dear brother. Why didn't he … ?"

"He didn't want … he was very protective."

Tears were streaming down Jesse's eyes. She rose, went out and momentarily returned with a handkerchief drying her eyes. She straightened up and asked Gladys, "How is your piano playing coming along? Harry used to praise your playing."

"It helps a little to pay the bills. Neely, too, is interested in music. We're into classics, mainly. For Neely, especially opera."

Jesse suddenly turned to Neel. "Oh my dear, music will break your heart. It will absolutely break your heart!" Jessie's eyes were watering.

Meanwhile, Neel had been looking at the large glass cabinets that contained an abundance of gold, shiny loving cups, shelf after shelf of them, each inscribed with Jesse's name somewhere in the inscription.

"What are these for, Aunt Jessie?" asked Neel.

"Oh, my dear, those are the awards I received for controlled driving. I competed all over the country."

"Jessie is known for her outstanding driving skills in national contests," offered the doctor who Gladys and sons now realized has more to say than "yes, yes."

"You must be famous?" chimed in David.

"Well," she replied, "I had to prove something to others and to myself."

The ensuing silence seemed to ask, "Prove what, Aunt Jessie? Prove what?"

Now the water-works turned on full force. Jessie wept aloud.

"I'm so sorry, Jessie," said Gladys, deeply sympathetic.

"Oh, my dear, we all have our devastating losses," murmured Jessie, doubling her fists, trying to control her emotions.

It was soon time to turn in, considering that Gladys and the boys were leaving Camdenton the next morning. It was the only time in the visit that Jesse was unable to fully recover her composure.

The next morning, the five of them spun off to the bus stop. When they said their good-byes, teary-eyed Jessie disappeared the moment after. Stevie was fascinated by the sound of the Pierce Arrow firing off and soon spinning around the corner onto the gravel road and out of sight.

"Mother," Dave asked, leaning around his seat, "Doesn't Jessie cry a lot?"

His Mother nodded, "Yes. Jesse is quite lachrymose."

Stevie who wanted to know words so he could be like his big brothers jumped on his mother's answer. "What's lack-a-moose, mother?"

She smiled. "La-chy-mose. mose, a long 'o'. It means tendency to cry. Yes, Jessie is very emotional.

"Why does she cry so much?" asked Neel over the top of his seat.

"Well, it was before you boys were born when your Aunt Jesse had her tragedy."

"Trage-- ..." uttered Stevie.

"She lost her only son."

Neel shook his head. "Aunt Jessie had a son?" He had never heard a son mentioned.

"Yes, her only child. Her pride and joy. He was only 16 years old when it happened. They lived on Lindell by Washington University. The college was having a major function. Her son was on his way to get his tux at the cleaners. He was at an intersection, crossing the road. A car came speeding around the corner and struck him. He was killed. And Jessie has never been the same since. You saw, by all the trophies she's won, she has become a driving expert."

Their bus pulled out, and soon they were humming along. The young family was on their way to Springfield, where Dave and Stevie had never been and where so much had ended and begun,

Epiglimpselogue Eleven

"Aunt Jessie was an interesting person. Did she really suffer a case of ... lachrymose?" Ben smiled when he said the word.

"Yes. About her behavior, Steve remembers this quite well. One moment, she would be quite up, excited, happy, laughing that loud laugh of hers, and the next moment she would be crying like a baby."

"And she lost her only child, the victim of a speeding car?" inquired Rupert.

"Yes. And she was never the same, their mother explained," James replied.

Sally shook her head in disbelief. "And the word lachrymose?"

"Their mother was a spelling whiz. She had top speller awards from school. Relatives have verified this. 'Gladys could spell anything!' they would say. This word, after all, has a rich tradition behind it. It is a Latin word, likely picked up from the ancient Greeks. When we speak of Greeks, we think of Niobe, as Shakespeare says, 'Niobe, all tears.' Why so? All her beloved children were shot dead by arrows. It happened that Niobe was too proud of her fourteen children, and Apollo and Diana, outraged at her bragging, shot them all dead with arrows. All Niobe could do was cry, cry, cry. Niobe, all her darling children, dead! That is poor Aunt Jesse. Her only child. Her dear son, dead at age 16.

"'It's not right to cry,' Steve's brother Dave would say. But Dave was a guy's guy. He thought crying was sissy-like."

"On the contrary," said Sally. "I think on occasion it could be quite manly to cry.

Glimpses Twelve

A WIDOW'S SUITORS

During the next several years, the widow had three suitors. The first was a manly looking fellow named Ward Kent; actually, his last name was not Kent, but he had a face like Clark Kent, and that is who the boys regarded him as. He dressed manly, like a soldier, and he always wanted to take the boys and the mother on long hikes. "Come on, boys, let's stomp in the woods!" The boys liked the idea, but hikes in the country was not their mother's idea of a great time. She smiled a lot in his presence, but she had her own thoughts. She was, or became, more the sit-at-the-kitchen-table, have-a-cigarette, a-bottle-of-beer and a-chat kind. Ward Kent's last words to the Fulbrights were, "Well, boys, I'm off to the Andes!" Stevie thought, "Up and away!"

Then there was Mr. Firmer—Mr. Firmer was a man firmly rooted in the soil. And Mr. Firmer was so when

plain ol' Ward was good enough for good ol' Ward Kent? But "Mr. Firmer" might as well have been Firmer's first name. With the boys, he had no other. Mr. Firmer this and Mr. Firmer that. And Mr. Firmer had a cabin way out in the country. Next to his rustic cabin, a natural spring flowed. The stream had been dammed up to form a beautiful, clear, deep pool and a wonderful waterfall. When Mr. Firmer drove the mother and boys out to his "little place" for a weekend, it was a most memorable experience for the boys. They couldn't wait to take their shoes off and walk out into the water that flowed like silk over the dam. Once barefooted, they waded. Oh, was it cold! Their feet turned blue. As hard as they tried, they could stand the temperature only a minute or two; then they would run to the lawn, plop down and rub their numb, aching feet. But it was heaven.

"What are those!" asked Stevie pointing to the water insect darting about with incredible speed.

"We call those 'Jesus spiders'—they walk upon the water," responded Mr. Firmer.

They certainly weren't like the creepy spiders at home, that was sure, the kind that spun webs to trap flies and bugs and hid in dark corners, the kind that'd dart out across the floor when you least expected.

"Water spiders are quick and graceful," said Mr. Firmer, "and they're purifiers. Wherever you see them, you can bet the water is clean enough to drink. Watch," he said. Mr. Firmer took a dipper off a nail in a post, dipped the water, and drank. "Ah, now that's good water."

"Me, too!" said Stevie, and Mr. Firmer handed him the dipper, and Stevie drank too. "Umm. That's good water," said Stevie. Mr. Firmer was pleased.

Imagine that, thought Stevie. The very water that the spindly creatures run on, creatures that could dart about so fast on the water that it made the water clean enough to drink. Did the spiders corral the grubby stuff? Did the grubby stuff ripple to the edge and out when the spiders ran? Or had the water spiders little scrubbers on their feet at the ends of their long legs? Could he take some spiders home to put into a pitcher of creek water from out the back of the house to make the water clean? Could he put some spiders in the creek in the woods back home to make the water clean enough to drink?

"Mother, can we take some Jesus spiders home?" Stevie asked.

"Heaven's sakes No!" she retorted.

"Why, Mr. Firmer, is the water always this cold?" asked Neely.

"From deep down, it comes right up and out of the ground," Mr. Firmer said. "It is very cold down deep in the ground."

That was a mystery to Stevie, for he had heard the ground was warm down deep? Even hot. Somewhere before you come to China. Once at home in his front yard, a man came by and looked down into a deep hole he and Stevie's friend were digging.

"It's goin' to get plenty hot down there! Don't you know that the earth's core is molten lava?" Wouldn't that make the water warm? So water this cold coming out of the ground at Mr. Firmer's didn't make sense. Still, that water in the spring, bubbling up so fresh and clear was definitely cold.

He loved to look at and feel that fresh water bubbling up. It bubbled up from the ground to form that beautiful pond, and the extra water, smooth as silk, that flowed over the dam. And the water that spilled over the dam flowed, sparkling in the sun, on down a quarter of a mile to the river which could be seen if you looked from just the right spot a little higher up the hill and down through the trees and thickets. There was nothing this marvelous at home!

Mr. Firmer was a nice person, but that friendship with Gladys, too, was short lived. Gladys explained it as "who's interested in a woman with three young boys to raise?" But really, wasn't it that Ward Kent and Mr. Firmer were outdoorsmen? This suited the boys. But such was definitely contrary to Gladys' life style. Growing up on the edge of town, she spent most of her time indoors, playing the piano, doing schoolwork, or playing teacher.

Why couldn't Stevie bring some nice water spiders home? The

answer was quite simple if you knew about her. Unknown to Stevie at the time, Gladys suffered from a case of arachnophobia. Once at home, she stopped in the middle of teaching a piano lesson and shouted to any of the boys who were home, "Quick! Come kill this big spider on the screen door!" Stevie was into spiders and all kinds of creepy creatures he could spot on his local safaris.

Stevie came running, expecting to find an enormous tarantula or maybe even a black widow, certainly some highly venomous foe. Instead, it appeared a simple garden spider, no bigger than, fully stretched out, a penny. Disappointed, he went up for a closer look to see if there was anything about it that would horrify a person. No, it was just an ordinary type. Boring.

"Watch it! It'll jump on you. Kill it! Kill it!" shouted his mother.

"Uh-huh." Stevie yawned ostentatiously, opened the door flicked it out with his finger and strolled away. The mother's arachnophobic stories became familiar. Stevie heard that when she was a girl growing up in Arkansas, she and her little sister Dot, on a mission to bring a jar of preserves up from the storm cellar used to maneuver a long stick to hook into a jar's wire holder. If they did this just right, they could hoist a jar out of the cellar and up through the open doors without having to go down into a cellar. His mother often said, "the cellar was crawling with spiders!" Outdoors-woman she was not.

The next gentleman-suitor was Dr. Collins, the dentist. He was a widower with a son and a daughter, but the son and daughter were older than Neel, and the addition of three younger children to raise, especially three boys, could be apt to prove too tedious a job. His own son and daughter were perfect. "Yes, sir," "No Sir," they always said to their father. Neely, Dave and Stevie always said "Yea" or "Nah" or "yeh" or "Nope" to whomever, including the King of England had he confronted them.

Clear enough, Gladys's three boys were, by comparison, (Faulkner's) the Snopes. Still, Dr. Collins was a nice man and maybe could be helpful to the widow if it weren't that he was a bit <u>too</u> nice a man. He did not smoke or drink and looked upon these habits with tolerant disdain. If Gladys could have been persuaded to change her habits, then he might have been nobly tempted to help raise another man's children.

But the main problem was Gladys. She could not or would not change her roaring 1920s style. Someone who would expect her to change would be a "Mr. Snooty." That smacked of the snooty Russellville religious "hypocrites." Certainly, she liked the dentist, as did the boys, but it didn't work out. Still, this male-friend lasted longer than the earlier two.

Gladys's long work hours and incessant smoking and two beers a day with no physical workouts took its toll on her appearance (and ultimately her health). She was looking less and less attractive as years went by. Who could blame her for drinking and smoking? Humphrey Bogart and Lauren Bacall did it. Besides, Gladys' two jobs and three rambunctious boys put so much stress on her that she was mentally and emotionally drained by the time she finished each day; she had little time to enjoy herself. Home time was spent doing the washing, cleaning up the house and, when she could, sitting at the kitchen table having a well-deserved beer and cigarette.

She had other jobs, as well. She played the piano at odd times on the radio to promote the sale of Baldwin pianos. The boys would tune in on their gothic radio.

"And now we present Gladys Fulbright playing on a new low-priced Baldwin grand piano Rachmanonov's Prelude in C# minor."

When the war started, the music scene was dominated by dance music like the fox-trot and the jitterbug, Glen Miller, Artie Shaw, and Benny Goodman style for the soldiers, so Gladys played piano in Al Burk's All Girl Orchestra. The band practiced in the neighborhood twice per week at night in Al Burk's basement and played for dances on Friday and Saturday nights in dance halls for the soldiers and the local women. Stevie and his friend, another waif in the neighborhood, used to lie down on the ground and watch and listen to the rehearsals through Al Burk's subterranean basement windows.

Still, Gladys' combined income was not enough to sustain her family. Almost but not quite. As Dickens' Mr. Macawber says, making one shilling over expenses means happiness, but making one shilling less than expenses means disaster. Little by little, Gladys was falling behind in payments of necessary expenses, rent, food, utilities, clothes, repairs, busfare.

This is when the forth suitor made his appearance on the scene, the least of the suitors, one Jim Rice. He was a short, tubby man, big stomach, and white hair, what there was of it; character-wise, he was pretentious and narrow-minded. When opportunity occurred, he would burst forth in song, with the harshest voice imaginable, the most tuneless talent, doing so probably in some desperate attempt to prove he was Irish. Had someone said once that since he was Irish, he must sing? He had no special Irish folk songs, just the conventional "When Irish Eyes Are Smiling" or "Mother McCreedy"—surprise, surprise, a major part of his repertoire!

Compared with Super Ward's up-and-away and Mr. Firmer's water spiders and Mr. Collin's "yes, sir and no sir [your Majesty]," this guy was a loser. A decent enough fellow, but a stale and stodgy bore. He was a short man, red faced, pompous, egotistical, narrow-minded wimp. But Jim was destined to be around for many years. Why? He picked Gladys up from work and brought her home one or more nights a week

Was Gladys mercenary? Certainly. And he bought it. He helped the widow and her three children to survive. And he didn't mind at all sitting at the kitchen table having a glass of something himself and chatting about the day's events. But above all, on an occasional Friday night, he picked her up from work, took her shopping, and even paid for some of the groceries, before taking her home. Most importantly, Gladys liked him.

"Will Jim talk about Mr. Fleshhole tonight?" asked Stevie.

"Mr. <u>Fleishel</u> is Jim's boss. Now you be nice to Jim. Jim's a good friend of the family."

"Does he always have to talk about Mr. Fleshholel?"

"Sh-h-h-h! Now behave yourself. There are times when—well,

we just couldn't make it without Jim's help. Understand? And he's taking Neel to Norwood Country Club Saturday to caddy and earn some money. So be nice. Okay?"

"Okay." But Stevie knew when Mother was out of earshot, Dave would mock Jim with, "Well-sir, I say to Mr. Fleshhole, I say, we can sign that contract and stick it ... " and they would howl with laughter.

When Neel came back from Norwood Country Club Saturday evening, he didn't look so good. He went straight to his bed and didn't say anything to anyone. Mother mentioned to Jim that poor Neel must be worn out from carrying the golf-bags for so long.

"We stopped off to buy some ice cream. I bought him some ice cream. He made three-and-a-half dollars, you know. Did all right for a boy his age. Got a tip. He'll make a fine caddie. He's a little rough around the edges, but he's got good eyes and watches the ball. That is a great help to us golfers."

"Neel, honey, don't you want some supper!" Neel shrugged.

She repeated it three times before she received a firm "No."

"Come and tell us about your new job." There was no answer. Again he shrugged. When he left the room. she mummed, "I guess he's too tired to talk."

"He's a strong boy. He can take it."

"Yes, he's strong ...," she shook her head, "but he's a sensitive boy too. He worries me sometimes. Four years and he's still not over his father's death."

Jim put his hand on her shoulder. "Does he talk about it?"

"No, and that's what worries me. When it comes up, he doesn't say anything. His lips tighten and he looks off into the distance. He feels his father's loss very deeply. It's nice that you've taken him under your wing like that. You're a good friend, Jim."

"I like to do what I can to help. He's a fine boy. Fine boy. And a handsome devil."

"Did he say anything about caddying?"

"No. But he'll make a fine caddie. He's a fine boy. Handsome devil. The girls take to him, I bet, with his dark complexion, that handsome head of dark, curly hair, that cleft in his chin—looks like Cornel Wilde, and his build. When he's a man, what a handsome dog he'll be."

She sighed deeply, "I don't like him to take things so to heart. He loves music, you know. Good music."

"He ought to appreciate his mother there. He takes after you."

The following two Saturdays were replays of the first Saturday. Jim took Neel to caddie. They came back late, and Neel went straight to bed. And in another week, Neel found a different job. He said to his mother, "I can't caddy anymore. I got a job as carryout at the A & P."

"Oh, Jim will be disappointed."

"Yea? Well, keep the fairy away from me."

"Neel, why do you say that?"

"Because he's always asking me questions."

"Like what?'

"Oh, about school and everything. He's not my father, okay?"

"Well, Jim doesn't have a family of his own. I think he would like to adopt us. I know Jim can be, at times, rather intrusive, but he means well. Jim has been a good friend to us. We never ..."

Oh well, she thought, Neel would always be nice to Jim. Neel was always respectful to adults. She needn't worry that he would hurt their relationship, she reassured herself. Besides, she could not expect Neel to ever accept someone else in the place of his real father. Again, with memories fading, of the three boys who knew their father the best, it was Neel. And there was so much that Neel, regardless of his young age, understood about her.

Epiglimpseloglue Twelve

"Neel really dislikes Jim Rice," said Rupert. "What do you suppose that is all about?"

"Why didn't Steve's mother get married when her children were young?" asked Sally.

"I don't know, but maybe her relationships never grew into that kind of maturity; otherwise, she was quite attractive enough. Jim Rice probably would have married her, but although she admired him, she found him a bit too old for her. When Harold LeMert came along, Steve was sixteen and on his way to self-sufficiency."

"Were LeMert and Gladys a good match?" asked Lilly.

"I don't know. Right away Mother and 'Pop'—the boys called him—they seemed to bicker a lot. Hal LeMert, Pop's son and friend of Steve's since the fifth grade, and Steve were often annoyed by this. They'd go out and sit on the front lawn until they figured the bickering had passed which it usually did in a short while."

"It was funny that Jim, the Irishman, didn't drink or smoke," said James.

"Yeh, That is surprising. Yet he quite tolerated such in Gladys?" inquired Lily.

"Yes. He seemed to simply enjoy Gladys' company. In the evenings he was satisfied to sit at the kitchen table with her and chat while she smoked and had her beer."

"So their mother never did give up beer drinking?" inquired Rupert.

"True. After a heavy day's work, it was calming and relaxing.

"So Neel's caddying days were short lived?"

"True, but now a young teen," replied James, "Steve became a caddy with Jim Rice's assistance. And he caddied for some years. Here's where he lost his interest in the game. He always felt the golfers were too grumpy to make the experience pleasant. He spoke of one Mr. Nablock, whom he says was a fine gentleman, the only one of the lot that he could tolerate. Unlike his brother Neely, he never took up golf, probably because of this early disdain. Yet the few times he played, he scored low enough to be competitive. Neely, on the other hand, took up golf with a passion in later life."

Glimpses Thirteen

STEVIE REDEEMS HIMSELF

Gladys' friend Ellen called Gladys and asked if she would like to join her to see "Merry Widow's Waltz " at the Muny Opera Saturday night. Ellen's youngest sister was in the dancing chorus and wanted Ellen to come and see the performance. She had given Ellen two tickets, and Gladys was welcome to the other.

"I'd love to, but although my older boys are on a Scouts' overnighter, I don't like to leave Stevie at home by himself."

"Bring him along. There'd be no charge, and I'm sure he would like to see the pretty lights."

"Well, if you don't mind him coming along."

"Not at all."

On Saturday Gladys spiffied Stevie, not yet eight, all up in his short pants sailor suit, and they took a bus from Natural Bridge to Midland to Delmar and there, transferred to a bus that took them to deBoulavere. They walked into the park and on to the Muny. They met Ellen at the fountain in front, as planned.

"Sally wants us to come to her dressing room at intermission. What do you think?"

Gladys glanced down at Stevie. Ellen hastened to add, "And Stevie too. He can come and see all the lights, dresses and make-up in the dressing rooms. Would you like that, Stevie?"

"Guess so."

"Sure you would, wouldn't you," said his mother. "He has hardly been to the Muny. After Stevie learned to walk, his father got so sick, we didn't have a chance to come anymore. Before his daddy's illness, we used to see all the shows."

It was still daylight when the show began, but before the intermission, darkness settled in. Spotlights from behind, up high, were shining over their heads and down, lighting the stage brilliantly. Smoke filtered up through this blinding light. Stevie had never seen anything like it. Thousands of people all around sat motionless, silent, transfixed. The performance was lively and colorful. The words were funny, and suddenly the crowd would burst into laughter and applause.

The music was catchy; the dancing, lively. One song played over and over in Stevie's mind: "singing girls, girls, girls, girls, girls … " In the waltz scene, the ladies were in the most colorful full dresses. Stevie longed to be on the stage with them, one of the escorts, strutting about, dancing, singing with these pretty ladies. He could wear a fancy suit and be the handsome tenor? He could, he could!

At intermission, they went backstage, and there he saw dressing tables and mirrors with their surrounding lights in a straight line as far as he could see, table and chair, and table and chair, mirror after mirror, and lights so bright he could go blind staring. And the ladies! The ladies! At different moments of dressing and making up. Some were in undergarments, and some were in multiple gowns of rich colors. It was beautiful. They were beautiful.

"Hi Stevie!" they'd say, one after another. "What a sweet little boy."

Oh, how he was in ecstasy!

And back to the performance, the girls sang, danced, swirled in their beautiful dresses in the spotlights on the glowing stage beneath the darkening sky under the emerging stars. And when his mother and he returned home, Stevie, hummed, "girls, girls,

girls, girls," suddenly stopped and said, "Mother, can I have a sister?"

"Why on earth did he ask you for a sister?" said Aunt Dot at Sunday dinner.

"I don't know, but maybe it's because he doesn't have a sister, and all he ever sees around the neighborhood are boys.

"And Robert and Benny too," she said, adding her two sons. "You're right. Nothing but boys in Stevie's life." And after a pause she said, "You don't suppose he's discovering girls at his age?"

Gladys flinched. "Really, Dot, six is a little young to be discovering girls."

That night when Stevie was in bed with his mother, long after lights were out, he moved up close behind his mother, right up against her; she instantly moved away, and the next night, she made up the couch in the parlor for him to sleep on.

"From now on, Stevie, you're old enough, you should have a bed of your own."

At school, in the middle of class, (kindergarten in a temporary building) a lady came, called Stevie and Stevie's new little friend Tommy out, and told them to report to the room to the left just inside the door of the big brick building. "Can you boys find it? Mrs. Hanson's room right over there." She pointed.

"Yes, Ma'am," replied Stevie. Stevie liked to be responsible.

When she left, Tommy cried.

"It's okay, Tommy, we're being promoted. We're going into the first grade with the older kids."

But Tommy wasn't listening. Stevie was the grown-up one. He took Tommy by the hand and led him to Mrs. Hanson's room.

Now Mrs. Hanson's room was a whole new world. This was no longer play; this was school. Real school. And Stevie was proud. Yet he wasn't too sure.

Stevie boasted to his big brothers that night that he'd been promoted, but the next day in Mrs. Hanson's room, he didn't feel all that good. He was told right away that he'd have to work on his letters. "Your letters won't do!" Mrs. Hanson said. "You need to open them up and make them clear so a person knows what they are."

So Stevie worked on his letters for quite a long while, but suddenly he realized something. It came as a shock. He had to go to the bathroom. In the kindergarten room, the little boy's bathroom could be entered right from the classroom. What did he do here in Mrs. Hanson's room? She was such an old sourpuss. Did anybody go to the bathroom in Mrs. Hanson's class? Was that what being older was, being able to hold it longer? Mrs. Hanson didn't put up with any nonsense, like going to the bathroom before recess or when you had to. "You're just going to have to wait," he commanded himself as in her voice. But this was bad! What was she to think? His first full day in her room and right away he had to go to the bathroom. And already she was glaring at him.

He shouldn't have to go so soon. He should hold it. She still glared. She didn't like him. He'd have to wait. He would wait until recess. But—oh—it got worse. Move! he told himself. Go to the bathroom. Tell her. Just go.

But he couldn't. He waited too late. Oh, no. It was coming. It was coming. It was awful. It was warm! He had wet his pants! He had wet his pants like a baby.

Did anybody see? It was all over. Everything was over. What could he do? He pretended nothing had happened. But for how long? Suddenly, a fat girl who sat next to him got up and went to Mrs. Hanson, pointed to Stevie and said something he couldn't hear. This was it! Mrs. Hanson knew Stevie had wet his pants! She wrote something and said to the fat girl, "Now, Patty, take this to Mr. Soddern."

The recess bell rang, and Stevie waited until everybody was out of the room, including Mrs. Hanson who left, he felt, pretending not to notice him. Then he slowly stood up. Eww! It was getting cold.

It smelled bad. It made him all alone. All alone. He stood there like a statue.

Then his big brother Dave came in with a friend.

"What did you do, Stevie?" Stevie knew that disgusted tone in his brother's voice.

"Over there," said his friend. "I see a shiny seat!" He hee-hawed!

"Oh, I got to take little brother home to get some dry pants. Come on, Stevie."

Stevie looked at him with tears in eyes. "Can we go out the back?"

He thought he'd like first grade, but he wasn't sure now. That girl who sat beside him, she was fat and had blocked-up-high hair and acted like she knew everything. Patty Field was somebody Stevie wouldn't like in a million years. And it was hard to pretend she wasn't there when she sat right next to him with the wall on the other side and the chalkboard in front. So sour-face Mrs. Hanson was too often right in front of him, and clinging Tommy was in the seat behind him, so there he was. Surrounded. And with no fortress walls.

So wouldn't you know the nice children were seated on the other side of the room. He soon learned the names of those nice children he would never get to play with—others' names he couldn't remember, just the ones he'd never get to play with; there was Johnny and Jimmy, Sharon and Delores and Albert. They came to school every day scrubbed and in nice clothes. Johnny wore shirts with collars. Jimmy and Albert had creases in their short pants. Sharon wore pretty pinafores; Stevie's favorite was pale violet with bright yellow daffodils.

But the nicest of all the children he'd never get to play with, the prettiest girl he'd ever seen in his entire, complete and everlasting life, Delores! She wore sweaters (his favorite was green) and sweet little pleated skirts. Now Stevie developed a thing about pleated skirts. There was nothing in the world like a pretty girl in a pleated skirt. It fell nicely when she rose and walked, and it folded nicely when she sat down. And Delores' hair, coming down near her shoulders and flip at the end, was dark brown and as soft-looking as duck down.

It made him sick, she was so pretty. There could be no doubt about it: Delores was another kind of being entirely. He would never know how to act around her anyway because she was from another planet. She talked with spiffy Johnny and played with Sharon and Albert. She and the other nice ones sat on the other side of the room. And Stevie was stuck with Patty Field, the class snitch, Tommy the crybaby, Mrs. Hanson the grouch and the rock-hard wall.

It was hopeless anyway because Stevie didn't have any nice new clothes like Johnny and Albert. In fact, Stevie had to wear the same old clothes, Neely and Dave's hand-me-downs, every day. He tried wearing one of Neel's old fancy collar shirts to school one day. Stevie couldn't imagine why he hadn't noticed how small it was. What was he thinking! It was miles too small. The sleeves cut him under the arms. The collar, which he felt had to be bottoned, choked him nearly to death. "Neel must have been a baby when he wore this," he thought. When Mrs. Hanson asked Stevie a question, he was too choked by the tight collar to speak.

And he "borrowed" a pair of Neel's new creased pants. Before he tried them on for size and wore them to school, hadn't he noticed how big they were on him! He found he had to twist the waist belt over and over to keep them from falling down. The otherside children came to school nice and spiffy and happy, but Stevie's big pants and tight collar were never going to get him in with the children he liked best, especially in with Delores who wore the pretty pleated skirts. All he'd have is the wall, dummy Tommy, Mrs. Hanson the hatcheter, and fatty Patty.

Day after day, he lived with it. He'd try not to notice Delores walk by. How could he be with the other-siders? They were so clean and nice, and he was so messy. He could ignore fatty Patty, but he couldn't ignore clinging Tommy. Tommy liked him. He was okay. But the other-siders didn't seem to like Tommy, and at recess, Tommy would always come to Stevie to play, Stevie liked having a friend. It was like nobody wanted to play with Tommy because nobody liked him. Tommy and Stevie soon discovered that they lived in the same direction, so after school Tommy looked for Stevie to walk home with.

One afternoon, they headed down Ravenwood Road and discovered a familiar little girl walking far up ahead of them. She had long brown hair, wore a white blouse and a green pleated skirt. When her companion had gone into her house, the girl had just been left to walk on home alone. Stevie would know the girl in the green pleated skirt anywhere. Stevie started walking faster with Tommy tripping behind, so he could catch up to walk with her, Delores! But when he nearly reached her, another boy cut across the street in front of them and joined Delores. "Rats!" thought Stevie.

But suddenly, the other boy grabbed Delores' pencil box away from her and jumped up on a lawn near a high hedge. "Gotta catch me!" he yelled to her, tauntingly, waving her pencil box.

"I don't want to," she replied.

"Then I'll keep it! Ha, ha, ha."

Stevie came up along side of Delores. Tommy stayed behind, stopping in his tracks.

"He won't give it to me," she said, looking like she was about to cry.

Stevie turned to the dark-haired boy who was about his own size, a boy he did not know.

"Aw, come on. Give it back to her."

"Jump in the lake!" he said. He stuck out his tongue at Stevie and waved the box tauntingly in front of her.

Stevie, quick as fox, snatched the pencil box, swung his open hand at the boy's chest, pushing him into the hedge. The boy lost his balance, fell all the way through the hedge, and flat on the other side. His face wrinkled and he set up a loud bawl. " Wa-a-a-a!" He got up and ran away.

Stevie stood in complete amazement. He had no thought of the boy falling over and through the hedge, nor of his running away. Stevie continued to look in the direction of the runaway for several moments. Delores stood by his side. Then he looked at her in complete silence. "Oh," he said, finally. "Here's your pencil box."

She accepted the prize and smiled at him. His amazement grew. He would never again in his life find someone so pretty. Now without a word about the feat they began walking and talking together. Tommy faded out. Stevie noticed a robin hopping along in front of them. It was a lovely spring afternoon.

"My name is Stevie."

"I know," she said. "Mine's Delores."

"I know," he said.

"You're in Mrs. Hanson's class."

"Yep. You too." He felt he sounded stupid. They both laughed. They laughed because he sounded so stupid. He felt he had to say something smart.

"I like airplanes." Now why did he say that? He'd never been in an airplane in his life, and maybe Delores didn't even like airplanes.

"You do?" she said. "Do you fly in an airplane."

"Nah. I just make model airplanes, but someday I'll fly an airplane. I wanna be a pilot."

"You do?"

"Unhuh."

They were near his house. Stevie called "Curley" and a little brown and white dog came running from around the side of the house. He jumped up on Stevie and Stevie kneeled and let him lick his face. "This is my dog Curley. He's part Spitz. My big brother Neel brought him home on Christmas Day. You can pet him if you want."

She laid down her box and petted Curley, and Curley licked her hand. "Oh!" She withdrew it. "He licked me."

"Sure. He likes you."

She smiled. "I got to get home now." She picked up her pencil box and started off. A few steps away she turned with a smile. "Bye."

Stevie continued to pet Curley and watched her walk on. "Bye!"

That evening, big brother Neel's friend came to their house and pointed to Stevie. "Hey, did you know your little brother bopped some kid, knocked 'im clean over the hedge!

"Huh?" Neel looked at Stevie as if he saw him now for the first time.

"Yeh. The kid was messing around, and Stevie went WACK and over the kid went, right into the stickers. Kerplunk! Yeh, and the kid went 'Whah-h-h' and ran home bawling.".

Dave just happened in and picked up on the bawling. "Yeh? No shit. Stevie did this?" He looked at Stevie with approval. "You showed him, didn't you, Stevie!"

Stevie felt good. He did it for Delores. And what's more, his brothers knew he did it.

Neel's hands went up on his hips. "Well, I'll be," he said, barely audibly. That was Neel's way. He spoke quietly even when impressed. Stevie knew it and liked it.

Epiglimpselogue Thirteen

James hastened to add, "In Stevie's early years, his brothers were models of grownup-ness. He envied them and, not often but occasionally, emulated them. They were the standard of manhood—since he had no father and no older man to look up to."

"So when he got his brothers' approval, it made him feel especially good," said Ben.

"True. But early on, they were out of his life. He was solely on his own."

"Figures," said Rupert. "But fancy telling on yourself that as a little kid, he wet his pants in class."

"Yes, in the first grade when he was thinking he was getting grown up like his brothers. Getting grown up was not that easy."

"True," said Sally. "He wasn't going to get there just walking across the hall."

"But helping Tommy and rescuing that girl's pencil box put him on his way," said Ben. "And I bet he never wet his pants again."

'Nope. Never," said James.

"And all those girls, girls, girls in the dressing room. Did he turn out to be girl-crazy?" asked Lisa.

"Yeh, like most guys!" replied James.

GLIMPSES FOURTEEN

WAR TIME

It was the Sunday that all hell broke loose—December 7th, 1941. The family was glued to their staticky gothic radio. Even Grandma was there and couldn't tear herself away. Her face was more than usually somber. "Well, I declare!" And when Stevie met his playmates, they were excited.

"Did you hear about it!"

"The Japs bombed Pearl Harbor!"

All through the school yard Monday morning, the children and adults were abuzz with it. President Roosevelt's words rung in their ears: "a day that will live in infamy." What did *infamy* mean? What was going on? The answer was repeated everywhere. The unexpected bombing at Pearl Harbor had caused the deaths of thousands of young American men. It was the worse calamity anybody could imagine. And the words "Remember Pearl Harbor!" became the battle cry of all true Americans. And spoken frequently, too, was, "those sneaky Japs!" No longer was Stevie, the class marble champion, interested in games of marbles. No longer would he rush home after school to play plain ol' cars with Arthur Summers or make houses and roads in Carl Johnson's sandbox. The country was at war. Somebody had to kill the sneaky Japs. In fact, he wondered, could he grow up fast enough to go kill some sneaky Japs himself?

Everyone said that the U.S. and England were far behind Japan and Germany who, in fact, had been preparing for war for years. The business of America now was war. War bonds went on sale. Rationing came in—Stevie was impressed, especially by—Oh no!—sugar rationing. This was serious. No more frivolous fudge-sickles. With his pennies and nickels, Stevie bought victory stamps for his stamp book at school that later, when he had enough, could be exchanged for a 25 dollar war bond. That was a fortune he could enjoy after the war, and for now, it could be used to help beat the Japs. Collection centers were set up for metal and silver paper which the young boys could collect.

Older boys, boys in his brothers' range, were lying about their ages and signing up for the army, navy, and marines. Saturday nights, his mother was playing the piano in a dance band to entertain the troops. She had wonderful hands. How her fingers could sweep error-free across the keyboard in perfect rhythm "to help the men in uniform."

The area the big lumber company had left vacant when it burned down last summer—that is, when one night to the east, behind the houses (like Stevie's) on the hill, deep red flames leapt into the air, and large heavy clouds of black smoke billowed high up into the sky—that large area on over to Goodfellow Boulevard became a giant military small-arms plant, one of the largest in the world. And farther away and to the west, the Curtis-Wright Company at Lambert Airfield became a principal employer of thousands of defense workers when it began manufacturing war planes. So Americans went to it—all Americans! Thousands of workers including women like "Rosie the riveter," went to work in the factories. This was everybody's war, little kids included.

After school Billy said, "Hey, Stevie, let's go play at the vacant lot."

"Okay." A favorite play area, this was a large double lot that had been left just as nature had made it (namely, for the neighborhood boys) a primeval jungle, a vast entanglement of trees, vines, thickets, and weeds, straight weeds, with sticky fuzz on their stalks, weeds taller than the tallest of the boys, and it was their own jungle; it belonged to the boys in the neighborhood because they took it over. Before the war, this was their land of Tarzan. They made the tall weeds that had pointed roots into their weapons—spears, that is, to use against the bad guys—who were greedy white men come to steal elephants' tusks and such.

But times had changed. The bad guys were not white guys, but yellow, slanty-eyed Japs, and weed spears were out. Guns and grenades were in—guns and grenades of all kinds. Guns were makeshift rifles and Lugers, usually made of wood, and grenades were made of bags of dust and mud-balls (like "snowballs" with dust cores. Old brown jackets with insignias and stripes sewn or pinned or glued on were in. Big brother's cloppy old boots were in. "This is the army, Mr. Jones!" Oh yes, John Wayne and a whole Hollywood brigade were in!

Billy and Stevie started up the path through the dense thicket, where an eerie silence ensued. When they had reached about the middle of the jungle, suddenly a half dozen males with blackened faces jumped out at them. "Stand where you are!" They wore—there it was!—their make-shift, quasi-military attire, boots, khaki shirts, heavy belts, cheap five-and-ten cent store helmets with weeds stuck in them. Each carried a weapon, mostly wooden rifles, but one, their leader, who wore an army shirt with sergeant stripes, older and taller than the others, held a real rifle, a hunting rifle, which he aimed at Stevie's face.

"Who are you!" shouted one.

He was nudged aside by the leader. "Well!" he said sarcastically, "Aren't you a stinking, yellow-bellied Jap! Don't you move, you!"

Stevie was dumbstruck.

"Yeh, he looks sneaky to me, Serg," said the shortest one who began circling around Stevie with his pointed wooden rifle that was as long as he was tall. "Pro'bly stick a knife in you if you turned your back on 'im."

"Shoot 'im!" said one whose blackened face contrasted with his red hair.

"Put 'im in jail," said the short one. "And torture 'im."

"Git in there, you," said their sergeant, still pointing his rifle in Stevie's face and motioning to some lair in the thicket.

"What for?" said Stevie, who was shaking like a leaf.

"Cause you're a sneaky Jap," said the short one.

"My eyes aren't slanty!" Stevie snapped around.

"Then you're worse! You're a Jap spy," said the sergeant. "You're a yellow-belly." When Stevie turned back, the sergeant poked him in the chest with the end of his gun barrow. "Get in there!"

"You're a spy yourself!" said Stevie, afraid to move.

The serg started to hit Stevie with his rifle butt. "What'd you say!"

"I'm no spy!"

Serg lowered his gun and shouted, "My brother's a marine! An' you're a spy!"

"My big brothers," said Stevie, "are going to be marines soons they're out of Normandy High School."

"You got big brothers?" asked the Serg whose voice now softened a tad.

Billy chimed in, "Yeh he does. He's got two big brothers. They play football." Stevie thought about how Neely's hand could grasp a football, and how his fingers lined up across the lace, and how he could spiral a ball eighty yards down the field.

"Football?" said the Sergeant, straightening himself. He looked back at Stevie. He pondered a moment, keeping his rifle trained on Stevie. "You got big brothers?"

"Yeh, and Neel's going to be a cap'n in the marines."

"A cap'n higher than a sergeant," said the short one to the Serg.

The Serg looked confused. He lowered his rifle. "Okay, you jus' git out of here. I'm letting you go, see, but you better watch your step, or we'll torture and shoot you for a spy. Now git out o' here."

He motioned to the others. "Com'on. We gotta kill some more Japs." They disappeared into the vacant-lot jungle.

The World War was heating up in both theaters. The Allies were fighting across North Africa and up the Italian boot heel, and U.S. forces were engaged in island-hopping campaigns in the Pacific. The big brother of Stevie's friend up the street was killed storming the beaches of corregidor, and Stevie's cousin Wesley, radio operator, was killed when his plane dropped into the Pacific off the Aleutian Islands. Gladys' sister, his mother, sent a snapshot of Wesley which showed the face of a clever young man. His fingers were on a simulator dial.

Neel invented the game blanket-island strategy. Soldiers were represented as beans (or buttons), and the island to be recaptured from the Japs was a large blanket from the big bed, which would be placed on the floor; the floor was the sea all around, and the blanket laid out and bunched up so that its flats, folds and humps would be beaches and mountains of the Pacific island. Sheets of paper were folded into boats or launches to carry invasion troops. The peas were divided to represent the U.S. and Japanese forces. Sides were made up. Neely was key at the command center; he always became the commander of the U.S. forces.

Stevie would place his beans out first, that is, separate them into small units and locate them in little pockets to protect all parts of the island from invasion, and then he would stand back to admire his defenses. "Ready."

Before long, Neely would sweep up a neat handful of his troops and launch an invasion of the island. Then he would begin removing Stevie's beans from action.

"Ra-ta-ta-ta! Boom, boom!"

"What are you doing?"

"I'm winning," said Neely.

"But my men are shooting your men too," said Stevie. "Ra-ta-ta-ta, boom."

"I know but I'm winning." Neel replaced more of Stevie's beans with his own.

"I take yours out too!" said Stevie.

"But I'ave more men. See. Twice as many as yours."

"But—"

"Ra-ta-ta-ta. Booom. And I'm winning 'cause there's more of us and not enough of you."

They "fought on" and suddenly, Neely took <u>all</u> of Stevie's beans in that spot away and shouted, "Principle of mass! Ra-ta-ta-ta."

"Huh?" said Stevie.

"I have more men than you do here, so I win the battle."

Then Neely with another handful launched a new attack on another beach spot of the island. "Ta-ta-ta-ta. Boom. Boom."

Quickly Stevie began amassing troops over to the new battleground. "Princ-ple of Mass!" he cried. "Ra-ta-ta-ta. Boom!"

"Wait!" shouted Neely. "You can't do that."

"Why not?"

"Cause <u>I</u> have the Principle of Surprise."

"Why can't I have a prin-celp of 'prise?"

"Can't cause you got the island, dummy! Can't have both!" Then he would sweep more of Stevie's beans out of the game. This would go on until Neely won the whole island. Stevie's troops were all gone.

Oh well, thought Stevie, my guys are just the Japs, as Neely was quick to point out.

One Saturday morning, Stevie walked out the front door on his way to the street car to go visit Carl Johnson, who lived back on Ravenwood where Stevie used to live. Suddenly, he was startled by a loud noise, as if someone had slammed a door really hard. "Whew! Somebody's mad." He went on to spend several hours playing with Carl at electric train and troop movements, had lunch that Carl's mother prepared for them (with tomato sauce and lots of pasta, always the best lunch he would ever have) and returned home around three o'clock in the afternoon. He met his brother racing through the house.

"Dave. Where you goin'?"

"S'been a plane crash. Haven't you heard." He rushed to the door.

"Where? I come too."

"Well, hurry."

It was a large open slope north of Elizabeth Road. There was nothing there except a few boys looking around the deserted field.

"Everything's been taken away," said a boy Dave knew. "They're gone. Took away in big trucks and ambulances—wreckage, bodies, stuff, everything."

"What was it?"

"A twin-engine recon plane. Lockeed. Had a crew of three—pilot, copilot, and navigator."

"What happened?"

"Engine trouble."

He showed them right where the plane crashed. A hole and several mounds of dirt—that was all. Hardly even any fragments. White powder coated everything.

"Lime," he said. "They covered the place with lime to get rid of the blood and pieces of bodies and smell and stuff." The boys scoured the ground.

"Here's something!" Dave bent over and picked up an object from the ground. Stevie dashed to see it. He cradled a piece of metal about the size of a golf ball in his hand. "Aluminum," said Dave. "See how light it is. Came off the plane in the crash."

Stevie could hear the twin engines way up high. Then he could hear one engine stop, then another engine stop. He could see, the plane take a nose dive, all the way down, down, and crash!—right into the ground. Right here.

"They said," Dave's friend continued, "that one of the men tried to parachute, but got his pant leg hung on something."

Looking all around the field and up in the sky just above, it was hard for Stevie not to relive the crash. As in the morning, he could hear the plane, its engines quit. Now he was inside the fuselage.

The three men were trying to jump, the plane was falling, falling; one man gets to the door, out the door, but his pant leg catches. His yelling cannot be heard, the plane is falling, falling—Oh God, too late! And smash, right into this field, this hole, right where the boys stood.

Stevie rubbed the fragment with his finger. He noticed it had had a coat of paint on it but the paint was mostly gone. The fragments of paint were khaki brown, the color used to camouflage army planes so the enemy would have trouble spotting them.

"Hey! What's this?" said Dave's friend. He had picked up something and was studying it. Dave and Stevie rushed to see it.

"It's a—!" suddenly he dropped it. He looked at Dave and Stevie, funny. He walked away as in a daze.

Stevie crouched down and looked at the object. He could see it had a curve to it. He could see furrows.

"My God! A man's finger! A piece of it," said Dave

"Just a little while ago, this morning," said Stevie, "when I was going to Carl's—this finger was on a live man. Where was his hand? Holding on to a control lever? Covering his eyes? Whose finger was it? Was it the pilot's? Steering the crippled plane? The copilot's, the navigator's? Was his hand on the wheel, his finger on a dial? A real finger. Did he point to the escape door? Was he yelling, "Out!" Did he yell "We're goin' down! Out, out!" And silence then--Crash! Stevie froze.

"Come on," said Dave. "There's nothing here. I'm going home."

Shortly, he turned his shoulder and headed back around to Stevie. "You comin'?"

Epiglimpselogue Fourteen

"They actually found a man's finger?" asked Lisa, shivering.

"Yes," James replied. "It was the same morning that the plane crashed in the lot. The brothers rushed over. They were quite shaken by it. The clean-up crew had been there, but had not found everything. They missed the bloodied end of a man's finger."

"The brothers were shocked?" said Sally,

"War seemed glamorous until they saw this bloodied finger that had that morning belonged to a living human being, a finger like their own," said James, interpretively.

"Reality sets in," said Rupert, himself always the realist. "Now a glimpse of, shall I say, real war."

Glimpses Fifteen

WAR IN PEACE

Early in the third grade Stevie and Deloris were making eyes at each other across the class room. They had begun walking home together after school.

One day Gladys answered the door bell.

"We're the Merthers from down the street." It was Mrs. Merther, an attractive lady in a floral dress, who spoke, and beside her, her husband in an open collar and a light-weight, light-blue jacket. "Our Deloris is in the same class as your Stevie. Deloris told us about Stevie retrieving her pencil box from a mean boy one day after school . There's such a scruffy lot that are moving into the neighborhood . This change does not really please us." She looked Gladys straight in the eyes. "You know what I mean, I believe."

Her pause seemed to be waiting for Gladys to make some confirming response, but the arrival of the Merthers at her front door on a Saturday morning in the middle of a piano lesson threw her into confusion. She simply smiled an uneasy smile and ventured nothing. Mrs. Merther looked around Gladys and saw the student at the piano, waiting.

"Oh, I hear you're a piano teacher. How nice. We could use more culture in the neighborhood. We won't intrude except to ask if Stevie would like to go to the airport with us and Deloris this evening to have an ice cream soda. The children love to go to the airport and see the planes landing and taking off at night."

"Oh, I'm sure Stevie would like that very much. He loves to watch the planes take off and land."

"Wonderful," said Mr. Merther in a low, mellow voice. "We'll come around seven-thirty and have him back before ten. And the treat will be on us." He nodded a pleasant smile. The two departed.

After the lesson, Gladys called Stevie in from outside and told him of the evening plans for him and Delores. Stevie couldn't believe his ears. He was going to get to see his favorite girl in all the world. This was going to be a real good day.

"Okay, you guys," said his brother when Stevie returned outside. "See this?" he held up a large, flat, black rubbery ring.

"Hey," said Dave, "where'd you get that old inner tube from?" He grabbed a side and examined it.

"Yeh. Where'd you get the inner tube?"

"It's got a big hole in it!" Dave stuck his finger into it.

"Know what we're going to do?"

"Sure," said Stevie. "Fix a tire."

"No, dummy. We're goin' make guns!"

"Guns!"

That was perplexing. How, wondered Stevie, could you make guns out of an old tire inner tube?

"Let's get the scissors—in the kitchen." They entered through the back door. From the other room, they could hear their mother's student playing notes; the student was fingering her way through "Fur Elise."

"No, no. That's a G-sharp played with the three-finger. Again! No, no, that's the G-sharp!"

In the kitchen, Neel began cutting away. Multiple circles, like over- grown rubber bands. Carefully and evenly. Soon, a pile of heavy bands was covering the kitchen table.

"Hey, Dave," said Neel, the commander. "Go down to the cellar and get that saw and one of those old bed slats. Cut it into foot-and-a-half -long pieces."

Stevie picked up one of the cut pieces of rubber. "These are big for rubber bands." Neel didn't say anything, just kept cutting away.

"Stevie, go out to the clothesline and get some clothespins."

"We goin' ta wash some clothes?"

"I told you. We're making guns, now git goin'!"

Stevie returned with both hands full of wooden clothespins.

"No, we don't need but three, three for six triggers. Take those others back and put 'em where they were, or mother'll wonder where they went when she's hanging up clothes, and she'll get mad at us."

Before Stevie was finished replacing the pins in the line bag where they were, Neel and Dave came out back with their hands full of rubber rings and pieces of wood, a chisel, and a hammer and nails.

"Okay, now give me those clothespins" He took one, and with the hammer and chisel split the clothespin lengthwise, turning one clothespin into two long pieces of wood, each with a flat side. "Now hand me those bands, Stevie. Come on, Stevie, take those bands off your arms and give them to me!" He worked diligently, holding and stretching. "Now another." Then he took the hammer and nailed a nail into the narrow edge of the wood close to where the clothespin was held tight by double bands stuck down about three inches below the edge.

"Now!" he said, holding the wood like a gun, the nail and the clothes- pin piece serving like squeeze triggers. "Now the bullets. Tie those narrower bands with knots like figure eights. See. Like this."

When he finished, he pulled one rubber eight over the end of the stick gun and doubled the other loop together and placed it to be held by the tight clothespin against the wood until the marksman was ready to release it by squeezing the half clothespin with the nail. Now Neel held the woodstock up, took aim and squeezed. The knotted rubber ring flew out, struck a flower pot sitting on the porch landing. It fell to the concrete step below and shattered. "Oops."

Soon they had two more long guns and a small gun.

"The little one is Stevie's luger"

"Aw. It won't shoot very hard."

"It's a little German luger. Neat, huh?"

"I don't want a you-ger. I want a big gun like yours."

Neely loaded his long gun again and fired it at Stevie's bare legs.

"Ow!" A red mark appeared where Stevie rubbed.

"See. It hurts," said Neely with satisfaction.

"Hey, what're you guys doin?"

It was Don Pfeiffer, Neel's friend, calling down the stairs. Stevie knew it. Right away, Neel gave the third, only other long gun to Don Pfeiffer. Stevie was stuck with the little gun.

"Common, you guys," said Dave, "let's make a fortress!"

They scoured around the steps. The basement was a fright—filled with such treasures as broken furniture, pieces of all kinds of lumber, including two large sheets of old plywood, a half dozen old suitcases, empty cardboard and wooden boxes, a large old clothes hamper. "Now," said Neely, "bring on those Japs!"

This wealth of material kept the four of them busy all afternoon, assembling them strategically, meticulously—one might almost add *artistically*—into not one, but two structures on opposite sides of the basement. The results of this shifting, arranging, piling were miraculous. ""Now," said Neely, Increasing his volume, "bring on those Japs!"

These two distinctive forts were created such that they had walls, lookout towers, gates that could be opened and closed, parapets, shelters, and escape hatches. Eight feet of nothing in between, "no man's land," separated the fortresses. A lookout person on either side could sit up high, look over his shield and zap an intruder or invader from his strategic vantage point. Gates were such that if one were so bold as to enter, he could be gunned down with vengeance. Further, the weaponry was not sufficient for the general. Neel, one-man research and development department, made himself a machine gun by taking a three-feet-long plank, cutting four notches in it for a strip of cloth to be run, by which he could hook the bands, then pull up on his strip and release four bullets (stretched rubber rings) in succession. Pow, pow, pow, pow, he demonstrated. He fixed himself a shielded seat up high on his fortress where he could let fly his bullets at any target he so chose.

Now it was approaching evening, six-thirty, and not one serious skirmish had taken place. But this was fortunate for their two cousins Rob and Ben arrived just in time to go on the sides: Neel, Don, and Ben opposing Rob, Dave and Stevie. They began settling in for the skirmish, but suddenly realized it was still too light to have a proper military engagement.

"Wait, wait, wait! Got to cover the windows!" Neel shouted. Things had to be right. They quickly improvised coverings with rags, tacks and tape and—at last—the battleground was ready. Again, they situated themselves in their opposing fortresses, but who was going to turn out the light? The switch was at the top of the basement steps. And when the light were to be turned off, the battle would begin.

"Stevie," commanded the commander, Neel, "Go turn the light off."

Stevie knew what this meant. If he turned the light off, he'd be zapped before he got to the bottom of the steps. "Nah," he said.

"Yeh," said Dave, "that isn't fair."

"Okay," said Neel, "after he turns the light out, I'll count to ten."

"Huh-uh," said Stevie

"Right again, Stevie," said Dave. "Who counts to ten? You could count to ten before he gets to the bottom of the steps."

"Okay," said Neel, "we'll all count to ten."

"How fast?" said Dave.

"Oh, for cryin' out loud. We'll never get the show on the road. Okay, like this. One-Two-Three," he counted, sarcastically slow.

"Make it twenty," said Dave.

"Geeze! Okay, okay, we'll count to twenty."

"We'll ALL count to twenty," said Dave.

"Well I'll be—," said Neel, "For Pete's sake, let's get started."

"Go ahead, Stevie," said Dave.

"Okay," said Stevie. Up the steps he went, nervously. He hit the switch and the light suddenly went off and back on again.

"I didn't mean--!"

Neel groaned. "Do it right, Stevie, or I'll come up there and knock your block off."

Stevie turned the light off and immediately stumbled.

"One-two-three—"

He recovered and went down several steps. *But gosh, it was dark!* He stumbled again at the bottom and fell to the floor.

"Seven-eight-nine—"

He scrambled to his feet and tried to hurry, but ran into a fortress wall.

"Fourteen-fifteen-sixteen."

He felt his way along, but couldn't locate the gate.

"Seventeen-eighteen-nineteen—"

He felt the edge of the opening and swung around.

Zing-kersplat. A bullet hit the wall next to him. Zing-kersplat. He could feel the air current through his hair.

Someone's strong arm grabbed his and pulled him down. Zing-kerspat. That one hit the chair shield in front of him. He was safe. Dave had pulled him out of danger.

Okay, thought Stevie, *it was time to show these guys a thing or two.* He got his gun and peeked up over the wall. Now he was going to be a hot- shot holy terror. His big brother would learn a little respect for a guy. He looked around but couldn't see anything. *Phooey. How I am going to shoot anybody if I can't see anything?* Then he thought he saw some movement across the way. He took aim, but suddenly felt a sharp pain as lightning struck his right eye .

"Yeow!" he yelled and set up a horrendous howling.

The lights went on. "What's going on down there?" shouted Uncle Art.

Stevie continued to wail.

"Come on up here, all of you!"

His mother's voice and then his Aunt's came into it, and the battle was over. He heard his uncle saying, "It's going to be quite a shiner!" The war was over. Peace was formally declared. Don Pfeiffer, Ben and Robert Dugger all went home.

At seven-thirty, Stevie had his first date ever and with a darling of a girl. Doloris's parents drove up, picked up Stevie, drove them to the airport to have an ice cream soda. Little did they expect that their small Robinhood-Flash Gordon would turn out to be such a total scruff himself—with one whopper of a black eye. Stevie would thereafter remain on the wrong side of the classroom. Still, he had proven himself. He was tough. Sort of.

Epiglimpselogue Fifteen

"So poor Stevie won the battle of the schoolyard but later lost the battle for his little lady-love?" said Sally, more confirming than questioning.

"True," responded James. "To look at him, Stevie himself was one of the neighborhood scruffs."

"I'm sure that didn't go over with the Merthers," added Lisa.

"Most likely not. But the Fulbrights were soon to move from Ravenwood to Adele, twenty miles or so away, a different community farther out in the county, and Steve would often wonder what ever became of cute little Deloris."

"Alas," moped Rupert mockingly. "Whatever became of our childhood loves!"

Sally shrugged, "And our Robinhoods?"

"Oh," said Ben, holding his hands out wide, like a performer. "We make an appearance now and again."

"Sounds like Steve was girl-oriented from day one," said Lisa.

"You could say that," responded James.

"So what is the point of all this stuff about Neel and his military stratagem?" asked Rupert.

"We shall shortly see this as working out to be one of the notable shortcomings of politicism."

GLIMPSES SIXTEEN

STEVE'S CHALLENGES

What could be more important to a person's life—here focusing on young Steve—than belief and career? The first is naturally belief. With his mother having unobtrusively rebelled against small-town "moss-backed narrow-mindedness hypocrites," and then being burdened with three young boys to raise by herself, four-year-old Steve was not compelled to attend a church or any kind of religious body. A father might have supplied this lack, but ... by way of a divorce, the opening of an exulted career of a legal profession, moving to the city, starting a new family with a young wife, Harry led the five of them on an entirely new journey.

Harry and Gladys had broken with tradition. Gladys had already taken up playing with a modern, for its times, band. Transportation had improved leaps and bounds. The war was over, and the doughboys were coming home. Factories flourished. Being a world-supplier, U. S. factories and businesses after the war years continued to expand. The media, too, expanded—newpapers, magazines, and radios—including news and comedy shows. Harry drove a Ford. Occasionally, in the early months, Harry and Gladys went to taverns, to dances, took up drinking beer and smoking cigarettes. If there were any scorn for such rebellion, it was put down by the progressive thought 'keeping up with the times.' Who could blame them? And then with Harry's untimely death, Gladys, now left solely responsible for the three young boys, worked in a modern office, so coping in the mainstream and teaching piano in the evenings and on Saturdays.

The boys went to public schools and chose their friends mostly from the neighborhood. Weekdays were busy (with Gladys always hard working) for all four, and mostly routine. Sundays were the only times Gladys could clean house and supervise the boys at such, do the family wash, get her own and the boys' clothes ready for the coming week and pay the bills. For the most part, her relaxation was that occasional bottle of beer and a cigarette. Most likely, and perhaps mainly, due to their impoverishment, beer and cigarettes were rarely if ever excessive. When the boys got into trouble, which fortunately was not frequent, so many limitations made it especially difficult to handle.

There was the time (alluded to above), right after Harry's death, when Gladys had to move them to a tenement building down in the North city that the boys were playing ball in the narrow back-yard. Their ball went over the five-foot high, wooden-slatted fence and into the next yard. "I get it!" said four year old Stevie. He ran to the alley, around a storage garage, and into the neighbor's yard. He pitched the ball over the fence to his brothers and turned back. The neighbor's boy, years older than Stevie, whom they had never seen before, came at him suddenly with a half brick in his hand and from just a few feet threw it at Stevie's face, missing his eye by an inch. Stevie ran back to his yard screaming, holding his hand over the profusely bleeding wound just below his right eye. Blood streamed through his fingers and down his face. It was severe enough a wound that he would bear the scar for the rest of his life.

What harm had he committed to the strange boy that would prompt such a vicious act? Would it leave other marks besides the one on his face? Stevie's mother moved them from the city within weeks as soon as she could afford to rent a small house in the county located in a better neighborhood.

But better neighborhoods do not guarantee nicer neighbors. Brother Dave was not known for discretion in choosing friends, especially in these younger years. He was about ten when he befriended one Hamilton McKinsey. Apparently Hamilton's father was into tough-guy stuff which included fire arms. They lived in the upper-story apartment a few houses from the Fulbrights. One day when Dave was in the back yard behind his house, Hamilton called to Dave from the outside second-story porch those few doors up from the Fulbrights.

"Hey, Dave! I want to show you something! " Dave hustled over there. "Come on up!" Hamilton said.

"Yeh. What is it?"

"Come and see." Suddenly he pulled out a handgun, pointed it at Dave's face and fired.

This was supposed to be fun because although a real pistol it had a blank shell in it. Apparently, no one informed Hamilton—he hardly suited his name—that a real gun firing a blank shell spews red-hot powder out the barrow that could burn a person's eyes out. And if the eyes survive, the powder burns could give the hapless victim blood poisoning. In any case, the splatter would cause severe burns, and Dave was staring straight into the barrow. Being suddenly splattered with its fire, he spun around, tripped down the stairs, and ran home yelling and crying, his face peppered with multiple burns.

He had to be rushed to a hospital emergency room for treatment which included shots for blood poisoning. Were there more marks than the ones on his face? Their mother had always been more frightened of firearms than burglars. Therefore, although their doors were seldom locked, their mother forbade them ever to have guns in their house. "Many more people are killed by 'unloaded' guns than by burglars!" she insisted frequently. Another move and another neighborhood?

So what was life all about? As Steve grew, the question became more pronounced in his mind. He began to ask questions, seldom this kind of question to his mother, but sometimes to his brother Dave who would usually make some kind of a joke out of it. Steve witnessed other boys going off to some church or other on Sunday mornings. Steve had friends to ask, and he was more fortunate, or maybe more select, in his quality of the neighborhood friends than was Dave.

There were three he made friends with. The boy who lived behind him on the other side of the creek was Martin Hoffman. His family was devout Lutheran. He was not going to lead Steve down any darkened path to misadventure or bad habits. Other than the way Martin and his quiet family lived, however, he was not a mentor of outstanding values or living a meaningful life.

Then there was Arthur Summers, across and up the street. This little boy of eight or nine was a talker. He had answers for most everything. Steve noted that he attended church regularly on Sundays and sometimes during the weekdays and even on Saturdays. It had long been a desire of Steve's to go to church, but he had no idea what church to go to, and all churches seemed to be so far away. They had no car; wherever Steve went, he had to walk. Outside of playing the organ for church (any church that paid), his mother made no effort to influence her boys religiously one way or the other. She left it up to the boys to make their own choices.

Steve found that Arthur Summers was quite ready at any time to tell about his church. One day, Arthur turned to Steve in all sincerity and said, "You know don't you that you're going to hell. That's where people burn for all eternity."

"No!" Steve responded emphatically, "I'm not going to hell."

"I've not heard you ever say that you've been to confession."

"What's confession?"

"You go to a priest and confess your sins."

"I don't have any sins."

The look on Arthur's face registered total disbelief. "Yes, you do! Everybody has sins."

"Well, I haven't."

"Yes, you have. Everybody commits sins. And every sin you commit puts a black mark on your soul." Arthur spoke in such sincerity there could be no doubt but that he was right.

Steve shook his head as if some nasty insect were buzzing around him. "So then what happens?"

"Each sin puts a black mark on your soul, and when you die, if there are any black marks on your soul, then you go to hell and burn forever."

In no way did Steve want to believe this. What had he done to burn forever in hell? Was this fair? And he didn't even know about it. But he remembered his teacher said once, there are many things that you must do, and not knowing about them is no excuse. This haunted Steve for several days. The next opportunity he had with Arthur, Steve asked his friend what he could do to get rid of these black marks.

Arthur was more than eager to help. "Well, you have to confess your sins to a priest."

"I don't know any priests."

"You'll have to go to church."

"What church?"

"Crimony! Don't you know anything! St. Anthony's up on Jennings Road. An' you better get there as soon as you can because your soul is as black as soot, and if you should die before you get forgiven, you're going to burn in hell."

"But I've never been …"

"Well, you better get goin'. Now I got some prayers you can say. That will get rid of some of the little black marks. But that's only the little ones. For the big ones …"

"I don't have any big sins …"

"Oh yes you do! An' they'll put you in Hell quicker than anything. You gotta go confess to a priest to get rid of those, or you'll go to Hell for sure."

It worried Steve deeply. He better do something right away. He knew roughly where St. Anthony's was, but going there and doing something—what?—who were the priests? Would he know them? Would they see his black sins and scorn him? Steve was puzzled.

That evening his two brothers were home, and he thought—but wasn't sure—maybe it would be best for him to ask them, both of them while they were altogether. Again, should he? It wasn't easy for him to decide. But Hell's fire was there waiting, and he better find out. He took the plunge.

"Neely! Dave! Gotta ask you something. I got big black sins inside me on my soul, and I'm going to Hell if I don't get to a priest, confess, and get rid of them, but I don't know … ?"

"Oh for cryin' out loud. Who have you been talking to/" said Neely.

"I talked to Arthur Summers, and he says …"

Dave bellowed, "For cryin' out loud! He's Catholic!"

"Yeh," said Neel. "The Summers family is all full of Popery!"

And as far as Catholicism and religion in general went, that was it for Steve. Nothing else was said among them about priests and confessionals and sins and black souls, then or ever. And Steve felt he needn't bother with priests and confessions, who and which completely mystified him. Maybe he could just find a church around somewhere, a church that looked friendly, and go in and look around and do what everybody else did. Maybe there he would find God, or maybe God would find him. That should take care of it.

It seemed, now, that Arthur avoided him, or maybe he avoided Arthur. Anyway there was a big church up on Natural Bridge Road. It was at least a twenty-minute walk from home each way through several neighborhoods that he was not familiar with, but that didn't matter if he could find God.

The next Sunday, he put on his best hand-me-downs. They were like most of his hand-me-downs, which were too big or too small for him, but they were the best clothes he had, and off he went by himself to church. Natural Bridge Road was the busiest street anywhere around, but it was Sunday morning, and if Steve took it slow and easy, he could make it across the road. Right in front of the massive church, Steve hesitated. The front entrance was high up the steps, and people were entering by the half dozens.

"Well," he thought, "here goes." Those entering, outside of babes in arms, were all adults. He thought he would see some neighborhood or school chums. Not a one! Inside, he found a seat on the side near the front and waited for the magic to happen. He was sure it would.

The ceremony began with some mentioning of Sunday School and an open-hand motioning to an entrance from the side "doors of youths." So that was it, he thought. He had heard of Sunday school for young people, so that was what he was supposed to do here, attend Sunday School and not the adult church service. Now, he felt totally out of place. Prayer came and went. The preacher preached a sermon. And there Steve sat, looking around and wondering what he was supposed to do. A plate with money and small envelopes came around, but all he could do was pass it on. Why hadn't he brought some of those pennies he had at home in a jar so he wouldn't feel totally inadequate? The organ crescendo-ed and everyone sang from books. Shouldn't he be singing too? But he didn't know what to sing. Psalms? Song books? Where was God? Had He left it up to the minister? When Steve headed out the large front doors where the minister stood smiling and shaking hands, the minister looked right past young Steve as if there were no one between the last person and the next. Not one person said a word to him the whole time he was in "God's house." So much for winging it.

Shortly thereafter, when the Fulbrights moved to Ferguson, it seemed to be a whole different season. He met Jim Poor, who went to the Episcopal Church. He met Harold LeMert, who went to the Presbyterian Church, and Robert Warren, who went to the Methodist Church and, across the street, Tom Mottin who went to the Catholic Church, all which were no more than three blocks from Steve's house.

Bob Warren said, "Steve, you have to come to my church's Sunday school and to the services and meet the minister. We call him Uncle Billy."

It was true. When he came to know Uncle Billy, Steve was amazed that Uncle Billy could not walk down the streets of Ferguson without greeting everyone with a great hello, a smile, a question about their health and family. For several years, Steve went to this church. Further, he passed the church on his way to school, the 5th grade at Central Elementary, and it made him feel at home.

But Steve was not sure he was making contact with God. He would, on occasion, visit another church with a friend or by himself looking for answers to the old questions. His life was a big question mark. Who was he himself? Where did he come from? Ultimately, where was he going? And then, not the least of the questions was what would become his life's work?

Epiglimpselogue Sixteen

"Did Steve continue the religious quest right up until now?" asked Sally.

"Off and on. He was never satisfied that he had found the answers. His quest for a career eventually settled to be a teacher, a field where he could continue to search for knowledge and understanding. Always, he has been the student."

"And Steve came across Thomas Hardy?" queried Rupert.

"He likes knowing the truth, not something that he wants to believe just to feel comfortable."

"I agree with him there," nodded Rupert. "Most of the stuff

people believe, they or someone equally unknowing makes up in their heads."

"Yes. Steve wanted truth. Evidence. Humankind is in a bind. In human history, we see masses of people say you must believe what I believe, or else. The consequences are dire, often inhumane."

Part II

Life, With Hopes Mixed In

Glimpses Seventeen

RAVENWOOD TO ADELE

"Gladys, this is a nice big house, but isn't it a bit far from your work?"

There it was again, thought Gladys, that old knack Dot had for striking at reality. "It takes another half hour to an hour to get back and forth to work, but it'll have to do for a while until I can find a job closer to home. Mr. Wilson says Ferguson is a nice community, a better place for the boys to grow up. Of course, Neel is being allowed to finish out at Normandy High School—he'll have a longer way to go, too—but he graduates from high school in a few years, and he wants to do it. He has his friends and all. Dave will start into Ferguson High School. Stevie finishes out fifth grade at Central and then goes over to the junior high."

"I know you are happy to get away from that old neighborhood," said Dot.

"Dave was falling into the wrong crowd over there."

"What was it that happened to Dave that you never told me about?"

"That McKenzie boy. Two doors over, had a gun. He was standing only a foot away from Dave when he shot him in the face. It had a blank in it, but that boy didn't have enough sense to know that those guns spew burnt black powder into the skin. And for all he knew, that gun could have had a real bullet in it. Even so, aimed a little higher and it could have blinded Dave for life."

"Doesn't that beat all!"

"I had to rush him to the emergency room."

"Is he all right?"

"You can still see the marks of powder burns. They gave him a tetanus shot. Cleaned him up. I guess he's all right. I never allow guns of any kind in my house. But I'd had it with that neighborhood."

"Land's sake, I don't blame you."

"Of course, Stevie is not happy about leaving his friend Carl Johnson, but then his parents promise to have Stevie over to see Carl sometimes."

"What about Stevie's little girlfriend?"

"Girlfriend? Oh, little Deloris. Stevie's shiner from the boys' rubber gun fight seems to have ended that little romance. We became some of the scruffs of the neighborhood. Anyway, the Merthers moved away last summer."

Dorothy looked all around the room. "Well, Gladys, I'm happy for you that you are in a quiet neighborhood and have a nice big house to bring the boys up in."

"A house that needs a lot of work done on it!"

"Yes, but you can take your time with that. It's quite livable."

Stevie dashed into the kitchen gasping to catch his breath.

"Stevie," said his aunt, "How do you like your new home?"

"Neat. We got a creek and all in the back. Crawdads and frogs and little fish, sometimes."

"That's nice."

"And a garage I can play in. And know what? We can follow the creek way, way up to woods and fields and all."

"Well, be careful up there. It could be a little wild." said his mother. "Mr. Wilson said that there was some country and farmland north of here." She sighed, as if to reassure herself, "One of the advantages here is Stevie's school next year is only two blocks from here. She pointed, "In the opposite direction of the woods."

"Oh, isn't that nice, Stevie."

"Guess so."

"I won't worry as much when I have to leave for work so early. But right now, his school, Central, is across town. He walks it—about twenty minutes."

"Do you like your new school, Stevie?"

"Uh-huh. Don't know anybody 'cept Jim and Bill and Harold and—oh mother, I met a guy named Carl, only he's Carl Jeske."

"That's nice. And you can have Carl Johnson over sometimes this summer."

"Goodo."

"How about the girls in your new school, Stevie?"

"Yeh, they got girls, too."

"His teacher said they were preparing for parents' night production. Tell your Aunt Dot what the children are going to do."

Stevie looked down at his feet and scratched his forehead. His voice dropped. "Oh, a, they're going to do a dance or somethin'."

"What's that?"

"They're doing the Missouri Waltz," said Gladys. "I'm sorry I'll miss it. I've piano lessons to give," said his mother.

Stevie brightened up. "That's okay."

"How nice! Won't dancing be fun, Stevie!"

"Didn't you say, Stevie, that all the children are going to dress up and dance the Missouri Waltz across the stage?" said his mother. "Didn't you, Stevie?"

Stevie looked at the door, distracted. "Guess so."

"Will you dance with a nice girl?"

"Boys ain't too happy."

"Don't say 'ain't', Stevie."

"Well, I think that's just wonderful," said Aunt Dot. "I didn't learn to dance until I was twenty. Did you, Gladys?"

"Not in Russellville, Arkansas. Those moss-backed hypocrites didn't approve of anything. Remember, I had to be chaperoned just to play piano at the dances in London and even then, tongues wagged about how disgraceful it was for Mama to let me earn money playing for a dance."

Dot laughed. "Uncle Bud had to take you and bring you home."

"I wasn't allowed to even talk to anybody at the dances."

Stevie looked around, wanting to end the interrogation. He eyed the refrigerator. "We gonna eat soon?"

"In about half an hour. Stay in ear-shot."

Stevie bolted out.

The evening of the elementary school's 'open house' arrived that following Thursday, and behind the stage curtain, the little boys in suits were tugging at their ties, and the little girls were in their prettiest, full party dresses.

Stevie peeked out between the curtains. "Yikes!" He saw that the gymnasium was filled with people—parents, neighbors, teachers, friends—he'd never seen so many people in one small space to watch the young ones perform something.

Mrs. Hunt said, "Now, Stevie, take your place over there by Lois. Now, children, all your parents should be in the front three rows." She peeked out between the curtains at the audience. "Where's your parents, Stevie?" Mrs. Hunt had Stevie by the sleeve. "They should be near the front. Where are they?"

"Um …they couldn't make it."

"Oh dear. I'm sorry to hear that. I so wanted to meet them. I wanted all the parents to be here."

"He don't got a father, Mrs. Hunt," said Carl Jeske. Carl was from a poor country family that lived on a five-acre farm on the outskirts of town. Stevie befriended him because he always passed Stevie's house going to and from school and stopped to notice Stevie's dog, and he felt some kind of kinship with Carl. He, like Stevie, had a big brother, who passed on to him ill-fitting clothes, obvious hand-me-downs.

This night, Stevie was wearing Neel's pants, which Neel had worn to seventh grade graduation. They sagged rather around the waist except where the belt gathered them in and they sagged in the crouch and were a little too long in the leg, bunching up at the shoe. Still, wondered Stevie, did everybody know that these pants had a fancy zipper, which he'd never had before?

"Stevie has no father?" responded Mrs. Hunt, shaking her head in pity.

Why did Mrs. Hunt sound so funny about Stevie having no father, wondered Stevie. Still, that's all right, thought Stevie. And he thought, too, that at least he was lucky that Neel and Dave weren't in the gym to watch him. The less they knew about his dancing with girls the better. He had been prepared for weeks to tell them, if they asked him, that dancing was sissified, and he did it only 'cause he had to. Of course, he liked being close to a girl, a pretty one that is, in a pretty dress, but Lois Barkley was no Lois Lane, though when he tied the strings of his mother's slip around his neck so that it dangled at his back and jumped from the dresser onto his mother's big bed (when no one was home, of course), he was surely Superman. Here he knew practically none of the girls backstage. Some were in another class, but they looked pretty just the same. He had hoped Deloris was among them. He saw them all. She was not. Nor any girl like her.

Mrs. Hunt called them together behind the stage. "All right, children, now get with your partners. Over here. You with Allison there, Freddie, and Dale get over here with Teresa. Stevie, you lost? There's your Lois over there. Now, children get ready to dance. That's right, Jimmy; you and Sharon lead off. Your hand at her waist and your other takes hers. Now. Okay, get ready. There's the music, the curtain. Now go!"

She pushed each couple out on the stage at intervals. Stevie and Lois were near the end, so they had to wait a long time and get the jitters before going out onto the stage in front of everybody—so they could get it over with. Suddenly the spotlight was on them, and Stevie danced Lois around and around, and suddenly, he thought he was on the stage at the Muny and thousands of people were watching the square and the whirl and the square and whirl—and it wasn't so bad after all. Not at all. Yet he could hear himself saying to Dave and Neel, "Old Mrs. Hunt made us do it!"

It was a brief performance. A few class skits and the Missouri Waltz while some of the children sang: "Way down in Missouri where I heard that melody ... "—the song played over and over in Stevie's mind—and all too quickly, it was over. The big lights went down, and the children began leaving the stage.

"Stevie," said Mrs. Hunt at the gym door. "Is somebody coming for you?"

"Yes, Ma'am," he said although he wasn't sure.

And later, with practically everyone gone, Stevie was still there, standing outside the gym door opposite the playground. It was a moonlit night and the stars were out. A few parents were lingering to talk to teachers. Shortly, Mrs. Hunt came over to Stevie.

"I see you're still here, Stevie."

Jiggers, thought Stevie, I'm noticed. "I'm leaving in a minute, Ma'am."

"Who's coming for you?"

"Oh, my brother Dave, Ma'am."

"I can take Stevie home," said a nice man in a blue suit. "Lois says he could use a ride."

"That would be nice, Mr. Barkley. Thank you."

"You don't mind a ride, do you, Stevie?" Mr. Barkley smiled.

"My brother Dave is coming." His face reddened.

"Your brother Dave, you say. We'll wait anyway for a few minutes just to be sure. We don't want you stranded here and have to walk home alone in the dark."

Mrs. Hunt and Mrs. Barkley talked on as Stevie became more and more antsy. He had to go to the bathroom, and he was afraid if he went in to the boys' room, his brother would come and go. He waited and waited some more. Meanwhile, another pair of parents joined in the conversation. Stevie decided he could wait no longer to go to the bathroom. He had learned his lesson about things like that, so brother or no brother, he was going to the bathroom. Back into the gym he went. He found the gym door to the locker room locked. That meant he had to go into the school hallway. Once there he had to go to the other end of the building to make it to the one washroom he knew. He hurried.

When he finished, something was caught. He couldn't get the zipper of his brother's pants to go back up; they were, after all, his big brother's pants, and although they were a size too large, he'd worn them because he didn't have anything else to wear. Besides, they had creases in the legs. But now, how was he to get the zipper up? Damn. None of his clothes had zippers. His other pants had bottoms, and he could just button them up. He hated zippers. After a struggle, he gave up and folded the material under his belt. It looked funny, but he had to hurry. When he had walked the length of the hall and grabbed the knob of the gym-door, suddenly all the lights went out.

"Geez, I gotta hurry!" He turned the knob, but nothing happened. "Door's locked!" He turned around. The hall was dark and forbidding.

"Mrs. Hunt."

Gotta talk louder. "Mrs. Hunt." No answer. Better shout. "Mrs. Hunt!"

Awful silence. What should he do? He'd never seen a school so silent and so dark. He started trying the other doors. Locked. Locked. Locked. Unlocked! But it was a closet. Brooms and folding chairs and stuff. Another door. Locked. All classrooms locked. And the principal's office locked. The front door. He ran to the big doors that faced downtown Ferguson. The outside light was fast fading. He tried the large doors. Locked too! He could see through the glass squares the street lights had come on. He could see lights in some of the homes on the other sides of the streets. But these were far away.

"Mrs. Hunt!" he shouted.

Then through the window squares, he saw two figures coming around the walk to the back of the school. They were young people, like his brothers. Wait! One was his brother.

"Dave!" he shouted and began rattling and pounding on the door.

It did the trick. They turned. They saw him.

"Hey," said Dave, "the little squirt is inside the closed-up school."

In seconds, they reached the door. "Come out of there!"

"He can't," said his friend Tom. "He's locked in."

"Locked in! The little squirt. Hey, Stevie, try the doors!" Through the class panes, Stevie was doing a dumb show of helplessness. "What a jerk!"

"His face is looking funny," said Tom.

"Hey, ya like school so much ya wanna stay there all weekend?" shouted Dave.

"He's funny! What a face!" shouted Tom. "Can he hear anything we say?"

"Ha, that's him crying," said Dave. They watched for a few minutes. Then Dave said, "Guess we should get him out of there." He looked around. "Let's try a classroom window. We'll tell him."

Dave began tapping on a window square, pointing down the hall. "Down there. Above the door! If you can climb up there, you can get into that classroom. Down there! See it!" He kept tapping. Stevie looked back and forth, from down the hall and back to his brother again.

"Up!" said Dave. "Over the door!"

Finally Stevie saw it, stopped crying and pointed, too.

"Yeh! Go down there, dopey! We'll go around to that classroom. We—around to the room! See you there! Okay! Get something to stand on. Climb up." Dave made a motion like he was climbing. "Stand on something. Climb up and through that thing over the door. Okay, we'll see you round the side."

Stevie ran down the hall to the door in question. He started jumping up and down under the transom, but soon he saw it was useless. He looked up and down the hall for something to stand on. Nothing. Then he remembered the broom closet. He ran to the door and swung it open. There was a light cord there, and he pulled it. He grabbed a folding chair and some boxes. He began hauling the windfall to the classroom door. Soon he had a pile high enough to allow him to reach the transom, but the pile was shakey. By this time, Dave and Tom were coaxing him from the outside windows across the classroom.

"That's it! Climb up now! Get through that opening!" But their words were useless. Stevie could not hear them. Still, he struggled to get atop the pile while Dave and Tom watched with amused interest.

"He made it," said Tom. But no sooner had he uttered these words then the structure collapsed. Down went Stevie, out of sight!

"Oops!" said Dave, trying not to laugh too loud.

"Now you see him, now you don't." Tom had no scruples.

At first, they didn't know if he would get up or not. Then they could see just the top of his towhead, then his sad face, and then his shoulders and arms as he scratched his head.

"He looks like a junior Stanley. There's Stanley of Olie and Stanley!"

"Hey, you numbskull!" shouted Dave. "Try it again!"

Without hearing the encouragement, Stevie set to trying it again. First the folding chair, then a wooden crate, and then a double cardboard carton. When he finished, the structure didn't appear to be much firmer. Yet Stevie climbed up slowly and got his hands and head through the transom. But the transom wasn't big enough for the rest of him.

Tom and Dave were really into the action.

"Turn the handle!" cried out Dave. "The handle!"

"Over there next to you! Look!" They pointed with exaggerated gestures.

"Over there! Turn the handle!"

Their dumb show worked. Stevie looked, saw the handle and pulled it. At first the wrong way and the window tightened on him. Ow! Then he turned the handle and lifted the other way, and it opened wide enough for him to fit through.

"Hooray for the clown!" shouted Dave.

"Goofy did it!" shouted Tom.

Now Stevie crawled through, twisted around, and with his hands holding on to the upper frame, he dangled there.

"That's it. Now drop!" shouted Dave.

"Drop!" shouted Tom.

"Why doesn't he drop? Hey, drop!"

"He's just hanging there, like a monkey. Let go, you monkey!"

"He's gotta drop sometime." Dave shook his head. "Uh-oh. There he goes."

Stevie dropped. They could hear the clump! He disappeared below the desktops.

"The little jerk killed himself," said Dave.

"No. He's up! He did it. He did it!" said Tom as if he were watching a motion picture thriller. "Here he comes!"

Dave shook his head. "What a clown!"

When Stevie reached the window which Tom and Dave were pressed against, they pointed to the lock and shouted, "Open it! Open it!"

In seconds, Stevie was free. They slapped him on the back. "Hooray for Stevie!" they shouted.

"Wait," said Tom. "We can't leave things like this. We gotta put that stuff back in there."

"Why for?" said Dave.

"Yeh, why for?" said Stevie.

"They'll know something happened here, and they'll get the FBI and they'll come out and take fingerprints and—and Stevie will go to prison."

"Geez," said Dave. "Don't you think we'd just better get the hell out of here?"

"Heck no," said Tom. "We gotta make it look like nothing's happened."

"Cops'll get us sure, if we don't git!"

"Come on. It's only the right way to do it. Come on." With that, Tom quickly climbed inside and headed for the door. Dave followed

Tom. This was hardest for Stevie because he never wanted to go inside that school again for the rest of his life. But Stevie didn't want to hang around out there by himself, so he followed Dave.

Now, being inside a school building by their own will made the event into an adventure. But Stevie was not so brave. "Do we haffta?" said Stevie three or four times while he followed.

They made it to the classroom hall door and unlatched it. Tom and Dave picked up the boxes, and Stevie folded the metal chair and put it on his head like he saw natives do to carry things in *Tarzan* films. Just as they started down the hall, a light flashed from outside the front doors and sharply beamed down the hall towards them.

"Jiggers, the cops!" shouted Tom, who instantly dropped his box and swung around. Dave dropped his, swung around and bumped into Stevie. Stevie fell backwards and his chair legs crashed through the classroom-door windows, making a terrible racket, with glass going everywhere.

"Geez, what'd you do that for, Stevie. Now we're in big trouble." But there wasn't time for them to discuss it. They ran back through the classroom and dove out the window. Across the school grounds, they sprinted like three scared rabbits.

"Hey, you boys! Stop!" It was man's angry voice. He had just turned the corner of the school building. "You hear me! Stop!"

They were spotted in the flashlight beam, but nothing was about to stop them. Stevie was sure he was going to hear machine gun fire like he saw in a prison-break film, where the prisoners, all except one, were mowed down in the searing light. If he didn't run faster, he knew he'd be mowed down.

They reached a fence, climbed and tumbled over it, ran around a house, over the yard, across the street and up a hill onto the railroad tracks. There they hid in bushes next to the terminal to catch their breath. Were they being chased? A train whistled in the distance.

Down below, a police car came spinning around the corner, spotlight sweeping the hill.

"Behind the station!" shouted Tom, who had grown up in

Ferguson and knew every nook and cranny. When they reached the platform, they saw the train in the distance. He pointed. "Come on, over the tracks to beat the train." He took off. The Fulbright boys followed.

"Hey, where are you boys—!" The stationmaster had come out of the station too late to stop the boys." He missed them as they flew over the tracks. "Stop! You want to get killed!"

The police car sped up the terminal drive and screeched to a halt just as the train's engine came rumbling through. Two policemen jumped out. They and the stationmaster stood together watching the boxcars rattle by.

The stationmaster shrugged his shoulder. "Damn kids!"

On the other side, the boys ran down the hill behind the shops and followed the creek under the bridge and on to home.

"Neato!" said Dave, which was his way of complimenting Tom for his lead in the get-away."

"That's nothing," said Tom, wiping the sweat from his brow. "We've had closer calls than that. You should have seen us when we snow-balled a copcar and got chased through the lumber yard."

"Yeh?"

When Stevie came in through the backdoor, it was dark in the hallway. His mother, grandmother and aunt were there.

"How's the big dancer?" asked his mother.

"Huh?"

"How's ol' Fred Astair!" said his Aunt. "I bet you did some fancy footwork."

"Huh?" Stevie was self-conscious about his escape attire.

"Sorry I couldn't make it," said his mother. "My student just left. Did you dance well for the parents?"

"Huh?"

"Come in the kitchen and let Dot and Mama see your clothes."

"Don't want to."

"Come on, Stevie. Don't be bashful. Come on." She pulled him into the light.

"Oh for heaven's sake, what happened to you? Your clothes are dirty and torn. I hope you didn't look like this in the show."

"Huh … ?" He sputtered. *How could he explain his appearance?*

"Is that all you can say, Stevie? 'Huh?'"

Stevie disappeared up the stairs.

"Well," said Gladys. "Anyhow, we're in a descent neighborhood."

Epiglimpselogue Seventeen

"They were lucky they didn't get caught. All three of them might have been sent off to a boys' reform school," said Sally, amused.

"True. But they weren't bad guys. They just had a lot of imagination and a knack for a little mild mischief," responded James.

"I wonder how Al Capone behaved at their age in those times," said Rupert.

"They never shot anybody or stole anything. Nor got into booze and stuff."

"Yeh, but it sounds like they enjoyed their little mischief."

"True," said James. "They used to throw snowballs at cars coming down Darst Road. On one occasion, they loaded up and plastered a car but good, and it turned out to be a police car. That's when they really got chased. They weren't caught, though. They knew the area better than the police!"

GLIMPSES EIGHTEEN

"HORSE DOCTOR"

On Monday, the Great Bowl game now history, Steve settled back into school work at Vogt. His music class introduced the classics, including Tchiakovsky's "Waltz of the Flowers" and "Swan Lake" and Bach and Beethoven. On Tuesday, Steve started sneezing and coughing, and on Wednesday, he got an earache. It was bad enough to keep him moaning and groaning in bed all day. On Thursday, it was bad enough that his mother told him he would have to go see the doctor, Dr. Roy Johnson that is. Steve was stunned.

"Not that ol' horse doctor!"

Mother was out the door, off to work. If she had heard him at all, she had nothing to say about that. After she left for work, Steve lay in bed with the worst earache he had ever had in his entire life, and the thought of Dr. Roy Johnson, horse doctor, M. D., didn't help his ache any. Of course, Dr. Johnson wasn't really a horse doctor. That's just what the kids called him. That was because Dr. Johnson was not much into anesthetics. He was the neighborhood doctor, and when kids came away from his treatments, they were nearly always in pain. How could Steve face more pain?

When the next day came, nothing had changed before his mother left for work, his mother again told him that she'd hear "no more nonsense," that Steve had to go see that Doctor.

"Not that Frankenstein, Mr. Hyde, Boris Karloff character!" As if his splitting ear wasn't bad enough!

"Now he's a good doctor. When I get home, I want to know that you've been to see him."

"But do I have to ..." again, the door slammed.

Soon his brother Dave popped his head in through the bedroom door. "Hey, squirt, Mother says you got to go see the doctor, so get up!"

"That horse doctor! Ain't gonna!"

"Ya better!"

"You said your own self that Dr. Rob-Roy Johnson is an ol' horse doctor."

"Nah, I didn't say that. I said he was an ol' army doctor. I said he used ta saw arms and legs off guys who'd got shot up and grenaded in a battle."

"You said he was a horse doctor. 'Sides, I don't want nothin' cut off."

"I didn't say he cut off things. I said he sawed off things, like arms and legs. That's different."

"Nah it ain't. I don't want nothin' sawed off."

"Have it your own way, but if you die, I'm takin' your set of cactuses."

"Ain't cactuses. It's cacti. 'Sides, you leave my—" but before Steve could finish, the front door slammed. Dave was gone.

"Ow!" that ear hurt.

Now there wasn't much point in trying to go back to sleep. Steve was fully awake with his ear hurting a whole lot. He thought about himself getting up, putting on his clothes and shoes and his coat and cap and saying goodbye to his little buddy, his little dog Curley—as far as he could see, the only one that had sympathy for him—and then walking the three blocks to Dr. Roy Johnson's office. It wasn't that far, not normally. Steve could make that distance in a matter of minutes. But with an aching ear—that was different. It could take him forever because he'd be thinking of the horse doctor sawing off guys' legs and what it was he'd do to Steve when he got there.

His ear was aching all the more like there was some plot to insure that Steve would have to face the horse doctor. His thoughts drifted back to late last summer when, like now, he had to go to the doctor by himself. Not that he wanted to relive any moment of it. But how could he forget that day? For sheer pain, it was the worst day of his life. He just couldn't help it. He had stepped on a board with a nail in it at the old lumber yard a few days before and that morning, he had awakened to his foot in so much pain he had to show it to his mother and she said.

"Oh my God," she'd said, "Your foot's infected—bad! You have to get to the doctor right away this morning."

It was true. Steve had never seen anything like it. All around his toes, it was swollen terribly. Underneath, on the ball of his foot where the nail had entered, it was puffy with a small black mark. Then a black line extended several inches up through the space between his big toe and the next toe, and there it was swollen even more, and the foot ached like he could never walk on it again.

Steve wasn't going to be able to run and play ball with a foot like that. So there was no doubt about it. Steve would have to go get some medicine to take for the nasty-looking thing so it would go away, and so he could walk and run like always. He had to get to the doctor's right away. He rose up and realized that getting to the doctor's was not going to be easy. His foot ached more than ever now that he was standing, and he would have to get his shoes on somehow and walk all the way to the doctor's.

When Steve took his first step that morning, he nearly collapsed with the shooting pain. What was he to do? He would have to get a shoe on that foot somehow, and he would have to walk very gingerly to the doctor's.

He found he could move a little at a time if he held his right injured foot out a little and hopped tiny distances on his left foot.

"Ow!" Even the slightest pressure on his injury hurt.

He wished he had crutches or a walking stick or something that could allow him to take all the pressure off his foot, but there was no such item to be found, he knew, anywhere in the house. It was difficult and seemed to take forever just to round up his clothes and shoes. And when it came to putting on the right-foot tennis shoe, he found he had to leave it wide open, unlaced, tongue out, just to insert the foot into the shoe. Then he put the tongue up and laced it ever so lightly, doing so only to get the strings out of the way so he wouldn't trip.

How could he relive that day now? Yet the distance he had to go made him relive that foot day and that horse doctor he had to go see.

Going down the steps wasn't too bad because he could sit down and scoot down a step at a time. At the bottom, he paused and looked back up the steps and thanked God he didn't have to go up steps, for that would have been a dilly. Finally he left the house and the trek was on. His limping was so pronounced and so obviously painful, he thought that perhaps someone would come along in a car and offer him a ride. This was not to happen that morning, for it appeared that everyone had left for work or school already, and the streets were empty. Getting to the end of the street, which usually took five minutes, took half an hour.

And the pain was steadily getting worse. When he rounded the next block, he remembered, and he was about half way there, he wondered if he'd be able to stand the pain long enough to make it all the way or would he have to lay down right where he was and die.

Someone would come in the afternoon and find his body and see his foot the size of a basketball, all puffy and black and red and blue. Somebody would notify his mother, and she would arrange a funeral with flowers like his father's funeral, and everybody would come and weep except his big brothers of course, but nobody would expect them to weep. His brother Neel would say, "Well, what do you know about that!" and his brother Dave would move Steve's cactus collection onto his own window ledge. Maybe they'd play "Waltz of the Cacti" at his funeral.

In an hour, Steve finally came within view of the squat building that housed Dr. Roy Johnson's clinic or office or whatever he called it. But Steve had reached only the back gravel parking area. He still had to go across and up the drive to enter in the front door, for the back door was a forbidden entrance with a big sign that said so. Steve had noticed that such is always true when there's an emergency and torture of this kind.

The gravel stones of the parking lot cut into the thin, well-worn sole of Steve's left tennis shoe because he had all his weight on the foot, especially while he was hopping. At last the front entrance! Oh no. Two up-steps with no banister mocked him. He stood for a while, contemplating this forbidding entranceway. Several persons jostled passed him, nearly stomping on his poor foot.

"Excuse me! Excuse me!" Their voices rang with annoyance.

"Geez," thought Steve, "in the way again." He called after them. "Jus' hangin' out!" They disappeared around the corner.

"Ow!" This jostling made his foot hurt more than ever, and he was exhausted. He scratched his head. He pondered. He couldn't give up now of course, now that he had arrived. But he guessed the doctor wasn't going to treat him out there on the street. How could he get up those two steps and inside? He thought. He could sit by easing himself down into a sitting position onto the top step and scoot back like he did going down the steps at home earlier, but in reverse, and when he was far enough across the deck, he would swing his legs around and then climb up the door with the use of the door handle and, in that way, be able to enter the reception room.

Well, why not? So he turned around and eased himself down. "Ow!" the foot hurt. He prepared for his next movement when suddenly a scream came from somewhere deep inside the building, a loud blood-curdling scream. "What was that!" It was a Frankenstein scream, like from a haunted castle somewhere in Moravia. Steve wondered if his infected foot could turn into a Wolf-man's hairy foot with large hooked claw-like nails. Maybe the doctor would run away from him, scared out of his pajabbers.

"You're in the way, buddy." A large man came out the door and scowled down at him. He shook his head, like what kind of an idiot kid is this, stepped over Steve and went on his way.

"Could've used that claw," thought Steve, wiggling his seat around on the deck of the entrance. With his legs swung around and leaning on his left arm, he reached up for the door handle, grabbed it, leaned forward and began lifting himself.

When he was just about all the way up, he felt suddenly the door knob turn in his hand, the door swing part-wide open, and then wham!—he lost his balance and fell—down he went into and onto the floor of the reception room. A plump lady with a young girl about his age coming through the door stood over him, both agape looking down at him. Since Steve was half inside, several other patients in the waiting room looked over and down at him as well with the strangest sort of curiosity on their faces.

"My goodness, I'm sorry," said the lady looking down at him. The girl smiled a half smile. "Are you all right?" asked her—he assumed-- mother.

"Huh?" *What was Steve to say?*

"Come, dear. Don't get too close to him." They shifted around and disappeared out the door. What did he have? Leprosy?

"Ow!" moaned Steve. Did anybody know that his foot really, really hurt? Steve rolled on into the reception room.

"Ow!" Did he groan that out loud? Oh well, thought Steve, feeling a sense of accomplishment that he had arrived. He crawled to a chair and slowly raised himself into it and into a sitting position. Several continued to stare at him.

"Well," Steve thought, "they can gawk at me all they want. I don't care. I made it!"

"Over here!" demanded a nurse, seemingly oblivious to his plight, through the glass sliding panel, which had just been opened from behind the counter.

"Geez," thought Steve. "Here we go again." He struggled and rose on the chair arms and very slowly and very carefully hobbled to the window.

"What seems to be the problem, young man?" said the lady, barely looking at him.

"My foot."

She leaned over the counter and looked down at it.

"What's wrong with it?"

"It hurts."

"Hum," said the lady. "What did you do to it?"

"Stepped on a nail th'other day, and now it's all red and puffy—and has a black line and it—"

"Had a tetanus shot?"

"Huh?"

"Okay, no tetanus shot," the lady said matter-of-factly.

"Appointment?"

"Huh?"

"No appointment," she whipped back. "Sit over there 'til the doctor calls. He's very busy today."

"My foot apologizes," Steve wanted to say.

Hours passed. People came and went and every so often, screams would come from somewhere way in back. Steve couldn't run. So he waited and waited. Finally about noon, he was called, and he hobbled in through the door to the examining room.

"Let's take a look," said the largest, burliest man he'd ever seen in his life. Surely this man was a professional wrestler who moonlighted a medical practice.

"Aha!" the Doctor said as if with delight when he uncovered the spectacle. "A nail, huh! Ought to watch where you step, young man." He smiled a malicious smile. Steve certainly needed to hear that.

Suddenly, Steve was poked in the arm with a needle by the nurse.

"Scoot back on the table there," said the doctor, catching Steve's injured foot with his hand and dabbing it with something smeared on cotton.

"Ow!" shouted Steve when the doctor squeezed his foot and dabbed some more. Then from out of nowhere, a knife flashed in the doctor's raised right hand.

Steve cringed and shriveled. "Are you goin' to cut my foot off?"

The doctor ignored his question. Down came the knife, and slice it went as quick as lightning.

"Yeow!" cried Steve with blood and puss squirting everywhere. "Yeow!"

The doctor squeezed Steve's foot, and up went the knife and *slice* again it went. Steve couldn't look. When he looked back, was he going to find his precious foot hanging off his ankle bone by a piece of tissue or skin? Of course, it hurt like the devil!

"Yeow!" In all of creation was there ever anything so painful. "Yeow!"

The doctor dabbed something gooey on the spot and motioned to the nurse. "Clean him up and send him home." And away the Doctor Roy Johnson flew. Like an elephant bat, thought Steve.

When this was accomplished and the dressing and bandage applied, Steve was let loose to embark on his homeward journey. His only solace was that he could see his foot was still attached to his ankle.

"Oh God," he said. "How am I going to get home?"

But he did make it home, on his own. And once home he had the sympathy of his best little friend, Curley!

Steve shook his head as if to awaken himself from his memory, the pain, a horrible nightmare. How did he get home that day? It was only last summer, and yet he could remember only that somehow he did get home, and when he did, he cherished his house, his Curley, his bedroom.

But reality again asserted itself. Now he must go to the ol' horse doctor again and have his ear—so painful, so terrible—because he was back again causing havoc, would this time he have to have his ear cut off!

Hold on. He felt his ear. Could it be? It couldn't be. But it was. His ear didn't ache anymore. He shook his head. The earache was gone. Oh, had it subsided only for a moment? Would it hurt again? No. It didn't ache again. It didn't ache at all. He could feel all around it. It was well. He was fine. Had he cured himself thinking of the ol' army-horse doctor? He spun around and headed back home. Good ol' Curley was there to greet him. It never felt so good to be home.

He couldn't wait to tell his mother in the evening how suddenly his earache went entirely away. Nor wait until he could tell his brother Dave that he wasn't going to get his cactus collection after all. He pulled through. Oh, what a good day it was. No earache, no earache!

"Well?" said his mother when she arrived home that evening. "Did you get to the doctor?"

"No, mother, my earache went away."

"Went away?" Her eyebrows raised and her eyes narrowed.

"Yes, mother."

"What do you mean your earache went away?"

Sreve shrugged. "Jus' went."

"Well, I'll tell you this, young man. You're going to have those tonsils out, no matter what!"

"Are they cut off, Mother? Or are they sawed off?"

Epiglimselogue Eighteen

"So Steve kept his foot and kept his ear," observed Rupert. "We had a family doctor like that. Never heard of painkillers."

"Yes," said Lily, "Painkillers, anesthesia, are a more recent phenomena. At least Steve and his family were in no danger of Steve becoming addicted to pain-killers."

"That is a major problem today," added Ben. "When I came out of the hospital, after an operation, I loaded up on painkiller, very little of which I actually took. A friend of mine begged me for the leftovers, and I gave them to her, wondering if I did the right thing."

"Those things can be highly addictive," said James.

"They can damage your liver," said Lily. "You see, Dr. Roy Johnson, the horse doctor, wasn't so bad, now was he!"

"Steve's painful foot is preferable!" exclaimed Ben. "Anyway, if a guy complained about pain, they'd say, 'You're a guy, you can take it.' And then, guy-to-guy, the well-meaning doctor suffered the epithet, 'horse-doctor.' and worse!"

"But painkillers are modern progress," said Rupert.

"Huxley warns us about eliminating pain and problems," offered Sally.

"Oh, yes," nodded James. "In *Brave New World*. Get rid of all the frustrations. Isn't that what progress, namely the future, is all about?"

Glimpses Nineteen

"SUFFER THE PETS TO COME UNTO ME"

One day during the second week of school at Vogt—a hot summer day it was in early September—Steve stood under an oak tree on the edge of the school's playground, a playground that was not at the school, but down the road a block away. Several boys Steve's age who knew each other were throwing a football back and forth as Steve watched with envy. He could do that as well as they could, and he wouldn't care about the heat if one of them would throw him the ball. He would show them.

"Betcha can't swim," said a voice behind him that sounded like the projected voice of a poor ventriloquist.

Steve turned. The oddest voice he'd ever heard, one that combined sissiness with cockiness, belonged to a short, squat, tussled, brown-haired boy with a wry smile.

"Watcha say?" said Steve.

"Betcha can't swim."

"Bet I can."

The boy reached for a low branch and tried to pull himself up, but then he let himself fall back again.

"No, you can't. Not where I swim."

"Where do you swim?"

"Swimmin' hole. Where d'ya think. Only place I'd swim." He picked up several acorns and threw them in the direction of the railroad track.

"No swimmin' holes around here," said Steve.

"Is so," replied the high-pitched Charley MacCarthy voice of the somewhat blubbery figure as he half swung on the limb again with his legs doubled under. "An' you don't know where it is."

"Where is it?" Steve said casually as if he didn't much care. But he thought of when he was in Joplin a few weeks ago with Ben, Roland and Deeter. They not only swam in an old swimming hole, but they caught fish there too, cooked them and ate them.

"You couldn't find it," said the boy with a tuft of black hair falling down his forehead.

"Why not? How'd ya find it?"

"It's on the way to my house, o'er there." He pointed beyond the railroad tracks. Steve noticed the sleeves of his striped shirt were rolled up, showing his pudgy forearm. Steve knew that the area he pointed to was a wild area thick with trees and vines and all kinds of undergrowth. He knew because he and Tom and Dave hid over there once when they were being chased for throwing rotten plums at cars.

"Nobody lives over there," said Steve.

"I do."

"I looked around over there couple weeks ago. Didn't see nothin'."

"Ya didn't look right. I can show ya. But you can't swim no way."

"I can so as good as you, I bet." He'd watched once when his older brothers were being taught by Clark Kent, his mom's friend, and wound up doing his arms and legs as good as his brothers, said Clark Kent Ward.

The boy smiled. "Soon's school's out, then I'll show ya."

It was a challenge. "Okay."

"Okay."

The boy started back down the road to the school. He had a

strange walk, thought Steve, like nobody else Steve had ever seen, like he was some kind of a cowboy with one heavy shoulder.

"Hey!" called Steve.

The boy stopped in his tracks and looked back.

"What's your name?"

"James."

"James?"

"James Dempsey." Steve had a peculiar feeling he'd heard that name before. Not in a good way, but maybe it was in school for getting into some kind of trouble or other.

"See ya after school," shouted Steve, hoping it would cover up his doubts.

James' lips scrunched together an okay and off he swaggered.

In class that afternoon, Steve got to thinking he didn't want to meet James. He was too weird. Steve thought maybe he'd go out the opposite school side exit in a hurry before James would see him. The bell rang, and Steve exited quickly, but suddenly that peculiar voice called to him from the road.

"Come on," said James. "This way."

"Ya sure? It's kind of hot."

"Yeah. It's hot. Come on." He led Steve down the road, across the playground, then up onto the railroad tracks where they had a view of the "Match Factory," a large factory building with some warehouses and several driveways and parking lots with cars spread out to the right of them. In front and to the left was a large wild area, a place that couldn't have been more thicketed, thought Steve as he stood in silence, trying to figure out how not to go with James if he could do it without acting like something was wrong.

Steve wiped the sweat from his brow. "You sure you know where you're goin'?"

"You're comin', ain't ya?"

"Yeah."

"Jis' follow me," said James Dempsey, and he led the way down the black-gray gravel decline into the woods. Steve followed, but it looked like he was being led right into the stickeries and brambles. But suddenly—it seemed like magic—they happened right onto a path, a well-defined one. They followed it. It wound around and down and shortly came to a meandering creek, a sparkling creek, and a little farther—there it was!—a blue pool just as large as Ben, Roland and Deeter's swimin' cove way out in the country, but right here close to everything.

"You swim here?" said Steve in amazement.

"Lots of times." James started pulling off his shoes. "Bes' place to swim anywhere. Don't like swimming pools. Full o' stuff, bad stuff. They're dumb! This is the bes' water they is."

"How'd know?"

"'Sides, anybody can tell you, if they have a lick 'o sense. They's chemicals and stuff in that swimmin' pool water. I got vials I can show you at home." Now James was stripped down to his gray underpants. He went to the drop-off several feet above the water and straightened his arms over his head. "Come on." He dove in, which made a considerable splash in those quiet surroundings.

Steve stood, looking out over the water and up at the trees. Several jays squawked and flew away. A heron floated off between the trees in the distance.

James's head bobbed up in the water. "Ya comin' in?"

"Don't got trunks." Steve looked around. It certainly was hot enough for a cooling swim.

"Nobody that swims here do!"

"Don't know."

"Don't need 'em!"

"Well, okay." Steve stripped down to his underpants, but he noticed how stark white his underpants were, and they made him feel naked and embarrassed. He hesitated.

"Come on!" shouted James. "Water's jis' fine."

In the water would be better than standing there so white, thought Steve, so he held his nose and jumped.

Quickly he bobbed up, shuddering. "It's cold!"

"Nah, it ain't!" said James. "Spring-fed." He swam around, appearing to quite enjoy it. "Nothing like it—on a hot day."

It was true, Steve thought. He was hot no longer and getting to like the cold's freshness. "You come here all the time, I bet?"

"Yeh. Those dumb-dumbs get themselves poisoned in the public pools. I come here on hot days. 'Sides, don't pay no money."

Steve's feet touched the bottom and he felt the ooze of mud through his toes. He felt it was messy. "Say, are there crawdads and snakes and stuff in here?" He imagined a coil around his ankles and pinchers slicing at his toes.

"Sure. Lots of crawdads. Wanna catch some?"

"An fish too?"

"Sure. Not big enough to eat." Then he added, "Little ones that like to nibble your nipples."

"Yowl!" cried Steve. He touched his breast. "One jus' did it!"

"Yeh, they pinch and flutter when they getcha." James floated on his back, looking up at the tops of the trees. "Softest bed in the world," he said.

"Huh?"

"I said it's the softest bed they is. Two parts hydrogen and one part oxygen."

"Huh?"

"Millions of molecules rolling over themselves. That's what water is. It seeks its own level. That's what it does."

"Huh? Hey, how do you know so much?"

"Just 'cause I look into stuff. I can tell you what a lot of things is made of."

"Ya can? Like what?"

"Like soap and dye and gun powder and—"

"Gun powder!"

"Potassium nitrate and sulfur and—"

"You mean gun powder that you shoot in guns?"

"Sure. I can make it."

"You can make it?"

"In my chemistry lab at home. I got all the stuff. Wanna see?"

That was an invitation Steve couldn't pass up. After while, they dressed and took the path James said led straight to his house a short distance away.

Soon James said, "There's where I live. Pa and me."

"Where?"

"There! Between those trees behind which Arffer will be waiting."

Steve stared and moved closer. He didn't see it at first, but then he began to make out a mossy stone structure. It was a small house on the edge of the woods that was so surrounded by vines and trees, you could hardly tell there was a house at all. A large, old mongrel dog loped around the house and wagged its tail.

"Your dog?" asked Steve.

"Yeah, good ol' Arffie!" said James, giving his dog affectionate pats.

As scoungy as the dog looked, Steve could tell by James's affectionate pats that Arffie was as important in James's life as Curley had been in his. It was nice but also it saddened Steve.

"Nice dog," Steve mustered, despite the dog's scruffiness. Steve, too, patted him on the head and scratched him behind the ears. "I lost my dog Curley couple weeks ago. He was my best pal. When I came home from Mr. Wilson's farm, Dave, my brother, met me on the bike at the corner and told me not to whistle for Curley. Curley died."

"Your best pal? I know what you mean. What he'd die of?"

"Dave said they didn't know, but maybe he was poisoned 'cause somebody down the street didn't like him barking."

"Some neighbors can be like that."

"And when I wrote my essay for Mrs. Hendricks about Curley dying, she told the whole class it was silly that children think pets go to heaven. 'Pets don't have souls,' she said. I don't like Mrs. Hendricks."

"Yeah, she said that? That Mrs. Hendricks is a mean bitch." James continued to lead the way, Arffie trailing along.

"Come on. I'll show you my chem lab."

James ignored the make-shift wooden steps that led up to the back door of his house and instead, opened the lower door under the porch that brought them into the basement. He switched on the lights, several long flourescents that hung from the ceiling. There, spread out on several tables, was a sight Steve had never seen before. There were flasks, test tubes, beakers, Bunsen burners and glass tubing running everywhere. Behind these were shelves with row upon row of jars and containers marked sulfur, potassium nitrate, carbon, magnesium, and on and on.

"This is my lab," said James. "And look over here." All kinds of strings and small joiners and a carton, all hanging from the ceiling. "I'm fixin' an experiment. It's all ready to go, so's I can show you."

He fiddled with some strings, separating some and joining others.

"Now," he said. "I'll light the fuse. I made it all myself."

He struck a match and touched it to one end of a string. It turned red and smoked, burning slow at first. Then suddenly it sputtered and sparked and took off, racing along a line, catching two other fuses, which caught more fuses causing glows that now raced along in all sorts of directions. Then all the sparklings reached the carton at the same time and boom! Steve flinched. The carton exploded into a hundred pieces sending out a cloud of black smoke engulfing James' face, the master face behind it all.

When the smoke cleared, James' blackened face revealed a wide grin from ear to ear.

"Pretty neat, huh?"

"Yeah," said Steve. "Pretty neat."

The following, week when Steve reached the classroom before the bell rang, he went straight to his desk. Mrs. Hendricks was out in the hall talking to one of the other teachers. Then he saw what he had not noticed when he first entered the room. James Dempsey was at Mrs. Hendricks' desk, pulling a small object out of his trouser pocket. He put the small object on Mrs. Hendricks' chair. "Oh no," thought

Steve, "a tack." He looked over at the door. Mrs. Hendricks was still outside. "Hurry, James!" he said to himself. "Get away from there, or she'll catch you! Then there'll be all hell to pay!" James started to move away, and Steve started to breathe a sigh of relief when James looked back at the chair and stopped abruptly. Something was wrong. He headed back to the chair.

"No, don't go back!" thought Steve. "Not now!" James reached the chair, studied it and pondered. At that moment, Mrs. Hendricks entered the room. She stood right behind James while he re-positioned the tack with the utmost care so it would have the maximum effect on her rear end when she took her seat. Steve couldn't look. He put his head down and closed his eyes. He thought, "What a goof!" Still Steve liked James. James knew how certain things should be done. Little things. Particular things. James was—well, a scientist. That's what he was. A real scientist.

Further on in the summer in Ferguson when he went hiking back up in the woods to find the creek's source, watching and catching minnows and crawdads, he imagined that he still had his faithful companion Curley, who was getting to more and more prefer to stay at home, but when Steve went somewhere and didn't say "Curley stay!" Curley was by his side through thick and thin. But now and then, with larger obstacles, like a wider spot in the creek, Curley would stop and bark, and Steve would return and help him or carry him over to the next path. Even with Curley gone, in his summer outings, Steve felt he and Curley were inseparable. James the scientist could appreciate that. He wanted revenge for Steve, his new pal.

Epiglimselogue Nineteen

"Too bad Steve didn't take Curley to school with him," said Lisa.

"He would have, if they'd let him."

"So Steve appreciated this new friend, James, the science guy."

"Yes," said James the narrator. "Steve has always wondered whatever happened to James Dempsey. He was a Thomas Edison all right. In his small basement lab, he had test tubes, Bunsen burners, scales, the works. He knew science and had a favorite pet, a faithful dog. There are so many people around caught up in their own superstitions. James Dempsey was weird, but greatly to be appreciated."

"What happened to him with the tack on the teacher's chair incident?" asked Sally.

"James Dempsey felt he wanted to get even with her for what she had told the class—scoffing pets. He was sent to the principal's office," replied James. "Steve rarely saw James Dempsey after that. Apparently James was switched to another class, another teacher."

Shortly, James, the Club's narrator, added, "James Dempsey was not going to automatically accept what the world around him took for granted. He had his own values—a natural world, the world of the provable."

GLIMPSES TWENTY

THE FIRE STOKER

The large, breezy, wooden frame house at 123 Adele Street, located in the heart of old Ferguson, Missouri which was still a small town with a few miles of country yet between it and the sprawling city and not yet swallowed up by suburbia. In the summer, the old house was not particularly cool, and in the winter, it was extraordinarily frigid. Heating was the task of a large old coal-burning furnace in the basement. Coal came in a truckload and was dumped through the side window into the basement, making delivery days coal-dust days, sending the fine black dust up the stairs and ducts to cover everything in the house in its light but ugly layer. Fortunately, coal deliveries were infrequent.

To warm the house, fires had to be built from scratch on the grate inside through the cracking furnace door with no handy fire-starters to aid in the process. Paper, wood from broken up dead branches of trees or wood splinters of smashed up crates, minute chunks of coal carefully placed were all needed to get the larger lumps of the most stubborn coal in all the universe to turn red and glow. When that happened, heat would rise up through the ducts and, eventually, warm the house.

Responsibility for fires rested on the shoulders of Dave and Steve since Neel was usually away on after-school activities or working at Food Center. For Dave's part, he was usually not available after school either. So Steve became the usual fire-maker by default. The necessity spurred a little pyromania in Steve, not untypical of boys, and usually he took to the task as a sense of duty. It was hard work, and often he'd find out after a half hour of searching, breaking, placing, stacking, lighting and fanning, the fire would not catch the sneering coal.

Then he'd have to set about the job all over again. Working at it and coming up with results was better than having his mother, the easiestly chilled woman in the universe, yell at and threaten them when she came home, which was usually between 7:00 and 8:00 p.m.; for after a full day's work, she was usually late getting home, having to give one or two piano lessons at people's homes before being allowed that privilege. Who could blame her for wanting to drink her beer and smoke a cigarette in a comfortable, warm house?

Being in the back of the basement in the coal bin with the black beetles made Steve feel as if he were the male counterpart to Cinderella; the more he worked to keep the house in shape and warm, the better guy he would be. Where did he get this idea? He couldn't tell you. It was another of his private myths like the one that made him think at four years of age he had killed his father by his ungenerous thoughts of other people (except that the killer-thoughts myth was much less constructive, to say the least, than the Cinderella myth).

The Cinderella myth meant hard and unjust work at home would make him stronger and more appealing in life, for example, on the football field and with the girls. Besides there was more to Steve than Steve-the-fire-builder and Steve-the-stoker. He dreamed it. It was Steve the Roman!

Steve had taken to history in the sixth grade at his new school. He was learning all about the ancient Romans. Roman soldiers marched through Gaul and Germany and stood upon the White Cliffs of Dover. Was he there in a former life? Another one of his childhood myths: reincarnation.

A patrician, a Roman consul, he imagined he was. The Romans conquered the known world and built roads and bridges and aqueducts and coliseums and even a forum. The Romans brought law and order to the world of what was otherwise barbarians and scruffs. Steve was order itself. (Or at least he wanted to be.)

"We inherited the Roman Empire," said his teacher with superb stature. "And we should appreciate that fact!" Steve knew at once he had inherited quality stuff from the Romans. He visualized himself a particular Roman, first as a soldier with a helmet and a shield and a short wide sword slicing up the savage enemy-intruders, himself in a chariot racing over the cobble-stone roads and marching dauntlessly across Gaul, and then as a senator in a toga walking up the great, wide marble steps of the forum and inside, making Mark Anthony speeches.

Surely, he had once really been a Roman. He had to be somewhere in those days before he was Steve. He felt that affinity with Rome, and Rome was where he was. He was a Roman!

But in class, after a month or so, Rome began to fall to disorder and chaos; with the winter coming on, the weather was turning quite cold in St. Louis in this twentieth century, and fires in the furnace at 123 Adele were becoming more and more a dire necessity. Since no one was home to stoke the fire all day, that meant a new fire had to be built every afternoon so that by evening, the house would be warm enough for their mother. After all she grew up in Arkansas and was never St. Louis acclimatized.

So who was going to build the fires? Neel always had an excuse, usually after-school activities or with his part-time work at the A & P. He came home at night to sleep! And by then, everything had happened that had to happen. Dave referred to Neel as mother's favorite because Neel seldom incurred his mother's wrath. Dave was usually out pal-ling around with his buddies and thus was unreliable at the hearth. That left Steve, who soon learned he was either to have the house warm by the time his mother arrived or ... or else.

On one hapless day in January, Dave had several friends over, and they got into a scuffle in the living room. Neel, who happened to be home, was puttering away at something in the dining room. Their mother came at six o'clock, a little earlier than the boys expected, and the stark horror on the boys' faces was clear guilt about what they had left undone.

She stood like a stark stone statue at the entranceway, with the front door wide open. All but one of the neighborhood boys ran through the kitchen and out the back way. The one exception, a varmint named Peter Pfeifer, found himself trapped on the far side of the living room with the piano for cover.

When Mrs. Fulbright opened the front door, instead of excusing himself like a young gentleman, Peter yelled "Giggers!" scrambled out from under the piano, jumped up on the piano bench, swung open the high revered stained-glass window (the only luxury built into the otherwise plain, ordinary house) and dove out! He landed in a sticker bush below— "Yowl!" and away he ran, bellowing.

The expression on their mother's face made it clear this was not excusable behavior and, for her thoughtless sons, was not going to pass lightly. While all three boys began frantically picking up clothes and litter that were strewn about—they knew the ritual well—she slammed the front door and shut and latched the ornamental window over the piano, stomped to the kitchen, closed and locked the back door, opened the oven doors, fired up the oven for quick heat, took a beer out of the refrigerator, sat down in the spare warmth, opened the bottle of beer, took a swig and lit up a cigarette.

That, Steve was hoping, would be sufficient to calm her nerves, but from the disgust on her face, he knew that this time it was only the beginning.

"All three of you! I want you in here this minute!"

The boys came sheepishly into the kitchen, one by one. Here it comes, thought Steve.

"I work my fingers to the bone to provide a home for you boys. But do you boys care? Do you turn one hand to help? No fire in the furnace, dirty dishes in the sink, beds unmade, clothes on the floor. A pig sty!"

She stood and went to the window with her cigarette between her fingers, smoke curling up to the ceiling. The reflection in the window showed she still wore her scarf and topcoat. Outside, even with the descending darkness and her reflection, she could see chimneys in the neighborhood—wouldn't you know—with smoke coming out of them.

"Other families have heat. But do we? Of course not! I can't expect you boys to lift a finger." She walked back to the table, sat down and had another gulp of beer. "Is it too much to ask to get a little help around here?" She drew in on her cigarette. It wasn't over, by far.

"I work all day long. I give lessons half the night and on Saturdays. I do the shopping. I wash the clothes. Do my boys help? No. They're satisfied with a pig sty. They're satisfied to live in their own filth." She drank deep from the bottle.

"Is it too much to ask you to help just the least little bit? No, we can't do that. No. We have to wallow in our own filth. We have to have a house that's so cold you can see your breath in it."

"Mother, I …," Steve ventured. Oops! It wasn't over yet.

"Do you know what it's like having some boss breathing over you all day long? Do you know what it's like to give lesson after lesson after lesson till you're so tired you can't move? No, you don't. You don't care. You're too lazy to do anything, too lazy to care even the least little bit!"

Steve and his brothers were getting the beatings of their lives. Beatings would have been easier. Yes, Rome was tottering. The enemies were rushing in. Now came the real lashes.

She drew deep on her cigarette. She drank from the bottle.

"Well, I'm beat. I'm too tired to do anything. I'm too tired to care. I was told to turn you boys over to an orphanage. That's what I should have done. That's what I should do right now! Is that what you want?" She stuffed the cigarette out in the ashtray.

"I'll make a fire right now, Mother," said Dave.

"Isn't it a little late for that? What good will it do now? It'll take hours to warm the house, and long before that, it's time to go to bed. I'll have to go to bed right now to get warm." She stuffed her cigarette out in a cup and lit another cigarette. Rome was dying.

"Some night, I just won't come home."

This surely could maim the weak.

"I think I'll turn off the fire in this oven, turn on the gas, and stick my head in."

"I'm fixin' the fire right now," said Dave, and he dashed down the stairs to the basement.

"I'm helpin'," said Steve, and he ran down after him.

In the coal bin, Dave smashed a crate and grabbed some old newspaper. Through the furnace door, where it was dark and cold, he wadded up the paper, stacked the kindling on top and struck a match. Quickly, the fire flared up. But when he fed the flames some small lumps of coal, the fire began to weaken. He blew on it. Steve scooped some ashes out of the bottom. Dave fed and blew some more. Together, they wadded up more paper and stuffed it under the grate.

Steve blew hard.

"I know why," said Steve.

Dave continued to feed and blow.

Steve blew some more.

"I know why," said Steve again.

Dave blew some more, shook his head like he was trying to get rid of some nasty insect buzzing around him. "What are you talking about?"

"Rome," said Steve. Dave jerked his head as if to say, "What the hell are you talking about?"

Steve blew again while Dave backed away.

"Fell down," said Steve.

"Where do you get that crap?"

Epiglimpselogue Twenty

"Well, Steve could hardly blame his mother. Did this tirade happen often?" asked Sally.

"No, not really. But it did happen more than once. And each time it was deeply taken."

"So most of the time they were growing up, did the boys feel the threat of everything falling apart as Steve said about Rome?" asked Lisa.

"Dave and Neel? I don't know," said James, "but Steve, yes. He felt it acutely."

"Well," said Rupert, "All had our hard times growing up. It's good for us. It toughens us up."

"Did the boys ever cry?" asked Lisa.

"Never!" exclaimed James.

"Oh, that's right," said Sally, with a tad of sarcasm, 'men never cry. Yet Steve was young; he could have cried."

James shook his head. "Not in their family! Do you know what it is like to stand against the might of two bigger brothers? Or what is worse, to fall under their scorn?"

"Too bad the Fulbright boys didn't have a sister," said Lisa. "A few tears might have helped."

"Do you think their mother ever came close to turning the boys over to an orphanage?" asked Sally.

"We'll never know. But Steve took it to heart. That was a whole different world. An unknown world.

When James hesitated to answer Sally's question, Rupert jumped in. "Of course she did. Thankfully, she had her cigarettes and beer. Right James?"

"Probably."

GLIMPSES TWENTY-ONE

"FRIENDS, ROMANS, COUNTRYMEN!"

"Friends, Romans, countrymen! Lend me you ears!" Steve was in the living room, practicing his Shakespeare for his English class. His English teacher Miss Claudia Nourse was an enthusiast for classical literature, and since the District had an unusually high percentage of college-bound students for a public school, she took her responsibility beyond anyone's expectations of a junior high teacher.

"Huh!" Neel looked up from the piano, where he was studying his choral music. "Scram, twerp. Get your Shakespeare out of here!" Steve had bugged them too much with his proximity runs.

Steve knew he had to find a private place to rehearse. Feeling his brothers and their friends didn't much care for the likes of Shakespeare, and realizing they were all over the place, it was hard to get away from them. Never mind. He would go upstairs to his mother's bedroom; she was at work and no one would go there. In fact, he could even go for a dress rehearsal. From the beginning of the assignment, Steve wanted to perform his lines in costume. In her closet, he found an old white bed sheet. He draped it over his shoulder and looked at himself in her dressing mirror. "Good." But he needed something to top it off. Back in the closet, he found one of her old hats. He detached wired artificial flowers. He bent them into a circle, placed it on his head and returned to the mirror. "Perfect!"

"Friends, Romans, Countrymen! Lend me your ears!" speechified Steve, standing on a footstool in front of the dressing mirror. Around his body, he had draped a bed sheet so that it swirled up across his chest and over his left shoulder. On his head was the circle that he cocked to one side. His so-there gesture started the make-shift wreath to slip over his left eye. He scooted the garland back to the top of his head, squared away his feet and stared straight into the mirror. He liked it.

"Hem. Friends, Romans, Countrymen! Lend me your ears!"

"Hey, guys! Get a load of Dave's kid brother!" Bill Trow, just out of the bathroom across the hall, had popped his head into the cracked open door to the bedroom. A storm of laughter came from several other heads that popped in around the door. Steve turned crimson. What are these guys doing up here? Damn!

Brother Dave suddenly appeared in the doorway as well. "Friends, Romans, countrymen," he mocked, "Lend me your money. What can you buy with an ear?" If there were a way to mock a serious piece of work, Dave would know it.

The door swung fully opened, and there stood three of his cronies and Dave in full view, hee-hawing away. Could Steve crawl under the bed, hide in the closet or jump out the window? What could save him from this?

And their words had to follow. "Is little Davy a lilly-dilly!" said Bill as loudly and as obnoxiously as a body could. If Dave's friends didn't bother to learn Steve's name, he came off as "little Dave " or "little Davy."

"Yeh, I think he's a sissy-girl!" said another. Steve glanced down at his makeshift toga. Yeh, it sure looked more like a sissy girl's raiment.

"What ya doin,' little cutie?" said the third in falsetto.

When the voices and laughter died down, Dave said coolly, "Steve's practicing a speech for his English class. Isn't that it, Steve?

Come on, you guys, I'll show you what I'm making for him, a bloodied Caesar." Dave had taken it upon himself to supply a prop for Steve's Anthony, a body of the butchered Ceasar, which included a discarded department store male manikin, a grotesque Halloween man's mask, some red paint, and a bowie knife, all designed by Dave's bizarre imagination to give Steve's class a real show.

"In the basement. Come on!"

Yeah!" they cried.

With that, they all scrambled out and down the stairs and left Steve to himself in his perverted attire. He plumped down on his mother's bed and collected himself. Now when he thought about it, it wasn't so bad because his brother had covered for him, the truth really, if anybody wanted to know, and sure, if anybody asked him, wouldn't he hasten to say that the teacher down right was making him do it. 'So there!" he could hear himself say to the scoffers. And then to close the subject, "Mind your own business!"

With this self-bolstering, Steve bounded up and back up on the stool, re-inventing his toga and setting out anew to convince the forum and all the world—who cares about those ignoramuses downstairs! Who cares if they think Steve is a 'trans-what do they call it? A trans-dresser. The important thing is that Brutus and his cronies deserved a comeuppance.

"Hem. 'Come I to Caesar's funeral. He was my friend, faithful and just to me." After all, wasn't Caesar Anthony's buddy? Dave, his own brother could be mean, but mostly he was a friend, that is, a guy like Caesar because the other day, when Steve's big brother Neel caught Steve spitting down the floor vent and in his disgust pushed Steve so hard that Steve slammed against the wall and slithered to the floor, it was Dave who shouted at Neel, "Pick on somebody your own size!"

"Oh, yeah," said Neel, and he shoved Dave. But Dave stood his ground and shoved him back. So back and forth they shoved each other until Dave tackled Neel and they fell to the floor together, wrestling and punching, upsetting the lamp table and causing knickknacks to fly across the floor. But it didn't matter because it was a fair fight. Not like this sneaky murder of Caesar, Anthony's buddy. There Neely and Dave were, scuffling on the floor, beating each other to a bloody pulp, when, what should happen but good ol' 'Get-the-butcher-knives Granma comes into the room as hurriedly as her limp would allow.

"What's all this here clamorin'?" Her hands were up on her hips, and she was fuming. "Lawdy! Stop that this minute! You boys are a-killin' each other! Stop it, ya hear me! Do you hear me! Stop that!" Her arms flailed about, but she knew she was too weak and they too big and strong, that she could have no physical effect. The scuffle went on, sending a chair flying over to bang against the wall next to slithered-down Steve.

"Stop that right now, do ya hear!" Of course, they paid no attention to her whatsoever and fought each other with all their might in renewed combat. This had come to the ultimate. Frustrated and completely overcome with emotion, Granma shouted, "So! That's it, is it?" She shouted her infamous, "Get the butcher knives! Get the butcher knives!" She ran around, appearing to get ready to head for the kitchen, flailing her arms and shouting, "Get the butcher knives! Get the butcher knives!"

Did this mean, "You boys, since you're not going to stop fighting and start behaving yourselves, then you might as well finish it once and for all with the butcher knives, by cutting each other to shreds?" That'd stop it, and each would get what he deserved.

Of course, that was not what she really meant. What she really meant in these times was, the thought of "butcher knives" used on each other—with all the blood and gore, such as in the assassination of Caesar—would bring them to their senses, just the thought that is, and they would stop fighting. Anyway, Steve had heard this protestation before (and now the whole charade seemed to make sense) and watched to see this work again. Both with red faces from exertion and headlocks, they backed away from each other. It worked. Granma prevailed again and stopped the fight.

And Steve was going to have to remember to keep his saliva and his Shakespeare to himself. Just one thing he had to find out: "Granma, did you know that the famous emperor of Rome, Julius Caesar, was knifed to death by Brutus, Cassius and their gang?"

"Laudy sake! No. What are you a-sayin'? Julius who?"

Anyway, Steve returned to his thoughts. Now back to Anthony: Caesar was Anthony's friend, and what Cassius and Brutus and all the other bad guys did to Caesar was mean and made Anthony mad. Anyway, with everyone gone from the bedroom, Steve latched the door and put a chair against it for good measure to prevent any more intrusions, re-draped the sheet over his left shoulder and began again.

"But the noble Brutus has told you Caesar was ambitious; if it were so, 'twas a grievous fault." Would Steve be able to get through this entire speech in front of his whole class way down to the part where Anthony says, "I must pause [because] my heart is there in the coffin with Caesar, and I must [wait] til it come back to me"? This part always brought tears to Steve's eyes.

"Oh, my God. Me and Aunt Jesse. All lachrymose. Wouldn't they laugh if they saw some real tears flowing from his eyes over some silly Shakespeare lines? If lines really were to bring tears to his eyes before the class, he could bury his head in his sheet-toga, then maybe they would not see his crybaby face, and they wouldn't laugh. If he forgot, he would be the laughing stock of the school. Could he memorize and recite down to that part in the speech and quit? But it was the best part. He must get to it or the speech wouldn't be right. With this strategy, on he practiced. If he practiced enough, maybe he'd get used to it, and maybe tears wouldn't well up in his eyes, and he'd be okay and not have to hide his face in his toga. Aunt Jesse never hid her crying. But she was a girl.

On Monday morning in class, Steve shook like a lone leaf on the branch in the wintry wind. Did Miss Claudia Nourse know this? Could the students tell he was so nervous he didn't know if he could utter a sound? Suddenly, Miss Nourse said, "All right Steve, let's get this over with." Yes, she knew he was nervous.

"Yes 'm," he said, not knowing if he were being the least audible, and he rose at his seat and cleared his throat. "Hem."

"At the front of the room, please, Steve."

At first, his legs wouldn't move him. When they did, he went like a condemned man to the wall before a firing squad. Now the whole class of twenty-seven young teenagers was watching his every move and gesture.

"Hem." Even his "hem' shook.

Out of a shopping bag, he took his sheet and home-made tiara. He draped himself and fidgeted with this toga with one hand and kept shifting his wreath with the other. He thought, why not say that he couldn't do it and sit back down? They would all laugh at him anyway. Let them laugh. If he could see himself as a comedy show, then maybe he wouldn't be so scared. If he didn't give the speech, later, his big brothers would ask him how it went, and how could he tell them he didn't do it? And they'd ask him why not. And he'd have to tell them he was too chicken. And Dave would start clucking. No, he had practiced it. He knew the speech—if he could just remember it in front of everyone. It came to him that he simply had to do it.

And good heavens! It was not a comedy. It was a tragedy. He felt it in his soul. That's why he volunteered to do it in the first place. That and to get some extra grade points.

Now, where was his prop? Where was Dave and the bloody body of Caesar? It was all planned and permissioned that Dave, waiting in the hall, would rush in at this point, lugging the Caesar manikin. It was time. Damn! Where was he? Steve had not seen the manikin when Dave and his buddies finished it. His brother was supposed to have already brought Caesar. Steve removed his wreath, put it back on his head again and re-wrapped himself in his toga. Students tittered. Still, he couldn't bring himself to begin. Students began to outright laugh .

"Well, Steve." Miss Nourse was tapping her foot. "Don't keep your audience waiting."

"I have a prop," he said very professionally, "but it's not here yet." He went to look out into the hall.

'His audience'? Miss Nourse is out-professionalizing me, thought Steve. But she *is* professional. Should he quit now? Could he? Could he? He couldn't. It was too late. They expected him to do it. It was too obvious. Besides he could do it. He could do it! Caesar prop or no Caesar prop, he had to do it. He cleared his throat again and reared back.

"Hem. FRIENDS, ROMANS, COUNTRYMEN!" It was overloud.

The class roared. "It's good, Steve. Go on," said Miss Nourse.

"Lend me your ears"—his voice cracked and weakly trailed off.

The class roared louder. "It's okay, Steve. Keep on," his teacher said encouragingly.

"The evil that—I mean." The class tittered. "I come to bury Caesar, not to praise him." Here he began to race. "Theevilthatmendolivesafterthem.Thegoodisoftburied with them,soletitbewithCaesar."

"Slow down a little," said Miss Nourse. "It's good, but slow down so we can understand you."

Steve cleared his throat. "Ahem. The noble Brutus"—the class laughed—"has told you Caesar was ambitious. So be it."

"So be it, Steve?" said Miss. Nourse. "Are you sure?"

"Yes'm."

"Well, go on."

"Yes'm." Here was Steve's favorite part that reminded him of his brother when he defended him against his older, and much bigger, brother. "Caesar was my friend, faithful and just to me."

Suddenly, through the classroom door, here came brother Dave on the run hauling a large sheeted creature-dummy, stuffed with rags and nearly the size of himself. He plopped the grotesquery down at Steve's feet—ker plunk!—in front of the class, a home-made mannequin with a bowie knife (a war souvenir sent from the Pacific by Bill's big brother, who was in the marines), stuck in the chest and with blood, the appearance of blood, streaming in all directions from that and several other supposed gashes. It was worse than any Halloween horror display. Dave darted out.

With "Oos" and "Ahs," the class rose in unison to get a good look at it. A better look brought more ooing and aahing accompanied by considerable irksome disdain. Even Steve cringed. Yet this was supposed to be the glorious and just emperor of Rome. "He was my friend, faithful and just to me," Steve spoke with a winkled-up nose. It didn't seem right. He paused.

Miss Nourse's eyes went to the ceiling. She folded her arms. "Go on Steve. Let's finish this." The class went silent.

"BUT!" said Steve, again, overloud. Several snickered.

"The noble Brutus has told you Caesar was ambitious, and if it were so it was a grievous fault and grievous-ly has Caesar answered it."

Sally Field raised her hand. "What's 'ambitious'?"

"Hungry, greedy for power," responded Miss. Nourse. "Go on, Steve."

"—and grievously has Caesar answered it," repeated Steve.

"You said that!" said Sally Field. "Oh, Miss Nourse, what is 'griev—'?"

"'Grievous' means sad, mournful." She nodded to Steve to continue.

"—and Brutus is an honorable man." Steve looked at Sally Field. "Honorable means nice guy," he said mockingly. The class roared.

Miss Nourse sighed. "Go on, Steve."

"Three times they tried to put a king's crown on Caesar's head, and every time, he said nope. See? Caesar wasn't a mean guy at all. He filled the treasury by bopping the bad guys over the head and taking their money."

"Stay with the script, Steve," said Miss Nourse.

"Yes, ma'am. Did this in Caesar seem ambitious? Ambition should be made of better STUFF." Steve thought it important to stress the word "stuff". At this word, the class became surprisingly quiet. Ah, that was neat. Steve liked that—bringing the class to complete silence all by himself. He strutted across the front of the classroom. Then he returned to look at the body. He shook his head. "My heart is there in the coffin with Caesar, and I must pause till it come back to me." Dramatically he raised his arm with the draping toga and buried his face in it. He waited in silence.

Finally the class broke into applause and hooting and hollering.

Steve was a success. The bell sounded. At last, recess. Apparently, the biggest success of the performance was the corpse. When other classes heard about it, students from everywhere wanted to see the corpse of Caesar, but right away, the bowie knife had to be removed and sent to the office. Miss Nourse eventually had to lock the mannequin in the cloakroom.

The next day, Steve and Miss Nourse were called into the principal's office.

"Must we have such bloody visuals with our—recitations?"

"Huh?" said Steve.

"I understand the victim was supposed to be Julius Caesar. With this bowie knife stuck in him." The principal waved the weapon in the air. "Where had Caesar been? Not in Rome but in the Philippines—attacked by the natives?"

"Huh?"

"A little gruesome, wouldn't you say, Steve?"

Steve remained silent.

"We must allow for a boy's imagination," said Miss Nourse..

"Well, I think we can do without this form of imaginative creativity. Return to the playground, Steve."

Steve swung the door open and headed out. Behind him he heard:

"Well, I must say," said the principal to Miss Nourse, "What I really couldn't abide besides the blood is the silly grin on Caesar's face."

"The catsup ...," said the teacher. Steve was away and out of earshot.

After school, Steve dragged the body home and stuffed it in a chest in the basement to be saved for another important occasion.

"How was Lawrence Olivier?" asked Neel.

Epiglympselogue Twenty-one

"Did that really happen?" asked Ben.

"For the most part," said James, grinning.

"I can't imagine the teacher—who was it? Claudia Nourse?—having the class of thirteen-fourteen year-olds doing Julius Caesar," commented Rupert.

"Well, it's true, she did. That had a life-time effect on Steve's future, I'll have to say. He became a teacher himself and specialized in recitations from great works of literature. Without ever looking at the play *Julius Caesar* again, he does Mark Anthony's speech from the memory of a thirteen year-old."

"Can Steve remember his teachers, James?" asked Lily.

"A few. And these quite well. We're coming up to one shortly."

GLIMPSES TWENTY-TWO

JESSIE FILLS IN MYTHOPOEICALLY

Mulling over the family history, James Stephen had to give Jessie Fulbright Schultz a little more play in the story than he had so far; after all, Jessie had a decided influence over her nephews, much more than James ever realized when he was growing up. There was this time, the time when Aunt Jessie and Uncle Billy came to stay with Gladys and the boys at Adele for several months. Why they came to stay with them was never explained to Steve. The house on Adele was an old house, true, but it was also a two-storey house that had three bedrooms and a bathroom upstairs, and there could accommodate, with Neely and Dave doubling up and Steve sleeping on the sloping porch, the couple with their own bedroom. Perhaps there was money involved; Jessie probably paid something in rent. So that would have helped the family a little.

When they arrived with their bags from the Ozarks, Jessie was mainly the same as she was seven some odd years before, but a little slower with age. Uncle Billy was a little spaced out, sinking slowly into senility. What happened to all the Schultz's furniture was not clear, not that the boys cared much, and this was never explained. Age precluded, most likely, that all the furniture be sold because the Schultz were never going to own and occupy any house again, let alone a big house like the one they lavished in on Lindell Boulevard.

What actually did the brothers experience in their psyches about their family worth which, of course, relates to their individual self-worth as well? Steve pondered this. He could see himself and his brothers:

The Schultzes had not even put their bags down before Jessie was already story-pontificating. "Ah, the fine young men, sons of Harry Wilks Fulbright, the distinguished Springfield lawyer, a Harvard man, a gentleman of the highest standing!"

The sons of that distinguished gentleman stood with their mouths agape. Not since their 'famous' trip to the Ozarks those seven years before (and then it was a kind of passing conscious memory though a basis for their myths to grow on) had the brothers heard anything like Aunt Jessie's glowing accounts of their family fame. They had not read or heard of anything about it.

And what was their assessment of dear Aunt Jessie? Although they knew family talk about her, mostly negative, they had only once seen Aunt Jessie in their lives, the Ozark sojourn; they lacked a "living" image of her. With a father, Jessie's brother, deceased and the boys' mother having to work all the time, and the three of boys, now ages 12, 15, and 17, scattered to the four winds of the neighborhood out of school, and otherwise separated to three different schools, they hardly knew they had a family, let alone such a one as Aunt Jessie gloried in.

"I could tell by just the look of you—the sons of the late, later, prominent St. Louis lawyer Harry Wilks Fulbright, my brother!" proclaimed Aunt Jessie, "and kin of the renowned Judge James Fulbright of Springfield—the youngest's namesake—the descendants of the great grandfather Fulbright who founded Springfield, boys! Yes, founded Springfield!" Her words were worthy of being spoken before the U. S. Senate.

This speech of Jessie's, remindful of that first day of acquaintance, getting off the Grayhound bus in Camdenton, was a bit much for the boys to grasp the full meaning of in one sitting, but there was no missing Jessie's pride of prominence.

Being the youngest, Steve was the most naturally curious. Besides, his older brothers were too old and too wise (for their age) to blunder with imprudent questions. Steve pulled big brother's sleeve. "What's *founded* mean, Neel?"

"Sh-h-h!" whispered Neel.

"One hundred thousand people of the southwest part of this fair state of Missouri are grateful for the service of our family, the Fulbrights of Springfield!"

"What'd we do?" Steve asked Neel.

"Sh-h-h!"

Jessie's brows knitted.

"Isn't that right, doctor?" she said, turning to her husband, who smiled his gold-tooth smile, then turned wide-eyed.

"Huh?" 'The doctor, William Schultz, M.D, ears, nose and throat specialist, was practically stone deaf.

She leaned into his ear and shouted, "I said, 'the Fulbrights are a distinguished family in Springfield'!"

"Yes, yes, yes," said the doctor, who had probably heard enough of this. If he didn't hear what was being said, it didn't show on the outside. Nodding, he was all smiles of certainty.

Steve was puzzled. Founded Springfield? Famous Fulbrights? He pictured his brother Dave sneaking out the window and running about the streets with the neighborhood riffraff—riffraff is what his mother called Dave's friends—the neighborhood war games: Neel making mud-cased smoke bombs for bombarding the other boys who comprised the enemy. Was brother Dave headed for Alcatraz and brother Neel maybe to fame as a great general or something one day, another Eisenhower or MacArthur to save America from the bad guys?

But talk about the awakening! Just listen to their Aunt Jessie, Steve thought, as she soapboxed the glories of the Fulbrights not only in Springfield but their glories from one end of the country to the other. Prominent this and renowned that! Those words of fame were born to them on that day and a few other days when they were in Aunt Jessie's awing presence. Steve felt that he and his brothers were naturally skeptical. Could the whole world know of such wonders about the Fulbrights, but the boys be totally ignorant of their—of whatever they were—heir to?

And it was style, too. Everything Aunt Jessie said was said like somebody famous speaking, like President Roosevelt on the radio: "Be proud boys. You are descendants of the famous Fulbrights, who founded Springfield?" was said just like Winston Churchill, "We shall fight in the streets ... and we shall neveh, neveh surrender!"

"Will we get lots of money?" whispered Steve to Neel.

"Oh for cryin' out loud, sh-h-h!" Neel had more sense of person than Steve, a sense that Steve envied Neel for, perhaps a sense of the supreme role of mythopoeia. Great armies, like great lives, were built on such.

The boys weren't going to get a lot of money, but what <u>were</u> they going to get from Aunt Jessie and her big talk? That was the puzzle. And whatever the real answer—even though they had been told that she was bonkers—they ran into a gold-fringed cloud bank of pride. And this meant they had much to live up to, when they thought about it which they couldn't help but do—sometimes. And who were they otherwise? The play-arounds of the neighborhood, that's who. Swinging from tree vines in vacant lots, fighting imaginary Japs through the high weeds in their imaginary jungle or, realistically, chasing around with street urchins after dark, doing all sorts of mischief, adventuring into vacant houses for spooks and running and hiding and kicking the tin-can off the curb, they grew.

They learned from this—Aunt Jessie's family anthem—that they were famous! "We are important!" each of the boys must have thought. "We are exceptional, smart, resourceful whatever that means—in short, we are the name-of-all-names, the Fulbrights!"

This Aunt Jessie of theirs was a lulu. Sure, she was their late father's older sister, but so what?—lot's of people have an Aunt

Jessie. Or do they? This Aunt Jessie knew every tidbit of history of the whole southern part of their state of Missouri and half of all the U.S. history to boot. She knew all the vital parts of the country, and the history of the Fulbrights all tied into it, and she knew the whole history of the Fulbrights since Noah's Ark, knew these histories better than anybody knew anything, so the boys were believing! Or so it sure sounded like it. And she herself? Jessie Schultz was none other than the wife of the imminent doctor William Schultz, formerly of St. Louis, resident of a fine house on Lindell Boulevard opposite the World's-Fairgrounds, Forest Park, now the doctor and Mrs. Schultz of Camdenton, Missouri, the Schultzes being those important people the boys and their mother visited in renewing family ties—at Jessie and the Doctor's rustic lake cottage in the Ozarks.

Aunt Jessie, stocky, in her sixties, possessing the energy of a thoroughbred filly, was thereafter known to the boys as "wild, whacky Aunt Jessie, into it!" whom even their late father—they'd heard their mother say—had found obnoxious and at times unbearable. But relations were good between Jessie and her late brother's family now that he was gone, for in earlier times when Harry was himself a young, struggling St. Louis lawyer, (the boys learned later) Jessie had threatened to sue him (and their two sisters)—and everybody else she could think of—over the family inheritance and this and that! But now the boys were to pay attention to their illustrious family history for Aunt Jessie was the voice of the true, one-and-only history, and in her own way, the voice of their father from beyond the grave (for all they knew). She was Aunt Jessie, the family sage and bard.

All this despite Neel's skepticism—in private, Neel would say to Dave and Steve, "This Aunt-Jessie stuff was just a covering up for a bunch of 'ol horse thieves."

"Horse thieves!" they snorted. Or was it "Rats!"

But the two younger brothers didn't buy the horse-thieves theory. They knew Neel didn't really think this. Dave laughed at anything he felt had the aura of a joke. In fact, Steve and Dave felt that Neel was swallowing Aunt Jessie's stories hook, line and sinker. Neel had had more contact with their father than they and quietly idolized him.

"Where *did* we come from, mother?" Steve asked at home when that time they returned from Aunt Jessie's. "Are we famous like Aunt Jessie says?"

"Oh, your Aunt Jessie!" she said. Their mother never denied anything about being famous, but she said, "Oh, your Aunt Jessie!" like don't bother me with Jessie's nonsense. Then Mother would change the subject or leave the room.

Another time the boys would not mention Aunt Jessie but ask, "Are we Fulbrights famous, Mother?"

"Well, your father's family had a lot of teachers, lawyers and judges among them, and your father knew the Senator's family, Senator J. William Fulbright. He used to visit them when the Senator was a youth at home in Fayetteville, Arkansas, growing up."

"Who are some of the famous people in our family, Mother? Were they presidents and senators?"

"Well, let's see, there is the Fulbright that founded Springfield, and there is the Senator from Arkansas, and Stephen Callahan of New York, and there is Judge James Fulbright of Springfield (Steve got their names) and ... I don't know, some others."

And Steve thought, "How neat! James was Steve's other name, his name sake. Maybe he was going to be a judge with a hammer and he'd pound a desk top and pronounce, "Case dismissed!" Maybe he would be "a founderer" of something or other. Something important. Then reality would set in: he had had no experience at being important. But he could imagine things—"Don't fantasize!" his teacher told him once. He grew fond of history, identifying with Julius Caesar, marching at the head of a legion, for example. But then in real life, he would do something stupid and lo! reverse the image!

But their mother did have an interest in family history and not just her own family, the Garrisons. "I wish you boys could know something more about your father's family. I know that the Fulbrights go way back in this country," said their mother on another occasion when she wasn't tired from work and felt in the mood to talk. "I know this. Your great, great-something-or-other grandfather arrived in Philadelphia off the boat from Germany in 1740." What were the boys to summon up in their own minds?

Steve wondered. 1740! Way back. A 1740s harbor, with tall sailing vessels? What a sight! Like olden times, one recently docks with passengers all lined up coming down the gangplank? Two of the immigrants are Germans, brothers, in old, worn farmer's clothes, one weaving from side to side.

"Country of origin?" inquires the customs official, seated and writing at a make-shift table with another port official seated at his side and a guardsman leaning on his musket-butt nearby, half listening.

"Deutchlands," says one who is clumsily making his way up to the table.

"What's wrong with him?" asked the other official.

"Is?"

The second brother says, "Min-neh brudde hast hard time mit der sea . He loose what he essen. He betteh on how-you-say-it, terra firma."

"Country?"

"Terra Firma," says the first brother, smiling.

"Huh?" The official, with a look of disgust, wipes the sweat off his brow.

"Nein," says the second brother. "Wir kommen ... Deutchland, across the waters. Germany," he says, looking over at his brother.

"Okay. Germany," the official writes. "Now your name?" the official asks the first brother.

The first brother stares at him blankly.

"He says," says the second brother to the first, 'wie heissen sie?'"

"Ja, ja. Wilhelm Volprecht."

"Isso," says the second. "He's Wilhelm Volprecht und I, his brudde Jacob Volprecht."

"Ah, let's see," says the official, "F-u-l-l—what is it?"

"Precht," says the immigrant second brother, showing his wide mouth and white teeth.

"Brite? B-r-i-t-e. Or maybe, b-r-i-g-h-t as in light." The official bends over and continues writing, then straightens up and looks satisfied with what he has written. "F-u-l-l-b-r-i-g-h-t? Yes?"

"Ja."

"Ja."

"Yacob und Vilhilm," says the first brother.

"Ja," says the second brother, "Jacob unt William in America." He smiles at his brother.

The first brother smiles back. "In America, vee Jacob unt William."

Satisfied, the official looks up at the line of immigrants past the second brother. "Next."

"Eins moment," says the second brother. He points one finger up. "Vee get verk right away, ja?"

"Go to the next barrow over by the tree," he points. "Next!"

"Bitte, eins el? ... please," said Jacob. "Long landts, short nammeh. Ja?"

"Ja, bitte," says the first brother, "eins el!"

"Yes, this is America, all right," says the official.

Both nodded. "Right!" said the official. He scratches out one el. "Eins el, I mean, one el in Fulbright."

Jacob looks over and down at the writing. "Gut. I like American one el." He looks at the official with determination. "Vee vork hardt unt buy farm unt make gut."

"Certainly," says the official. "Lots of land here. Jus' have to maybe fight a few injuns." He snickers. "Next!"

"Injuns?" says Jacob with a knitted brow.

"Next!" shouts the official. Reluctantly, the German brothers bump toward the tree and barrow.

When they are out of ear shot, the second official leans over and says to the first official, "These new-ones, immigrants, will have you speak their language."

"Ha!" says the other official. "They'll be lucky. We don't even sprecken English here!" He snickers. The other official snickers. The guardsman snickers. That's what Jacob Stephen—or rather J. Steve—surmises.

"We're D-A-R, you know, boys!" said Aunt Jessie, they recalled on that previous visit. "Absolutely. No question about it."

"D-A—?" the boys had asked.

Yet most of the time when the boys saw Aunt Jessie and heard her family bellowing's, they wanted her to be right, and although they snickered, in some strange way, they believed her, but sometimes their ignorance or natural skepticism prevailed. In her expostulations, her tendency was to become more and more bizarre.

"Daughters of the American Revolution. Original founders!"

"We are what?"

"Absolutely. We go way back, boys. Back to Captain John Smith and Pochohontus." Ah, that sounded familiar from the ol' Ozark days.

Steve whooped it up, "Yeeoow. Me Injun."

"That's right, Steve. Indians on both sides of your family! Pocahontas on your father's side and the daughter of a Cherokee Indian chief on your mother's; that was one Frances Polly Poole. One-fourth American Indian means a government pension, my boys. Has your mother done anything about that pension?"

The word "pension"—that sounded good. "That's money, isn't it!" Steve whispered to Dave. Hadn't their maternal Grandma lived on her pension from the coal mining company.

"A little," he said.

Jessie's look changed suddenly to deadly earnest. "Gladys, you must look into this at once. A pension would help you raise these boys and help you get them into the finest colleges in the country. The Fulbrights must attend the finest schools in the country. They're entitled to it by right of their original American Indian blood."

She looked earnestly into the eyes of the boys. "Your father went to Harvard, boys. Yes, Harvard, the oldest and finest university this side of the Atlantic!"

The Harvard part was true. They knew this although he went for just a year or so. Didn't finish his degree there. But this tale about Pocahontas—their mother and not even the boys could make that leap. The Cherokee, Frances Polly Poole, on their mother's side, yes, that was true. But Pocahontas on their father's side! Their father had been a tall, blue-eyed blonde, and brothers Dave and Steve took after him with their blue eyes and blonde hair. Maybe Neel could pass for part Indian. He took after their mother with brown eyes and dark hair. But the other boys! No one in the family photos on the father's side even hinted of Indian lineage.

This Pocahontas tale never went anywhere. The best they could figure was that Jessie's thinking was merely wishful thinking to counter the Garrisons with—their father's family, their mother's family stuff—but the story did make the Gladys Fulbright family, who had fallen on hard times, fantasize that they would suddenly have dollars flowing in from the U.S. government with apologies for having stolen their ancestral hunting grounds. A pension would have helped a poor family that received not a penny of social security in those days. Never mind. No extra money. Not a dime without working for it. All would have to work. To suffer. From their mother's side, the boys had heard from day one that "suffering builds character," and character was what it was all about. You bet!

In the late 18th century and early 19th century, some of the Fulbrights stayed in Philadelphia while others went south into North Carolina. A generation or so later, some of the latter North Carolinian Fulbrights, who had worked hard and saved enough money to purchase provisions, and a few slaves joined the real movement of the 1820s and went—West—into Tennessee. But there was greater promise farther West still, so a few of the men of the clan ventured across the river and over into Missouri, discovered rich land with a profuse spring gushing out the side of a stony hill, water that was cold, clean and pure and valuable that they were required to share with just a few (friendly) Indians living in the area. The men rushed back to Tennessee, gathered some forty-five of their kinsmen, hirees, and slaves, and returned to found Springfield, Missouri, where the springs still bear the name of Fulbright to this day—Fulbright Springs that supplies the major amount of water to this entire region.

Never mind those scalawags, the Campbells, who also claim to have founded Springfield. The Fulbights held the spring that made it all happen! After the Civil War the few remaining black slaves assumed the Fulbright name, moved to Kansas to find jobs as free men. Several of their descendants live there to this day.

Aunt Jessie wasn't entirely crazy. The Fulbrights settled in the Springfield area, early enough in the 19th century to be a prominent family in the generations to come. In the nineteenth century, some of these Fulbrights also settled in Arkansas (Fayetteville, mainly) and within a generation started the first newspaper in the area that laid the foundation for the Senator's influence and fame and, in time, a name prominent in international relations—note the Fulbright teacher-scholar exchange program.

Aunt Jessie clued the boys in on that which the boys already knew. The boys' father, Harry Wilks Fulbright, grew up with three older sisters on a farm in Marionville, Missouri, etcetera, went to Drury College, to Harvard, married, had two children, happened in on his wife's affair, divorced, completed a law degree at Washington University, remarried, a pretty young piano major, Gladys Jewel Garrison at Drury College, married her, lived in a log cabin in Marionville, where their first son William Neely was born, and thereafter moved to St. Louis where he went into law practice with Stanley Sydman, settled in to have two more sons.

Then he died an early death, at just 43 years of age, leaving the widow and the three young boys. So there were the three brothers who had the honor of being Fulbright heirs who inherited no house, no money, no pension, no social security, nothing of material value, had no Fulbright family interest in them But, perhaps more significantly, they had Aunt Jessie who willed them stories, myths, and pride.

"Neel," Steve one day would ask, "who is that other brother and sister we have?"

"Don't know. Never met them." Then he added, "Don't ever ask mother."

Steve didn't. His question was never answered.

But there was that time of Steve's rebellion—is that what it was? Steve had begun on the piano. He only had a few pieces of lessons. The last thing Gladys was interested in was teaching more lessons, especially to her own sons who might not appreciate it. Nevertheless, she showed Steve a book of Hannon's drills which Steve tried on the piano. One of the days when the Schultz were still at the Fulbrights, Steve played up a storm on the piano with Hannon's drills. Right in the middle of his 'recital,' Jessie ran down the stairs and exclaimed,

"Brilliant! Brilliant! You're a genius!"

Steve rebelled, the first time ever. "I'm not a genius! I'm not a genius!"

He did not know why he said that. He thought about it now and again over the years and never was able to come up with an explanation. Why did he say that? Why was he so incensed? He could never find the answer. But Jessie was hurt and never spoke to him again about the piano or—as he recalls—about anything else. The Schultzes soon moved out and were never seen again or spoken to again by the sons of Jessie's only brother, Harry. Steve's response that day was strange. And thereafter, so was Jessie's absence from their lives.

Epiglimselogue Twenty-two

"That is strange," said Lisa. "Were the family myths, as dramatized by their Aunt Jessie, too great a burden for the sensitive young Steve?"

"Could be," replied James.

"Sounds like Steve himself had a problem with what he might have taken as an overwhelming burden of expectation—that he was supposed to become something great, something exceptional, and it was so unusual for anyone to make a fuss over him, he had grave doubts about his abilities to measure up," said Rupert.

"Good point," said James.

"For many people," Rupert continued, " the problem is family expectations are too low to cause inspired behavior among its young. Matching family myth with a young family member's abilities is a problem."

"What is this word *Mythopoeia*?" asked Lisa.

"I can tell you about that," said Sally. "It's a belief system that is not based on reality or science that may powerfully influence behavior."

"It is possible then," responded Lisa, "that having lost her only child, a promising young man and, therefore, having no progeny, Aunt Jesse wanted to influence her brother's boys along the path of success."

"It is unfortunate, then," said Ben, "that Steve rebelled at that point."

"Perhaps," said Rupert, "he'd just had enough, as we have, of his Aunt Jessie's flair."

"That's true, but it is also noteworthy," said James, "that Steve had a lot in common with his Aunt Jessie. Though neither of them realized it. Take his regard for Shakespeare, for example. Now Neel's operatic aspirations were much more to Aunt Jessie's liking than Steve's 'I'm no genius!' Aunt Jessie teared up when she told Neel 'music will break your heart.'"

"Whether we realize it or not, myth-building is important to families," added Sally.

GLIMPSES TWENTY-THREE

NEEL AND DAVE

Steve remembers Dave and Neel as contenders from a very early age. At times, they would sass one another and wind up in a scuffle. But there was no doubt that they grew up close albeit in a very masculine way, never with any show of family affection. Heaven forbid! The contrasts between them were many. Although each was academically and physically capable, Neel and Dave pursued these capabilities irregularly and differently.

As kids, both Neel and Dave played sandlot football. For Dave, football became the one sport—football all the way. In high school, Dave played three years of varsity halfback, "scat-back," they called him. Neel went after baseball well before high school and continued baseball into high school, playing catcher and pitcher on the varsity throughout high school.

Ultimately Dave played football at Mizzou where he, one Saturday in a freshman game against the Kansas Jayhawks, by galloping long yardage for three touchdowns impressed Don Faurot who awarded him with a walk-on scholarship (although in the subsequent years it came to nothing).

Long before high school, Neel played baseball, (probably influenced in childhood by his dad) He played American Legion Baseball, developed a fine pitching arm which stood him well for catcher and pitcher on the Normandy High School varsity (athletically, one of the top schools in the city and state), and he played varsity quarterback his junior and senior years and his first year in the marines. Athletically, as in other ways, Neel was an inspiration to his younger brothers. Neel had the aura of knowing what was the right way, that is, knowing the right thing to do and how to achieve this goal.

Academically, although competent in math, Neel was more into humanities, literature and music, in high school; Dave tended more towards science and technology, especially after high school.

Further, in the earlier years Neel was more a participant than Dave. He was an Eagle Scout, went camping, went to jamborees. By high school and in high school, he fell in with a good crowd. All-around, long-term friends were Dick Houskins and Dick Hosketer. In football, he befriended one Rich Swyers, whose father was the pastor of a Christian Church on Kings highway Boulevard, and on Sunday mornings, Neel began attending this Church, doing a long walk from home to the intersection of Jennings Road and Natural Bridge Avenue where he caught a bus for the rest of the way.

At Church, he became a member of the choir. In high school he joined the chorus. His special interest was opera. He came to want desperately to be an operatic tenor. This was a particular challenge because from the earliest time, Steve remembers, Neel always had a natural base voice. He remembers asking his mother why Neel didn't pursue the role of an operatic baritone. No answer was ever forthcoming. It was a predominate family mode to let things take their own natural course although no one in the family ever objected to at least trying to turn a frog into a prince. Amazingly, as a tenor, Neel achieved the unlikely.

Dave, too, loved music, but he was a guy's guy. No fancy opera for him. Early in high school he joined a barbershop quartet group of young male teenagers and sang in front of the student body in assemblies.

Steve can still hear "She's my Coney Island baby/she's my own true love" with their rich bass and tenor voices, including Dave's baritone, his own rich, deep voice along with that of his friend Corky Plank who later sang on Broadway.

Otherwise, in those early growing-up years, contrast between Dave and Neel prevailed. If Neel were out late, after dark, there was a good reason. On the other hand, Dave loved getting out and staying out late at night, even as a boy of twelve and thirteen, meeting clandestinely with a bunch of guys in the neighborhood and tomcatting around, mainly "up to no good!" as some would say.

Steve, on one occasion after ten p.m., when they were supposed to be in bed, followed Dave out the window, up the alley, and into the street to join his friends or "Hoodlums!" his mother would call them. Steve was accepted, or tolerated, at first and hobnobbed with the mischief-makers, ringing doorbells and running, night-peeking in through windows, soaping car windows. Around midnight, he began to pull on Dave's arm.

"Dave, don't you think we better get home now?"

"Nah. Hey Ken, look over there!" and off they'd go on another escapade.

And soon, Steve pleaded again, "Dave, it's getting awful late."

Suddenly one of his buddies chimed in, "Why'd you bring your kid brother along! He's a pain in the ass."

Shortly, it was clear Dave was going to stay with the guys, so Steve left them, ran home, climbed back through the window and got into bed. He laid awake and wondered if Dave was going to get into some terrible trouble. This was a persistent concern of Steve's; he didn't want to see Dave get into trouble. Despite his lack of judgment in choice of friends, Dave was a neat guy. He rarely got into trouble.

When Dave did get into some unveiled mischief, his mother would say, "Every family has a black sheep!" Of course she cared about him, and he loved her; it's just that in those growing-up years of male-dominated relations, such a thing as affection of a son for his mother would never be admitted, much less demonstrated.

Rarely if ever did the subject of family bonding come up, but when it did, Dave would say, "Oh, Mother always likes Neel the best!" And their mother would say about them but with Dave clearly in mind, "a person is judged by the company he keeps."

Dave's friends were not the sophisticates of the neighborhood—that's for sure! Whether it was their influence or Dave's own propensity, he certainly was inclined toward mischief with the guys though never anything serious. In fact, Steve remembers Dave as the one out looking for a good time, but not at the expense of hurting someone else. He imagined Dave getting the guys together back behind a garage to see who could tell the funniest dirty joke. Dave himself was the funniest one in the family. His jokes were frequently not merely off-color, but nevertheless funny and sometimes clever. And nothing stood too sacred to be turned into humor. Nobody could mess up a lovely melody's lyrics like Dave. "My desert is waiting, please hand me a spoon ." but more typically, "Give me five minutes more with that red-headed whore!"

And it would come up again and again, "Oh, mother always likes Neel the best." If she did, it was because Neel rarely ever gave her reason to worry. She was too busy keeping a roof over their heads to give excess attention to any of the boys. Yet, ironically, in the adult years, Dave and his mother were closer than Neel and his mother.

But when growing up in teen years, Neel felt particularly close to his mother. Money was a family lack. Neel applied to the local A & P grocery store, was accepted, and worked whenever he could after school and on Saturdays. Steve remembers his mother often saying in those early times, "After working hard all week at school and at the grocery store, he would come home on pay night and turn his entire paycheck over to me." Indeed, Steve had heard his mother say this on numerous occasions, prompting Steve to feel, although he was dumbfounded to hear it, that his brother Neel was a Godsend to their family. For his athleticism, achievements, his acquiring devoted friends and his money contributions to the family, Steve, was unable to emulate Neel; in fact, in the latter years he stood rather distantly in awe of his big brother.

For Dave and Steve, their eldest brother the tenor and their mother the pianist determined their taste in music ever after. Classical! Puccini, Verdi, Bizet, Strauss, Beethoven, Bach, Mozart, Strauss, Tschaikovsky, Chopin, and on. The piano, records, radio—all classical. Filled with joy, delight, sorrow, tragedy, all were deeply emotional. Steve could hear Aunt Jessie's words, "Music will break your heart!"

Neel's seriousness about music was evident in those early years. It was typical for this to happen: Neel would be in the bathroom at the top of the stairs. He would hit a high note, stop everything, rush down the stairs and strike a note on the keyboard. "AAAAH!" He would repeat it several times and, satisfied, return upstairs to his toilet. Very little would take precedence over his voice quality and range.

This, Dave and Steve grew up with. And the tenor records began to mount up. Neel bought his own records whenever he could save up the money: Enrique Crusoe, Lauritz Melchior, Jussi Bjorling, John McCormack; songs from *Aida, Carmen, Barber of Seville, The Magic Flute, Don Giavanni*. How could one be exposed to such music and performers day after day without picking up the deep human emotions?

Here grew up a remarkable young man, Neel. In his early teens, in addition to his job at the grocery store, he worked as a caddy at Norwood Country Club, which helped him provide for a few of his own needs. Later in life, he became an exceptional golfer, some of which interest and skill were achieved by his acute observation, thanks to this period of his life. In his younger life, he was a considerably above-average student and athlete. He mixed with fine young men from Swyer's Church. He sang in the choir, in the chorus. In high school, he sang solos before the student body.

Then too, he was officer material with a natural ability in military strategy. He achieved A's and B's in most every course he took.

He was handsome in appearance, with dark hair and complexion, and a fine physique, often compared to Cornel Wilde, the swashbuckling handsome movie star. When Neel's name was read at graduation from Normandy High School, at that time one of the best public high schools in St. Louis and St. Louis County, with his accomplishments, his appearance, his stature in the opinions of teachers and students and even his name indeed were distinctive. The school board president read, "William Neely Halstead Fulbright the Third."

"Wow!" many thought. "Is that he? Really? With a name like that, you have to be someone special!"

The "if" factor figured into the family prospective behavior. Had the Fulbrights the money, Neel would have been sent straight off to Julliard. Even without that or some similar advantage, he was able to later sing professionally. But such expensive top schooling would never happen.

What else could advance a young man's career under more favorable conditions? This highly masculine young man, a varsity player as a quarterback in football and a pitcher in baseball at one of the top athletic schools in the state, a top merit badge earner in the Scouts, must go not just to any college, but he must go to the United States West Point Military Academy. No doubt about it. With high recommendations, administrators saw to it that William Neely had the application and all the paper work sent in to West Point. He was made for such a place.

Yes, his name came before the U. S. senators in 1945 at a time when our nation was winding down from one of the most destructive wars in history. The war taught this nation to have the best of the best ready for national defense, prepping the outstanding young men like William Neely Halstead Fulbright III.

But he was not selected! Were the four selected from around the state as deserving as he? We'll never know, but Neel's family, friends, teachers and administrators, all who knew him, were greatly disappointed. Several felt that Neel lost out because he had no close political connections in the state of Missouri. And since the death of Neel's father, even less so in national politics, considering that the Ferguson Fulbrights had no connection with the influential Fulbrights of Southern Missouri nor with the rising fortunes of the Fayetteville-Arkansas Fulbrights, who would, in a few years become a favorite son in the United States Senate. This is hardly the first time the family felt, in addition to the personal loss, the loss of Harry Wilks Fulbright, who was close to the Fayetteville Fulbrights, in his potentially potent career.

It might have been good had Neel picked up on the high and mighty family aura spewed by his Aunt Jessie. After all, that glow was not totally baseless. Although Neel tried at times to be more aggressive—wasn't he often told after his father's death that "you, Neel, are now the man of the family"—he was only nine at the time. Furthermore, he was more the modest sort by nature, perhaps enhanced by his awareness that powerful blows can come from sources like cancer of the lymph nodes, And this at a time when he, a boy, needed his father most. How many of his friends, classmates, scholastic, academic and athletic competitors lost their fathers at such an important early age of nine years and whose mothers had to work ten hours a day and all day on Saturdays—without inheritance or even social security (not yet enacted)—just to pay the ordinary bills. These were circumstances beyond his control. Perhaps this is why the dramatic operatic tragedies caught on with such potency deep inside him and with every member of the family.

A small scholarship allowed Neel to start college at Washington University. In his first class, algebra, Neel learned that a young man seated near him had not only purchased the class text but also had worked and solved every problem in the book. While Neel was working at A & P and bringing home his checks to his mother, this other young man could devote his entire time to getting ahead, way ahead of everyone in algebra. How was Neel to compete with that?

Neel lasted one semester there, quit and joined the U. S. Marines. In his position, this was a good move. After a few years of service, he could come out not only more mature, but also with the complete G. I. Bill, that is, with most of the rest of his college paid for. Further, his experience in the Marines was excellent. He became a sea-going marine, was awarded a marksman medal, traveled to Okinawa, the Philippines, Japan, and came out ready to attend a university. He picked Southern Methodist University in Dallas, Texas.

There he studied math, music and teaching methods, He met his wife-to-be, Babs Blaine, completed an advanced degree in education, married, began teaching, and working part time at his father-in-law's business, a bakery. Eventually he moved up the education ladder to become an assistant superintendent of schools, the superintendent's right hand man, an information provider, that is, a researcher. He and Babs provided a wonderful home for six children suited exceptionally to learning.

Unfortunately, family history repeated itself. Neel went into the hospital to be treated for pneumonia. It was discovered that he had lung cancer. Neel did not get to see his wonderful children grow up, except for one that is, the eldest, Dana Denise.

Made bald by chemotherapy, he lived long enough to walk her down the aisle to marry her young gentleman and long enough to see her drive off with her new husband on their way back to college.

How often do you, driving an automobile, following another car, expect that car ahead to suddenly come head-on straight at you? How can that happen? You were looking at his rear-end bumper!

On their way back to the university in New Mexico, Dana and her new husband were driving in West Texas when an unexpected freeze rendered the highway they traveled unpredictably icy. The car they followed suddenly spun around and slammed into them head on. Dana was killed instantly.

Neel received word that his eldest child never made it back to college, would never thereafter start a career and family of her own. The news was devastating. In less than two years later, Neel died of lung cancer.

David Stanley, Neel's two-years-younger brother, after winning a football scholarship from the sports' famous Don Faurot, inventor of the split T formation, however, had other plans. He dropped out of Mizzou to marry his high school sweetheart, the young Mildred Davis, the Comet's Queen's court attendant, whom he had escorted to the high school annual prom. He took a job in a T.V. service shop just off the main street in Ferguson, only a short distance from the high school that Mildred and he had attended. He took a few courses in electronics at Washington University, but funds were highly limited, and soon a family was on the way. Gail, her grandmother Gladys Garrison's pride and joy, was borne. He worked well and hard and soon acquired the shop and in a few years worked it into a successful business.

Having purchased a house two blocks from his mother in Ferguson, he was quite settled in his career. A second daughter, Laura, came along, Laura, and a son, Gary. Years later, a short time after his oldest daughter Gail was married to Tom Mines in the Ferguson Episcopal Church, Dave had a heart attack. He died at the age of forty-one. Brother Neel's death followed two and a half years later; Neel passed away at the age of forty-four. After all those years of working for, raising, caring for, and worrying about Dave and Neel, their deaths so close in time were devastating to Gladys. She, of course, would never get over it. Most of the rest of her life would be underlined with grief.

Steve, too, was struck severe blows by these deaths. And he has often wondered how he could make some small enhancement to Dave and Neel's having lived.

With Dave, that has been easy and fun. Now and again some witticism will come up, and Steve will say, "as my brother Dave would say ..." especially if the subject had some off-color aspect or implication. Such to the extent that his friend will say, "I wish I had known your brother Dave—what a character he must have been!"

Yes, Steve has always appreciated his brother Dave's wit as well as the fact that in those mysterious days of growing up, Dave protected Steve, the youngest and weakest.

Enhancement can occur if we review their lives and consider what worth we have received from this departed person? One message from Neel comes immediately to Steve's mind. When Neel was studying changes in the Dallas Public Schools that might improve instruction, help develop students in skill and in intelligence, he was challenged by his superintendent, who said (words to the effect), "but if we know what methods will improve education, will the faculty employ them?" and Neel responded, "In my observations and interviews, I find that the faculty is quite willing to make changes if they know what to do." So their method came to be pending and finally applicable, when they could navigate with each faculty member his/her methodology with clarity of purpose, goal, and fulfillment.

Epiglympselogue Twenty-three

"How old was their mother when she passed away?" asked Sally.

"Seventy-four," James replied. "In the last half dozen years of her life, her youngest son Steve would have a weekly dinner with her, after which he would ask her questions about the family's past and would record these by tape and notes. He encouraged her to write family history, to tell about her growing-up years in Russellville, Arkansas, papers he acquired along with photographs after her death in 1979."

"You said at one point that Gladys was a heavy smoker," said Rupert. What did she die of—lung cancer like her son Neel?"

"No," James replied. "She died of a stroke. Steve was not with her when she passed away—which he regretted. Steve always felt that she had a wonderful constitution—such that she would live to be a hundred if she'd give up her smoking and beer-drinking, and start to exercise. She would never do this. Smoking and drinking beer was too much of her lifestyle. Steve hinted for her to change, but she told him once that her doctor told her to give up smoking. Rather than do that, she gave up her doctor."

"Sometimes living a long life is not a priority," commented Lisa.

"Steve has mentioned that he speculates that his mother's smoking-drinking beer, non-exercising lifestyle was a connection to the past. He had reason to believe that she was greatly nostalgic. The glory years were behind her, years with her handsome, talented husband, and her three boys, the years filled with fun, excitement and, especially, filled with promise."

"How did she come to feel about "the Black Sheep of the family," asked Ben.

"After all," joined in Rupert, "didn't he establish his family just a few short blocks away from where she lived on Robert and Chancellor?"

"Yes, and not only that, but she worked for him part-time, and she worked for some years in the Ferguson Bank right across the street from his business. Dave and his mother were quite close."

"Even though he was always saying that Neel was her favorite?"

"True. One of her all-time favorite children in her later life was Dave's oldest daughter Gail. She gave little Gail piano lessons. She adored little Gail!"

Sally's persistent hand waved vigorously for attention. "But, back to Neel. Did he ever say anything to Steve about smoking?"

James flinched. "Yes, definitely. When Neel had only a few months to live, Steve visited him in Dallas. Steve remembers it vividly. The two of them were alone in his car; they had just pulled up in his driveway, behind his house. Completely unlike the Neel he grew up with, the Neel that went off to the marines and the Neel that returned to college, the Neel that was so striking in looks when he and Babs married, this Neel, bald-headed, white and sickly began to weep. Wanting to get the subject on something pleasant, Steve touched his shoulder and asked something inane. Neel brought up the subject of cigarettes. He said, 'I wished the damned things had been illegal!' indicating to Steve that he, Neel the marine, would have no problem following the law, but when it came to making the right judgment himself, for himself, this did not work. It was a part of the times. The times he lived in."

"Bringing back Oedipus, we have to suffer the real consequences whether we have the knowledge or not," pontificated Rupert.

"True," responded James, "But we can't sit on top of the mountain and peer down at those who did not know what we are fortunate enough now to know. Remember those marines were facing life and death situations and lighting up a cigarette was a small thing, but it gave some easing of the dire situation. So who could blame them? Wouldn't you and I have done the same?"

"And the science of the effects of nicotine had not yet been learned, so people did not know at that time was not yet conducted," commented Ben.

"And look at the choices people make now, even with certain knowledge," said Sally.

GLIMPSES TWENTY-FOUR

PARTNERS AMORE, MEMORY

Steve has a rich recollection of two ladies, Nancy Vogt and Patti White, whom he met in college, and the sum total of their relationships occurred during those two or three years of undergraduate college. He was attending the University of Missouri, Columbia, and they were attending Stephens College, also in Columbia. There was a third young lady, but he did not first meet her at Stephens College as he had the other two. He first met her, Rosann, in the 5th grade at Central Elementary School in Ferguson. (She will be told about shortly.) He saw her, occasionally in Columbia. They went out together there, but the denouement of their relationship came soon after her graduation from Stephens. The height of the relationship of each of the other two, Nancy and Patti, as stated, came during the young ladies' two years at Stephens College.

To more fully grasp the situation, let's take Steve back in time. Let us consider the *milieu* (one of Steve's favorite terms). Usually applied to historicity, the term here allows us to more fully examine the context, meaning that which surrounded the feelings, emotions, in short, the sense of presence and eventual loss.

Like so many college-university towns in our nation, the location where Steve would spend some six-plus years in (at this time, four of those six-plus years) Columbia, Missouri, was (is?) a bachelor's paradise. The University of Missouri, hereafter Mizzou, was of course open to both males and females, with many more males than females. But two colleges in the town of Columbia at that time were women's colleges: Columbia College on the north side of town and Stephens College on the east side of town. All the campuses were within walking distance of one another, easily accessible to male suitors. So with these thousands of young people, young ladies from all around the country, including young GIs coming to college on the GI bill, the abundant availability of the opposite sex was advantageous to the young ready to get a start on life.

Like so many other young men, eighteen-year-old Steve was frequently looking for a girlfriend, but not for a wife. He had seen several of his young friends get married immediately out of high school, but he saw himself as a young professional destined to have a successful career although the natural propagation tendency in him was, perhaps, as strong as in any healthy male. The difference between these two kinds of people, the immediate propagators and the delayers, was a matter of, one, understanding and, two, will. Understanding eluded those who could not see what they were getting into, a locked-in job for the rest of their lives or, if lucky, a rise in career and status, a way of life that could be shared with a family. And, two, the will, a determination to ride the whole thing out, to better prepare oneself for life. Delaying his masculine nature was not easy for Steve.

Let's not overlook or downplay the role of romantic dispositions. There was romance in the wonderful melodies and their accompanying poetic lyrics. There were the love songs of the era, a virtual renaissance of popular melodies with their lyrics. Nothing was more popular than *Show Boat*. These songs of love have not been surpassed: "You Are Love," and "Make Believe." At a very early age (ten to fifteen), Steve and his young friends after dark would stand on a neighborhood street corner and sing these songs—sing their hearts out. Although coming out in the late 1920s, Hammerstein and Kern's *Show Boat's* staging and songs continued to grow in popularity. Then more wonderful lyrics and melodies from Rogers and Hammerstein

And there were the love songs of the 1940s, the war years, when young men away from home were dying (in cases, literally) for their lady-loves, songs like Cole Porter's "You'd Be So Nice to Come Home To," Rogers and Hammerstein's *State Fair* songs, like especially "It Might as Well Be Spring" and songs from the early 1950s "When I Fall In Love," "Cry Me a River" and "Fly Me To The Moon." Ah Frank Sinatra and Nat King Cole!

And dances! There were all the "mixers," of course the fraternity-sorority mixers, the Columbia College mixers and, what Steve especially appreciated, the Stephens College mixers. Over the four years, there were many, many mixers, which Steve frequently attended and enjoyed. And after each mixer, he would return to his dorm room and fall asleep to the radio playing Nat King Cole singing songs like "Unforgettable" and "Mona Lisa." Where did those wonderful talents of musicians go? Where did those years go? Overcoming loss is a problem for all of us, no less than for Steve.

We'll consider Nancy Vogt first. This relationship became a quasi-tragedy. When Steve and Nancy met at a Stephens College mixer, it was love at first sight. Most of the desirable young ladies that Steve met at college were ready for marriage. Most likely, their parents had sent them off to Stephens, "the finishing school," to give their young daughters a little more time to mature, but they were physically ready for motherhood and, hopefully, for the matrimonial state with it.

Steve was not ready for matrimony. He had too many years to go before he could attain a position of intellectual achievement and financial security. He often wondered if the young ladies he dated or befriended while in that collegiate atmosphere ever fully realized that being of roughly the same age as the male was not appropriate for them because of the young man's need to gain the earning power and self-assurance necessary for providing a home and the basic needs of a family. The couple would have been better suited if he were twenty-two to twenty-five and she eighteen to twenty-one.

Nancy Vogt, eighteen, was exceedingly, overwhelmingly pretty. For several months, she and Steve went to dances, football games, coke-jukebox dates, the typical fare. Then came an open weekend in the fall when it was acceptable for her to go with him to his mother's home in Ferguson, St. Louis, and to become acquainted with his family, his mother Gladys and his stepfather Harold LeMert.

Nancy and Steve were quite compatible and proper. Once there, Nancy slept in one bedroom and Steve slept on the couch-bed in the family room at the opposite end of the house. When they went to a local bar-restaurant, they met a few of his former high school friends. When she excused herself to the ladies' room, one of his old high school friends Paul McKee said softly to Steve. "Say, does your Nancy have a sister?"

"Not here. A little sister."

"Nancy is gorgeous. I want someone like her."

"Yes, that dimpled brown-eyed smile quite takes a guy's breath away."

"You say she has a sister?'

"Well, yes. Nancy's family lives in Norfolk, Virginia. Her father is a Colonel in the Marines."

That's the way it went. Steve was the envy of all the guys he knew because Nancy was such a pretty and charming girl.

When Christmas came, she got permission from her parents to bring Steve home with her to Norfolk, Virginia, for the holidays to meet her family, her Colonel father and her mother, and her little brother and sister. Steve, of course, had little money, but with some finagling, he managed to come up with enough for a bus ticket, gleaned from his pittance of a savings and a little Christmas money from his mother.

Nancy, who would normally fly, opted to take the bus with Steve. It was a long, tough trip east. They rode all night on a Greyhound bus. In the early hours of morning, Nancy proceeded to get sick. Fortunately, they made it to a bus stop, where she could get to a ladies' room in time to throw up. After a difficult time, when they finally made it to Norfolk, Nancy was in no condition to do anything but lie down for most of the day to recover.

Although the Colonel's family seemed to approve of Steve, the circumstances were not conducive to joy for the first half of the holiday season. When the few-days visit was over, Steve had to return alone on the bus while Nancy followed later by air. They resumed their romance in Columbia, where they also resumed their studies to wrap up the semester.

Of course, Steve eventually would be getting a commission through his ROTC course and going into the Air Force so the military family life would be compatible with the way that Nancy had lived all of her life. She made a career decision at this point to become an airline reservationist. This way, she could begin earning money to help support the two of them while Steve was finishing up his studies that next year. Then he, as an officer in the Air Force, could support them thereafter. It was a good and serious plan. Steve agreed but with the proviso that if being an officer in the Air Force did not suit him, he needed to go to law school to qualify for a civilian profession.

"Oh," Nancy proclaimed. "I can continue my job as an airline reservationist."

The plans were settled.

The fly in the ointment came in the spring when her father was transferred from Virginia to Hawaii, which, as far as Steve was concerned, might as well have been a transfer to the other side of the moon.

Nancy's first reaction was, "No. I'm not going that far away from Steve. I want to stay while Steve finishes out his senior year and becomes a second lieutenant in the Air Force!"

"But once out there," her family argued (by letter and phone), "this is the most beautiful place in all the world. You don't want to miss it."

Her response was, "But I'm not coming out there. So forget it!"

Three or four more exchanges occurred as the spring flowers grew and blossomed. "Hawaii is the most wonderful place in the world!" and "you'd be a fool to miss it!" kept resonating.

Soon, Steve could see the handwriting on the wall. How could he ask Nancy to give up such an opportunity? What was he going to do? He had another year of college. He had not the money to go anywhere. He didn't even have enough money to buy Nancy a decent graduation present.

So what that meant was, when Nancy's girlfriends were all getting engagement rings for graduation, Nancy received her petty gift from Steve. When she unwrapped her gift and saw the cheap little 15-dollar bracelet to accompany the plain graduation card, Steve could see her otherwise captivating smile fade into sadness, disappointment and finally anger.

He surmised that, in her view, the idea was, *well, if you really loved me, you would have found a way to buy me an engagement ring.*

"Oh?" Steve inside himself responded. *"How? Steal it! How else could I have given you one?"*

So after graduation, Nancy boarded a flight for Hawaii. "We'll write. But I'm not staying. I'm coming back so we can get married."

"I hope so. I'll miss you so much," said Steve. But he could not help but wonder, *will I ever see Nancy again?* He was already having that feeling of deep and permanent loss.

A few letters came at first, but they seemed to grow cold. What in Heaven's name could he do about it? He knew she was on base with thousands of highly eligible marines. It was just a matter of time. Little by little, her indications of ever returning faded away. Although he had never been there, he knew well enough what was said about places like Waikiki Beach. He imagined the beauty of Hawaii, the paradise on earth: the wide, blue ocean, the long, sandy beaches, the waving palms—oh yes, and the eager young marines! Wouldn't it be easy for her to convince herself that Steve was not really that much in love with her, that he was not really interested in marriage?

And, looking at his side of it, what could he do, with no money and no time. If he didn't keep his nose to the grindstone, he would never be able to marry. He suffered with her growing coldness towards him in her letters. Oh, she glowed all right, but not over him as in former conversations, but over the glorious landscapes of Hawaii. His last letter to Nancy reflected his pessimism about their future together. He wanted her to come back with reassurances. No sooner had he mailed off the letter then he began to regret it.

Her return letter came immediately: "Your letter makes it very difficult for me to choose!" To choose! She had already chosen! No doubt about it. She would stay and marry a marine. What was there to choose between?

Then there were no letters from her at all. A month or so later, he received a bland card from her, which she signed as *Mrs. Something or rather.* Could it really have happened that soon? Could she really be that flippant? And that cruel? Sure, she wanted him to know that she had (quickly!) found someone else. So much for their plans! So much for promises! So much for true love! And human nature? Pathetic!

The other young Stephens lady, Patti White, whom he later, after the fading Nancy relationship, began seeing occasionally, he liked and admired her a great deal. She was from Marblehead, Massachusetts, and had the cutest New England accent. And she was smart. He could be really great friends with her. She was pretty, had a sweet disposition, made outstanding grades, was elected president of her class. With the campus political situations, he felt as if he were her, or she were his, counterpart.

They dated a few times, but Steve was not greatly physically attracted to her. He wished he were. She was a genuinely good person. Since she was a year younger, their ages were a little more compatible. Well, those things happen. She graduated when he did. When he was off to his first duty station at RAF Station Manston, England, he flew from Westover, Massachusetts. There in Massachusetts, before he left, he felt especially close to her. She represented his growing nostalgic feelings for the now forever-gone campus social and political times in Columbia. Before taking off for England and a whole new life, he called Patti and wished her all the best. She sweetly returned the wish. That was it, but he always wished he had kept contact with her, at least, as a friend.

Where are you today, Patti White? Did you, Patti White, wind up with someone deserving of you?

Epiglimselogue Twenty-four

James looked each member of the book club in the eye. "I speak of memory rather than history because for most people I have observed, memory is more personal than history, or so they feel. Yet history is so much a part of us."

The members could tell that James was just warming up to his subject. "To many, history is remote, something you have to study in school, which one may take to or not. These people do not realize history's magnitude and impact. So let us call this focus memory."

"May I jump in here?" said Rupert. "What are we without memory? May I say that we are nothing at all without memory. What is all happening, all feeling, all experiencing if it is not recorded in the memory? Why do we see Alzheimer's as the ultimate in human tragedy? Because our awareness, our total being, who we are and what we are is tied into memory. Memory gives us awareness and continuity. When someone we know intimately dies, we are stunned by the taking away of a memory. So much departs with that person that we cannot retrieve. As far as we know, so much in that memory is gone forever."

"I think we're of one mind here, Rupert, ol' chap," said James. "And of course what we do recall is potentially subject to forgetfulness, coloration, modification, distortion, imagination and, finally, interpretation. When we "re-write" memory, that is recall it, write it down, consciously or unconsciously embellish it, what do we have? To some degree or other fiction, intentionally or not."

"Lo!" said Sally. "We have our stories. Perhaps the best of ourselves, worthy of preserving for posterity."

"Yes. I feel Steve's broken heart over Nancy," said Lisa. "After their times together at college, dances, football games, coke-dates and at their trips to their family homes, their plans to spend their lives together, then their thousands-of-miles of separation, her sudden marriage to someone else---how Sad!"

Glimpses Twenty-five

RICHARD RODEN

One of Steve's very good friends was Dick Roden. What's in a name? Later in life, Steve's friend preferred to be called Richard, and Steve preferred to pronounce his last name like the sculptor Ro-din, accent on the last syllable. But Steve stuck to Dick Roden the way things were in the beginning of the story until near the end. Then Steve accepted Richard's wishes.

For one year (actually less than one year) Steve's mother moved the two of them from Ferguson (St. Louis County), Missouri, south to Dallas, Texas. Yes, Steve was interested in sports in those days, but he was aware of the need for scholarship too. He wanted to be Mr. Scholar-Athlete, or rather Mr. Athletic-Scholar. He had just finished football season at Ferguson and was starting into basketball.

His brother Dave wanted to stay at Missouri University, where he managed to get a walk-on scholarship (under coach Don Faurot) and to stay close to his high school sweetheart, Mildred Davis. Dave and Steve's brother Neel was now out of the Marines and attending Southern Methodist University on the GI bill, one of the great ways at that time for one short of funds to pay for the basics of a college education. Very soon, he met the love of his life Babs Blaine, his future wife. Neel's attending SMU was their mother's incentive to move herself and Steve to Dallas.

As for Steve, he was totally forlorn, leaving behind not only his prospects for a great high school basketball career (or so he thought at the time) but also, more importantly, his friends from school grades five through eleven in Ferguson. And what was Dallas going to be like? He had no idea. Yet nothing (including pleading and whining) could be done to change his mother's wishes to move. And move they did.

In Dallas, he attended Woodrow Wilson High School—"Sant Louie"—they called him, the total outsider: their accent, a charming difference, made him imagine he had just stepped into *Gone With the Wind*. "Whah I declare, Rhet Butler!"

And as for sports, he figured in such a sports'-minded environment, making the team was a sure-fire acceptance-getter—an inter-school sport, at this season, basketball.

Shortly, he found himself before the principal. Mr. Oberthorpe spoke authoritatively and, of course in Steve's mind, in accent. "Ya'al'll want to join the ROTC; we have the biggest and fi-i-i-i-nest in the whole country," *Was this out of a movie script?* Richer than Steve thought! Of course, this was no mere boast; it would later be confirmed by every new acquaintance Steve made at the school. "Yes, sir, the fiii-nest ROTC in the land!"

But at that time, he replied a snappy response to the principal:

"I'll think about it." To Steve, this seemed an intelligent response, the cool, thoughtful outsider mulling over the prospect, but Mr. Oberthorpe's scowls suggested that even thinking about it was a disgusting miscalculation.

In the next few days, while Steve was supposedly "thinking about it," the bulk of the school males went drilling and target practicing—Steve didn't know which end of the rifle to fire from and, too, most un-hemanly-like, wasn't the least interested in finding out. Without a husband for most of those years, his mother raised Steve to despise all firearms. And then, lodged in their memories was that incident in the city not long after their father died. For a lark, a neighbor's boy, the scruff of the neighborhood, shot Steve's brother Dave in the face with a gun firing a blank cartridge at close range. With powder burns all over his face, he was rushed to a hospital emergency room for treatment, scaring their mother half to death and costing money she didn't have. At first, there was fear that he might lose an eye and the fear of blood-poisoning. And this was only a pistol shooting a blank.

At Woodrow Wilson that first week, while the robust young men were target-practicing and marching, Steve was sent to the holding room with the cripples, unfit, physically inept and even riffraff, where he could—think about it. Such a "holding room" was totally unfair, of course, but as far as Steve could determine, there were no special programs for this variety of students. Seemingly, all dumped together as misfits. A war against this sort of practice had been fought recently, but that didn't seem to matter. They were there "to study," and most likely bemoan the fact that they were not up to what was determined the physical norm. Dumped there for the year meant a shared stereotype that would exclude Steve and anyone else so designated from varsity sports and very likely from social acceptance.

Steve got the message. This decrepit, wretched room was not where a big-time, athletic, macho, Texan male—totally lacking in humanistic empathy—spent even a fraction of his school time.

By the weekend, Steve no longer had to think about it. Monday morning, Steve sho' nough came around. From the moment he rendered his decision in the principal's office, at once Steve was ushered to the armory office and placed before a uniformed officer.

"Yes sir, Mr. Commandant, *"Ja-val, Herr commandant,"* he felt he might have said.

"Major Mackson, son!"

"I'll join up, Sir." Steve said as manly as he could muster. At least the boy had learned way back "up Nouth" in the Boy Scouts something about how to come to attention.

But Steve didn't realize that here before the distinguished Major, he was a little slouched until the Major's lips tightened and he said, "We teach respect her-ah, son." When he eyed Steve over and snorted deeply, Steve quickly straightened up. The Major looked at the clock over Steve's shoulder and seemed satisfied.

"S-ah-n hereh, son, on the dotted li-ahne and get ya uniforms from suppl-ah. We wear uniforms to school four days a week, Mondays through Thursdays. Ya hee-ah? Every Wednesday morning at eight, we march in parade shoulderin' riii-fles rii-ght he-ah on ahr parade grounds with evrabody comin from miihles around a-watchin'."

Then he smiled. "Now ah mean to tell ya, that was a rii-ah-t good decision ya-ll made the-ah, prii-vate, a—lets see ah he-ah—" He glanced down at his papers, "Priivate Fulbraht. Ya-al report to Sergeant Howker. Now, ya-al he-ah? Dismissed, prii-vate."

It seemed appropriate for Steve to spin around on pivot and beat a hasty exit. He would have cliqued his heals if he knew how to do it.

Before he dressed in the brown khaki issue, Steve was an alien. Now suddenly, he became one of them, all except for the Yankee accent. The accent spoken all around him in his new Dallas environment seemed quite appropriate as he, in other ways that he could muster, swam with the current. Even when a very cute girl he met, named Martha, looked at him smiling at her and asked, "Wahy ya'll smilin'?"

"Sorry but it's the way you speak. It's so ..."

"Wahy? Ah talk jis liike ya-al do!"

"Well, yes, I ..."

His classes were not all that appealing. His ignorance of their tradition cut him out of what might have been the better classes and the better teachers, at least from the student's perspective. It was the practice of Woodrow Wilson High to have the students on class roster day, day-one of the semester, run to the classrooms of the teachers whose courses they want to sign up for. Since Steve had not taken part in this custom in September, he was placed in the classes with the fewer number of students, which perhaps wouldn't be a detriment except with this system it meant that the smaller classes where the administration would place new students were the classes with the least popular teachers in the school.

Steve remembers especially his Spanish class taught by an elderly sourpuss named Miss Hardriff. Of all classes that Steve had to be dumped in (for that is what it was), he had to have Miss Hardriff for not only Spanish class but also for this period of the day which doubled once a week for 'Homeroom.'

At the beginning of the period, out of the blue, Miss Hardriff sauntered to the front and says, her words running together, "Who-wants-his-name-up for class representative?"

No one raised a hand or budged.

She spoke again, fast, running her words together even more so. "Everybody-knows-that-a person-who-wants-to-run puts his own name up for a vote," she continued authoritatively. "Now, who-wants-this?"

Again, no response. Steve was not sure. *Did I hear that right?*

"If'n no-one's-willing-to-put-his-own-name-up, then-we-won't-have a representative." That was the end of it! Steve couldn't believe it. *This was their democratic process?*. In his classes back in St. Louis, his classmates nominated each other willingly with their own classmates in charge—if someone were nominated who didn't want to serve, then that person declined the nomination in favor of someone else. The procedure was always explained in class, handled with great care by the teacher or a Council Representative before proceeding. Those accepting nominations had their names written on the board, a short speech was in order, and then a vote was taken privately, the ballots collected, counted, and the one with the highest number of votes served as the homeroom representative to the Student Council.

Steve knew the process well because he had served two years on the Council, and when he returned, he was nominated and voted in and eventually served as the student body vice-president.

But here in Miss Hardriff's class, the whole business was over in less than three minutes. Steve was not aware that anything else ever came of it. Apparently that was the beginning and end of the school's education in democracy, at least in Miss Hardriff's classroom.

Steve soon learned there was a power struggle going on between Miss Hardriff and the majority of males in the class. On one occasion when she turned her back to write on the chalkboard, spitballs flew everywhere. When one large spitball zinged past her ear and smacked against the board in front of her, she spun around and with an inhuman look of utter disgust on her face, she screeched, "If you ever threw anything?"

"We're all in for it," Steve heard one guy near him whisper.

"Who EVER threw anything?!" Steve noticed that often Miss Hardriff didn't say things quite right. Silence ensued.

"If you ever threw anything, stand up!" *What does that mean?* Steve wondered. Surely, she didn't say that right. Everybody has thrown something at one time or another. Yet, she repeated it. "Everyone-who-ever-threw-anything, stand up!"

One boy slowly took to his feet. Then another one. And another. Finally, Steve was the only male left seated. *Oh, well,* he thought. *I can't just sit here. The only seated male. The only Mr. Goodie-two-shoes. And she did say "ever."* So Steve rose to his feet.

Apparently, this was a shocker. She stared him down with horror and disbelief. "Did you throw something?" she blurted.

He shrugged his shoulders. Apparently, none of the culprits were punished that day because Mr. Yankey newcomer stood with them. *That might have helped my acceptance,* Steve figured.

Out in the hall, when the class was over, one of the boys came to Steve and said, "Whah did ya-al stand up? Ya-al didn't throw anything?" Even now Steve didn't know what to say. He just shrugged and said, "She said 'ever'!" He grinned and walked away.

In those first few days of newness, *Steve wondered, will I meet anyone here in Texas that I can be real friends with? Not unless I can understand what these people are saying and, of course, if I can shoot a rifle and march in a parade.*

But Steve's chance to gain acceptance came through basketball. He soon learned that the coach was an older man they referred to as "Pop" Kitchner who apparently had been there forever! His first question to Steve was have you played varsity basketball?

"Yes, sir. We were the B-team champs of the county."

That did it. Steve was first team varsity right off the bat. Of course basketball was not the prime sport of such a militaristic school, public school or not. Football was THE sport. Steve remembers the great star of the football team one Bill Forester. Probably he was the biggest, strongest guy in the school or of many another school. He had set all kinds of records as a fullback, and he would go on to play university and professional football. At Woodrow he was on the basketball team, but more as the big man in the center who took up a good deal of space in front of the basket rather than a skillful maneuverer and basket-dunker.

A few of the practice sessions Steve remembers especially well. When he and his teammates were not executing a play correctly, good ol' Pop Kitchner would redden in the face and turn to his student assistant and say, "Lummy, go get me the "minder." In a few minutes Lummy would return with the minder, a large razor strap. "Now let's run that play again!" he'd shout.

As soon as they did, he would call a player over and command, "Bend over." Then whack! He would rare back and give the player a hard, solid whack on the ramp with the strap.

Later, in the shower room, the guys would whoop it up, pointing at each other and shouting, "Pop sure gave you some good ones!" For Weeks many of Steve's team mates had red stripped back sides. But the guys seemed to like it, as if these were marks of distinction.

When Steve went with his brother Neel to the Blaine's elegant family home to meet Neel's intended for the first time, his brother and he stood in the entranceway, awaiting Babs's appearance at the top of the stairs. There was absolute silence.

Then he could hardly believe his ears. He heard Scarlet O'Hara call down from aloft, "Neeeel, is that little ol' cat down theah?" And when she came down, though Steve was waiting to see Vivien

Leigh, lo, it was Babs Blaine, also very pretty but in a different way. Steve had awakened to find himself somewhere in the land of Tara.

His first buddy he met at basketball practice was Dick Sanderson. They hit it off right away. He lived only two blocks away and had a basketball hoop in his driveway where they could shoot baskets at off moments. Further, Dick Sanderson, the only offspring, had free access to his mother's powder-blue, year-old Chrysler. And he was the one who introduced Steve to Dick Roden, who was to make such an impression on Steve's life, one of his all-time favorite people. Dick Roden and Dick Sanderson knew each other through their Church. Their United Christian Church had a basketball team and competed in a church league. Dick Roden didn't attend Woodrow Wilson until after Steve moved back North. But he was Dick Sanderson's good buddy from Church, and Steve was invited to join the Church team. The more game experience, the better so there he was, with the three of them, blond-headed chums—called cotton-tops—playing basketball and cruising about Dallas together in Dick Sanderson's mom's fancy Chrysler.

As usual Steve was always broke. So he didn't go anywhere fancy with them, but otherwise they shared games, activities, guy talk. On the teams Steve's alias "Sant Louie" prevailed; hence, "throw the ball, Sant Louie." And Steve would throw the ball. After all, he was a congenial team player, who desperately needed acceptance.

When Steve settled in at Dallas and felt quite at ease with his new friend Dick Roden, he took young-people speculation with him. Since Steve was very young and so new thereabouts, he asked questions, sometimes of the wrong people and-or at the wrong times. His new social environment seemed to be rather into religious belief. Unthinking, one day, being in a theological speculative mood, not unusual for Steve, he asked Dick Roden, "How do you know God exists?" This was sincere speculation on his part, not argumentation which meant, 'let's talk about religious belief.'

Dick's face reddened, flushing with anger. "Don't you ever say that!" He snapped. "Don't you ever say that!"

Oops. Wrong person, wrong time. Steve dropped it and never said it again to Dick. He was deeply sorry he had offended his new friend. He figured at the time that he had virtually ruined their newly found friendship. After the basketball season, Steve felt that he would probably, by Dick Roden's doing, never see him again.

How wrong Steve was. When summer came, Steve had a big break—thanks to Dick Roden. It happened his father was a foreman at John E. Mitchell Cotton-gin Machinery Factory located right there in the heart of Dallas. One day, coming as a complete surprise, Dick said to Steve, "You want a job for the summer, Steve?"

"Huh?" Steve's eyes lit up, wondering if he were hearing it right. "A summer job? You bet!"

Dick's father the foreman came into play. From Steve's impecunious point of view, the factory paid quite decent wages. Both Dick and Steve could work there for the summer, stocking the assembly lines with all kinds of metal parts.

And so it was, Dick and Steve were all over that plant loading carts with slabs of steel and manually pushing those massive carriers all over the plant. They had gloves that had to be replaced every other day because the steel, as it slid through their gloved hands, sliced them up, soon shredding the gloves to the point of uselessness and leaving their hands with faint slice marks, this way and that.

And the heat. Wow! Sure the factory had fans. Large ones. However, all these monsters did was blow the hot air around. Steve was amazed at the workers around him, a number of whom seemed quite adapted to this heat. Steve wondered if these workers, many of them students at a local seminary, had some kind of special divine dispensation. He came to admire their pertinacity in their work ethic and in their endurance of the oppressive heat.

After a few weeks of work, Steve noticed that he was breaking out under his arms and around his waist with ghastly red bumps. His ailment was growing painful. He needed to ask their boss about this condition. This was not easy to do. The boss was on the move constantly. One day, he caught up with him.

"Look at these." Steve showed his boss the red bumps.

The boss looked at Steve skeptically. "Have you been taking salt pills?"

"Salt pills?"

"Well, of course you haven't." He shook his head in disbelief. "You silly fool! What ya have is plain ol' heat rash. You're not getting your salt. Why do you think we have these salt-pill machines all around the place!" He swirled his pointed finger in the air. "Don't ya know heat rash when ya see it!"

His boss might as well have said to Steve, *"What kind of an idiot are you?"*

He pointed and commanded, "Hurry up and fill those bins over thah. Ya hear! An' then get yourself some salt pills." And off he galloped at breakneck speed. Steve had often felt that these men handling the monsters of steel were the masters of the range, and in a strange way, he envied them.

"Yes, sir," Steve said and then to himself, *"Oops, sorry. This heat rash is obviously my fault. I'll get salt pills at once. Salt-pill machine? Ah, there's one."* So Steve hustled over, put his hand out, pulled the lever, and there down dropped the magic pill. Promptly, he went to the drinking fountain and with a big gulp of water, he threw back the pill.

Ow! It hit his stomach like a bomb. Steve became instantly ill. He ran to the restroom toilet and threw up everything, it seemed, everything that he had ever eaten in his life. That was the end of the miraculous salt pills.

He resolved to suffer with the heat rash; after all, he was earning money, real money—for himself, for that time—better than mowing lawns, setting pins at the bowling alley, or washing windows. Besides, the summer wouldn't last forever, and by this time, his mother had made it apparent she was intending to return to Ferguson, St. Louis, at the beginning of September, that she was going to get married to the widower whose son, Hal Steve had met in junior high. In fact, Hal and he had introduced Hal's dad to Steve's mother about a year back.

Nevertheless, heat and all, Dick and he had a great summer. It was during that summer that Steve unknowingly did the greatest thing for Dick that he could have done. Dick had never been to a musical. And Steve learned that Dallas had a great open-air theater like his Muny Opera back in St. Louis, which he had been to many times, even as a child. He saw an ad that *Show Boat*, one of Steve's all-time favorite musicals, was going to be performed at the Starlight Operetta.

It had the songs that Steve liked so well, the songs that he and his buddies used to sing standing on the street corner of Hereford and Adele in Ferguson. They'd sing out 'Ol' man River' at the top of their lungs. Steve had often wondered since why the lot of them were never arrested and thrown into the tank for disturbing the peace. If they were singing, he guessed that people thought, at least the boys weren't up to mischief. In later days, reflecting their maturing interests, they sang the love songs from this and other operettas on more street corners, at their homes and at their parties.

"What did you say, Dick?! You've never been to your own Starlight Theater? I can't believe it. What you are missing!" Steve taunted.

"Let's go," said Dick, without hesitation.

So Dick and Steve went and saw *Show Boat*. And the next week they saw *Pal Joey*, and later *Oklahoma*. Steve had never seen anyone so enthralled as Dick. Something amazing was going on inside Dick's head and heart, but Steve didn't know about it. Not for many years.

Well, to jump ahead in time, Steve went back to St. Louis for the fall semester of his senior year. The next year he made one brief trip down to Dallas, and that was for his brother's wedding—Neel married Babs Blaine of course, one of SMU's campus beauties, who also happened to be very bright; she went through the University entirely on scholarships. Steve remembered once reading the same novel *The Scarlet Letter* that Babs was reading, and she finished it when Steve was barely a few chapters into it, and she said, "Heavens,

I finished that ages ago!" Not only was Steve by comparison a slow reader, but he liked to take his time and really live in the story! But Babs was not only a speed reader, she, too, knew the story she had read quite well.

During the weekend of his brother's wedding, Steve contacted Dick Roden. Steve had one afternoon to spare, so he said to Dick, we have to get together. Dick invited him to a tennis court, and it was there that Steve played his first game of tennis ever. It occurred to Steve that Dick was more the skillful athlete kind rather than the hard-nosed, power plunger that were so admired at good ol' Woodrow. Dick taught Steve tennis in that afternoon. After Steve left Dallas, he didn't play tennis again for several years, but tennis was in the back of his mind. In high school Steve was into what the guys considered macho sports like football and basketball. Years later, he changed his view, about twenty-five years later, and took up tennis in earnest when he was in his late forties, and he has been playing tennis ever since—and no basketball and no football. Dick was ahead of Steve's time.

Anyway, Steve returned to St. Louis, went to Mizzou, received an AB and a commission in the Air Force, served in England, came out, went to grad school, became a teacher, went on an exchange program to England, returned, earned a Ph.D. and continued teaching, now college and university level. About forty years after his last contact with Dick Roden, Steve came home from work and found a familiar voice from the past on his phone message machine:

"Is this Steve Fulbraaht who went to Woodrow Wilson in Dallas many years ago? This is Dick Roden. If you are Steve, give me a call … my number is …"

How extraordinary! After all those years, he remembered Steve and that he lived in St. Louis. He remembered ol' Sant Louie. Dick had checked out the phone book numbers and found Steve's name among about five Fulbrights and gave it a try. When Steve called him back, it was as if they had played basketball and tennis just the other day.

"Dick Roden? Is it really you? I can't believe it. How the Hell—I mean how are you?" It is a world for accidental occurrences and coincidences. Who would have thought Steve would still be in his thoughts. And another amazing coincidence was that Steve had just won a National Endowment for the Humanities Award to Princeton University that summer—and where was Dick? Not in Dallas, Texas! He was living in Atlantic Highlands, New Jersey, about thirty miles from Princeton, here his old Dallas-Texas buddy!

In New Jersey, he was performing on the stage (at that time mostly up and down the East Coast) and teaching school. Their other buddy Dick Sanderson, Dick Roden informed Steve, had graduated from law school at SMU and now was serving as a court Justice in Texas.

"And what is it you're doing?" Steve asked.

"Performing on the stage. In musicals."

"Hey, how great! Tell me all about it. I can't wait to hear."

So Dick and Steve made arrangements and got together that summer when Steve went to Princeton. He met Dick's charming wife Louise. They had dinners together. And he and Steve went into New York City to watch a play. They had a great summer.

And here is Dick's story during those forty years. After *Show Boat* at the Starlight Theater and after Steve went back to St. Louis, Dick gained a passion for music and performing. He graduated from Woodrow Wilson High which he had switched to, good ol' Woodrow Wilson. He went on to TCU and became a music major. He graduated and began singing professionally. He met Louise singing, fell in love, he a tenor and she a soprano. Also he played the guitar and she played the piano. For eleven years, they spent their summers singing professionally light operatic love songs on touring boats sailing back and forth across Lake Michigan.

Further, they went to perform all over the world. Louise's home originally was New Jersey. One imagines that her charming home won out over the heat index of the Dallas summers, and they wound up making New Jersey their home. They both became teachers though Dick, continuing to honor his passion for performing, was registered with the New Jersey Arts Council which had him performing in and out of state for years. As an actor, he performed scenes from Shakespeare, and as a musician he was the lead tenor in numerous musicals, including Gilbert and Sullivan's *H.M. S. Pinafore* and as a specialty, he performed a one-man show, playing a guitar and singing songs of Steven Foster.

In the following years, Sara—Steve's dear Sara— and Steve visited Richard and Louise in New Jersey twice. Among their activities were bicycling, touring (they remember as a strictly bicycle museum, Steve never knew any such thing existed) and dining at a charming Atlantic Coast boat dock. They had great times, unfortunately too brief.

A year or so later, Sara and Steve discovered a great place to bicycle in Ohio, a town named Xenia where one could bicycle out from the town in any of four directions on bicycle paths. Their favorite was the one West to Dayton, Ohio, where one eventually comes to the river, follows along its banks, and can have lunch on a deck overlooking the river and boat docks. The location of Xenia, halfway across Ohio, and roughly halfway between St. Louis and Atlantic Highlands, was perfect for Dick and Louise and Sara and Steve to meet and bicycle. Steve envisioned many happy rides, dinners and conversations.

That holiday season, Steve sent a Christmas card to Dick and Louise, a card that featured from Charles Dickens Mr. Pickwicke dottering in a Christmas scene. By return mail he received a brief note from Louise. "My dear Richard passed away recently. He would have loved the card."

Richard Ro-den!—in his very best French pronunciation— despite the short time they were able to pal-around together, Steve wishes he had told Richard, before the end, how much he enriched Steve's life as well. *May we meet again, dear friend,* Steve ardently wished.

Enjoying the coast at Atlantic Highlands:
Steve Fulbright, Sara Seymour, Richard Roden, Louise Roden

EPIGLIMPSELOGUE TWENTY-FIVE

"There you are, ladies and gentlemen," said James, "Beautiful and sad."

"I can see a few thematic possibilities," said Rupert. "Young Steve found himself in a foreign country, so to speak, and needed a way to survive."

"That could be," said Sally. "The story emphasizes the value of friendship. Maybe that was Steve's road to survival."

"True," said Ben. "What a shame Dick Roden had to die when he did. The couples should have had many more years of fun together, biking, hiking, going places together."

"Yes, Steve was totally unprepared for his death. No prior illness. No warning. Just gone. His friendship, an unexpected gift, his death, an unexpected, heartfelt loss."

"Wasn't Richard suffering from something?" asked Rupert.

"Yes, but who knew anything about it until it was too late. He had a melanoma on his back, his wife said, which he had probably had for some time but didn't know it," said James. "When he discovered it, he had it removed, but then he lived for only two months after that. Too late. Steve had a melanoma under his eye, but he was aware of it early on because he saw it whenever he looked in the mirror. Sara advised Steve to have it removed, which he did. No reoccurrence. The Answer is knowing about it and that means seeing it. Being alerted. And doing something about it."

"But the story," said Lisa, "What does it altogether mean? What are we to take from it? All that 'alien' business coming in?"

"Withhold judgment," offered Ben.

"True," confirmed James. "You never know when it might be the best experience of your life."

"And you often don't know what a major influence you might have on another person's life," offered Lisa.

GLIMPSES TWENTY-SIX

ROSANN: SOIL AND WATER

Late Wednesday evening, the 12th of January, 1999, Steve was reading an article about "The Grand Design" by Stephen Hawking when the phone rang.

"Steve? This is Lois, your old classmate."

"Hi Lois. What's up? Another class reunion?"

"Well, maybe, but have you seen the morning *Post-Dispatch*?"

"Some of it. Why?"

"Did you see about Rosann? On the second page news?"

"What about her?"

"You haven't seen it. Well, brace yourself. She's missing."

"She's what!"

"She's missing. She's been missing since Saturday. The police have sent out alerts. She was supposed to board a flight to Los Angeles, where she was to be met by family. But she didn't show up. Nor does she seem to be anywhere else. She simply vanished into thin air."

Missing? Four days?"

"Yes. She's missing. Vanished."

"Can't be. She's got to be somewhere. Rosann isn't the kind of person who goes missing."

"Have you any idea where she could be?"

Silence. "None. It seems to me that when she comes to St. Louis she is a complete recluse. I don't know who she sees here or talks to even. If anybody."

"Have you seen her recently?"

"I think it was last September, 1997. She seemed only mildly interested in getting together. Typically Rosann. I couldn't reach her by phone. I had no number but that of the old family home, which had no answering machine. I suggested she get one, but she balked. I decided in my mind that the next time I see her, I'm going to tell her to come with me: I'm going to take you down to a shop and buy you a telephone answering machine so I can leave you messages when you are out of town."

After talking with Lois, Steve finally assumed Rosann had never returned from Santa Barbara. The spring before, Steve had gone with Rosann to her mother's funeral. He felt really sorry for Rosann. So much in her life seemed to have fallen apart or was falling apart. But when Steve thought she would have returned to town, she never came. If she had come and been there when Steve called, she was not answering the phone. It seemed to Steve Rosann had no one else and loved the old homestead so much that she refused to sell it and lived totally on her Santa Barbara ranch. And Steve flattered himself thinking that because both were unattached, she would want to strike up their old friendship and maybe romance. Perhaps she did have someone else and simply didn't tell Steve.

Then Steve saw in the Obits that her father died. She did not call Steve and again, Steve could not reach her so he decided he would go to the visitation with the hopes of seeing her there, but no dice.

So Lois and Steve exchanged this information, and he concluded, "The whole thing is strange. Further, looking back, you know she never came to our class reunion. And that after she told me she was coming. As clear as day."

"I know. She told me too that she was coming," Lois said.

"I went expecting to see her. I was disappointed. I called her after our reunion, and finally reaching her, her explanation was that she was working on a law suit over a fire insurance company failing to fulfill their obligation—as she put it—to finish redoing the interior of her house, you know, the old family home out on Hallsferry Road. It doesn't seem to me that an hour or two break that evening to see some old friends would have thrown a kink into her plans for a law suit. Does that make any sense to you?"

"Not at all."

"And now this, Rosann is missing."

"She never got on the plane, they said, although she had a reservation."

A few weeks later, Steve called the County police and brought up the case to the sergeant. "Her purse was found in a parking lot on the East Side, at a casino, but there was no sign of her," he said.

"And her whereabouts is still unknown?" inquired Steve.

"Who is this?"

Steve explained that he was an old friend, concerned about her safety. Steve gave him his name and phone number. Steve tried the police again a few months later. Still no further developments.

It started Steve thinking about their past, he and Rosann her married name Stiegel, nee Rosann Hammer. In 1942 when he was in the fifth grade, the Fulbrights moved from Pine Lawn, close in to the city, out to the town of Ferguson. With a few miles of rapidly disappearing country in between, it was regarded as a part of St. Louis County, and young Steve was switched over to Central Elementary School, located about six blocks from his house and only a block away from Florissant Road, the main street through Ferguson, the busy street with all the shops.

Here in the fifth grade was where he first saw Rosann Hammer. She was a cute little girl with a darling face always attired in simple and charming little dresses. But she was quite taken up by other boys who similarly found her cute. Steve always noticed her, but the interest was not mutual. Steve remembers one little guy Clinton Rounds, who was most frequently with her and Rosann's family, a distinguished-looking father and an attractive mother who radiated propriety, and a little baby sister.

For the three years at Vogt Junior High and the ninth grade of Ferguson High, Steve saw little of her. They did not have any classes together, and her social life seemed to be taken up by Clinton and some Clinton (parent-approved) types and by cadets from one of the military academies. Steve learned the reason for this was that her father who worked at MacDonald Aircraft Corporation, had gone to Missouri Military Academy (or was it Wentworth M. C.?) and continued to have contacts there which coincided with his government-defense and military interests. Steve learned later that Rosann loved to see and be with boys in uniforms, loved to go to military balls, loved the swirling around in her pretty ballroom dresses with a young gentleman in uniform. Indeed she was pretty, shapely but not overly endowed, and had a certain charm in her feminine laugh and speech that attracted attention.

But the last two years of senior high school, with its proms, dances, and football games, attracted her attention at least some of the time. Steve and Rosann had an English class together in which they became quite caught up with literature, and soon a casual acquaintance between them grew into a teenage, boy-girl friendship with a strong hint of romance. Her family—which consisted of her father, Oscar, her mother, her sister Nancy, about two years younger and then a little brother Larry, ol' Dan'l Boone Steve called him from their hikes together, about four years younger, had recently moved out of Ferguson and northwest into the country, out a little over a mile from the Missouri River. She had learned to drive and now was driving her mother's light gray Chrysler to school. Those like Rosann with cars were the envy of the other students, including Steve who had no such prospects. Steve remembers one Laurence

Lucas, who had frequent access to a new Cadillac, which placed him at the top of the school social pecking order. The rest of the students who had no such access, nor any possibility of such, had to content themselves with invitation rides or simply with fantasies.

In addition to literature, Rosann and Steve shared an interest in music--she in the violin and the both of them in the high school chorus--and so were brought together in music class, rehearsals and musical programs. In 1948, Steve's brother Neel, now out of the marines, was working on a degree at Southern Methodist University, and now with Dave no longer living at home, Steve's mother decided she and Steve should move to Dallas, Texas. This approaching move seemed to make Rosann's heart grow fonder of Steve. They went to several dances together and formed a social group with a few other couples that included Steve's football and basketball teammates Jim Poor and Bill Quade and their girlfriends Martha Logan and Nancy Long.

The rivers, the Missouri and Mississippi, were their treasures. There were cruise picnics and dances on the Admiral; there were the musicals, especially *Show Boat*, and there were their moonlight rambles in the evenings after dark, out around the rivers, the confluence, areas near the Hammer farm.

The last night Steve was there, at the end of the football season, a going-away party was held in his honor, and he became the recipient of a charming engraved I.D. bracelet. Being likely her project, Rosann presented it to him amidst oohs and aahs, and he never felt so flattered and so sad that he had to leave his old friends and now, sweetheart.

He and his mother lived in Dallas for less than a year until the September of 1949, the beginning of his senior year. While in Dallas he had given the bracelet to a new girlfriend, one Martha, whose father owned a new car dealership in Denton just north of Dallas. This Martha was a cute little girl who had another boyfriend. When Steve and his mother went back to Dallas for a few days to attend his brother Neel's wedding, Steve joined up with his old friend Dick Roden, who drove them over to Martha's house to retrieve the bracelet. He would never see Martha again, but back in St. Louis he had renewed his relationship with Rosann, and knowing he would need to account for the bracelet Rosann had been so instrumental in giving him, he now saw it was appropriate to give the bracelet to Rosann as a symbol of their renewed romance.

Then came a dramatic incident that brought him better knowledge of Rosann. In their Ferguson High School Choral class under one Mr. Max Plavnic's direction, Rosann and Steve were in the large student-filled choral room together often eyeing each other across the room, from the bass section to the soprano section. One day, their singing was suspended and the period was said to convert to a study period instead. With that, Rosann and he swept over to two empty chairs together and began their socializing in their closeness behind literature books.

Horror of horrors! Mr. Plavnick's severe reprimanding voice directed straight at them rang out. "We'll have none of that in my classroom, you two! Return to your proper seats at once!"

All eyes turned on Rosann and Steve. What indeed was going on? "None of that" had severe innuendoes. They couldn't believe their ears. Rosann turned a bright shade of red—for she was very defensive of her reputation—first from embarrassment and then from anger. Steve had never seen her so angry, up until then or ever after. Of course, the two complied with Mr. Plavnick's command at once.

The next day, Rosann informed Steve of the events that followed that reprimand. When the class period ended, Rosann went immediately to the principal and complained bitterly. Later, all three—the principal, Mr Plavnick and Rosann—were brought together.

What were their classmates to think when ol' Max shouted out such a dictum. 'None of that in my classroom!' Sure! None of what? They could conclude nothing less than some obscene behavior.

Yet good ol' Max held his ground. Nothing less than a parents' conference would lessen the impact. But Steve and a few others concluded that dear ol' Max for some time had had his eye on his cute little violin protégé, and seeing her so unexpectedly in close proximity to a young man caused him to explode. How else could such outrage be explained? Some girls would have seen the event a kind of plus factor—see me. I'm desirable! But not Rosann. She was quite protective of her propriety.

Time passed. They made it to prom night and graduation. At the prom, he escorted Rosann, and she told Steve afterword that she was quite elated when they were announced in: "Next, Miss Rosann Hammer is escorted by Steve Fulbright, editor of the school paper and captain of the football and basketball teams." Of course he was proud of himself, but until she mentioned her feeling of esteem, it did not occur to him that the lady maiden would be so enamored! Steve was the knight before the royal crown and Rosann was his princess!

Some years later when the song "Moon River" came out, it reminded Steve of his days with Rosann Hammer. Did she feel it as well? The Hammers had moved out close to the Missouri River, and Steve and Rosann would drive out at night to view the steady flow of the great river and its shimmering lights—a memorable sight: the moon, the stars, the river, the crickets, the peacefulness. Their two hearts as one. Nothing seemed to capture those years as well as Mancini and Mercer's "Moon River". Ah, those vivid lyrics. Here, Steve can put this down from memory:

> *Moon River, wider than the sky,*
> *I'm crossing you in style some day,*
> *Ol' dream maker, you heart breaker,*
> *Where ever you're going, I'm going your way.*
>
> *Two drifters [that was us alright!] off to see the world,*
> *There's such a lot of world to see;*
> *We're after the same rainbows end,*
> *Comin' round the bend, Moon River and me.*

Especially "the two drifters" were undoubtedly Rosann and Steve soon to embark on the wide, wide world with all its happiness, thrills, and sadness.

Well, that was it for those youthful days before early adulthood. Back up to 2000, Steve had another phone call from Lois.

"Yes, Lois, something new on the Rosann case?"

"I'll say. Page three of the *Post*. It's too horrible to believe."

"Oh God no! Let me see. It's right here. Yes, I see it:

… Several months ago the body of a woman attached to a heavy object was pulled out of the Gulf three miles off shore by two fishermen whose lines became entangled… The body had been only just recently identified as that of Rosann Stiegel nee Hammer who had been reported missing … . The sweater the woman was wearing had the victim's sister's name on the inside tag … Recent developments in DNA have made it possible to identify this body as that of the missing woman.'"

"God, this is horrible!" Steve couldn't believe it. 'Soon after the woman went missing, her purse was found in a casino parking lot on the East St. Louis side of the river.'"

"It gets worse," said Lois. "Read on."

"'Forensics determined the woman's death was caused by two bullet wounds in the chest.' Lois, I can't conceive of such a thing. She was such a sweet person …"

"I know. It is too much to …"

Epiglimselogue Twenty-six

"Good God!" exclaimed Sally. "Horrible!"

"Did they find the murderer?" Rupert asked matter-of-factly.

"Not the last time Steve checked with the County police. It was all so tragic. What could have happened? What could have led to such a bitter, cruel, ugly end? To such brutality?" James replied.

Silence. Then James added, "Such is never easy to take. Especially when, looking back, as adults and as youths, they were so close. If circumstances and attitudes had been a little different, Rosann and Steve might have been married as you will see shortly in the next story."

"So were Rosann and Steve dating after high school?" asked Lisa.

"Yes. In college. I'll tell you that story next—it's heartbreaking!—including so many years later, the last time Steve ever saw Rosann alive."

GLIMPSES TWENTY-SEVEN

ROSANN, ROMANCE AND REALITY

In 1950, when Rosann and Steve graduated from High School, they were romantically involved, but not thinking seriously about marriage. They had too much ahead of them yet to prepare for, jobs and positions, before marriage and family. The aura of *Show Boat* and the moonlit river was always with them, but at that time they had to face practical matters.

Steve's immediate goals were to go to college for four years and get a bachelor's degree and search for a profession along the way. Steve was aware of his serious lack of money and had been all of his mature life. He felt strongly that he had to have a decent paying job to take care of a wife and children. Except for one of his jobs that he had in the past, he would be able to support a family; his first three, no way: a caddy at Norwood Country Club, and a pin boy at the Ferguson Bowling Alley, a member of a two-man maintenance crew at Walbash Park. The thought was ludicrous. The one job that was helping get him through college was at an auto plant, working on a Ford assembly line. The pay was good, but he would never last at this job more than another summer or two. Further, there was no money in the family pipeline for him, only that which he could earn himself.

As for Rosann, her ambitions at the max were a two-year degree, a short-term career of some kind, marriage and family. Figuring from the time of their graduation from high school, her time frame was half of his; hence, the time differences were critical. In fact, one could argue that Rosann was ready for marriage any time now that she was eighteen. Not so with Steve. His family thought he was cut out to be a lawyer like his father. This would mean six years of college at the minimum. And then, did Steve really want to be a lawyer? What had he learned about law from his father? Nothing. He was just barely four when his father died. And if he did decide to become a lawyer, there was the matter of, after law school, getting established.

Did Rosann's husband-alertness bother Steve? Yes, rather, but not that he wasn't used to this. Most of the young ladies he dated were his age or older, and most were clearly looking for marriage. Steve understood this as the natural way of life. After all, the financial burden was, traditionally, on the shoulders of the male and few were so acutely aware of his financial limitations as Steve, so unless the young bachelors were already well-healed, the young lady Steve's age was too old for him, or he was too young for her. After all, the lady's little baby factory is in a rush to birth babies. If she delayed too long, she may never fulfill her natural purpose. Steve understood this and appreciated the fact. On the other hand, if she were ready to work alongside her husband while he was finishing his education and was capable of sharing the financial burden for a time while he was getting established, then the more suited would be their ages. This would mean a willing sacrifice on her side. Many eligible couples take this route. It was humbling to Steve to confront too few women of interest willing to leap into this financial-burden-sharers scenario with him. Of course, such surmises of Steve were known only by innuendoes. It was rarely discussed per se.

In any case, at this earlier point, Rosann was in no rush to get to the altar. As she told him many, many years later, "I could have had any man I wanted." This was not just boasting. By looks alone, she could have. She was as cute as a button. But was she fully aware of her power at that time? One thing was clear at the time they were dating. She was ambitious. She was quite aware of status. Probably too much so. Wealth was definitely a factor. She was not going to settle for an unestablished, impecunious young man. To Steve, this was a serious drawback to the prospect of their ever getting married.

Both Rosann and Steve went to Columbia, Missouri, for college, Rosann to Stephens College and Steve to the University of Missouri. In those days, Stephens was a somewhat expensive two-year young women's college and nationally was well-thought of as a lady's rather posh, finishing school. Many ladies came out of the Northeast and to the far West to attend Stephens.

Columbia, Missouri, was a young bachelor's paradise. With the abundance of young ladies around, not just Stephens' girls but also university girls and Christian College girls, the young male students did not feel any hurry to lock themselves into matrimony and family. Steve dated Rosann, but only occasionally. Rosann on the other hand was quite pretty, sweet and vivacious and dated whomever and dated frequently.

On dates, mainly Coke dates, with an occasional dance to a favorite Juke box tune, they sat in a booth and both played psychological games. Hers was to find out what the male's prospects were. Did he have professional ambitions? On these dates, she often asked him about what he had planned for the future.

When he was noncommittal, she would say, "You really must become a senator."

Whether it was his family name-sake Senator J. William Fulbright of Arkansas, a second cousin, or his interest in campus politics, her attitude toward him was favorable. And his game was to appear masculine. After all, he was a high school athlete, captain of the football team, and that had impressed her.

"A senator?"

"Absolutely. You are meant to be a senator."

"Well, maybe, but I have a way to go before ..."

She liked to ask questions that would set him up for contender or doubtful prospect. He knew that game, yet had different ideas in mind when he "played" it, ideas that were different from hers.

"Describe for me an impressive picture," she said as she rattled her fingers on the table.

"Oh-oh," Steve thought. *Here we go again,* though he didn't want to say this out loud. He wanted to appear to be super masculine, so he made up an image, he thought that maybe Alexander Dumas would admire. "Well, let's see: A long sparkling sabre, glistening in the sunrise, against a tapestry of rich purple velvet."

"Ah, yes," Rosann responded. "I see what you mean. How about this? What are you like first thing in the morning?" Again, she rattled her fingers on the table. *That's an irritating gesture!* thought Steve.

Oh no, thought Steve, *Rosann the psych-digger again! Digging him out.* It happened that he had had a conversation with one of their macho friends Charley Chandler, and he said that when he is first awakened in the morning, he is ready to punch somebody out! So Steve said, "I don't put up with nonsense in the mornings!"

"In other words," she said, "you're in a foul mood in the mornings. Right?"

"You bet."

"Oh my!" she barely whispered, her fingers covering her lips.

Almost immediately, Steve regretted saying this. He was not at all in a foul mood in the mornings. He felt good in the mornings, even cheerful. Why did he say that? Why would he want to give her the wrong impression of himself? Especially a bad impression. If she were cross-examining him for matrimony, why would she want to marry a man who was mean and grumpy first off in the mornings? Could it be that his understanding of this "what do you imagine? And "What-if?" game was all wrong? She a pro, he an amateur!

Another time she tested his "what-if?" she suspected him to be a much too tolerant, highly liberal, attitude kind of guy regarding race issues. Apparently, she was aware that Steve, as student president of one of the college dorms, had rejected a dance reservation at one of the large hotel ballrooms because the hotel had a restricted policy regarding blacks. Steve's dorm had one black student. "If he can't come, then none of us will come," Steve was quoted saying in major newspapers throughout the state.

Rosann surprised Steve with the question, "Are you saying that you could marry a black girl?"

He replied in all seriousness. "Certainly, if I fell in love with one."

"Oh my," she whispered.

There's that "Oh my!" again, he thought. This brought to Steve's mind the Hammer farm that he and his male friends out driving around would refer to as the "Hammer plantation." The place, after all, did have a slaves' quarters, albeit a disused relic, out to the side back, which Rosann often (pridefully?) pointed out to visitors. Steve thought about this years later when he remembered her peculiar inquiry. He had never fallen in love with a black woman nor came close. He attributed this to the fact that there was so little mixed, if any, socializing in those days. One of his friends occasionally spoke lustfully about dating a black girl, but although Steve was very accepting by nature, the prospect was never a driving force to Steve. So again Steve had failed in the "game," resulting in her judgment of him.

When the Spring semester of their second year in college ended, Rosann began a career as an airline stewardess for American Airlines. She attended stewardess school in Oklahoma and in a few months began a regular job flying for American. She and two other young stewardesses rented an apartment on the beach in Santa Monica, California. When Stephen (she always called him Stephen he guessed because it was more posh-sounding) heard about it—wow, what a wonderful life!

Steve and Rosann's contact was at its peak just before Rosann's departure, but when Rosann's full-time job kicked in, their closeness began to fade. So when it appeared things had to happen or else, Rosann came home to her parents' farm on a job break.

"Stephen, would you like to come to have dinner tomorrow night with my family? My mother invites you," she said on the phone.

Not until that time did it occur to Steve that to Rosann he was Stephen. It seemed to him that she had always called him that. It seemed somehow to suit her that her friend would be a Stephen rather than plain Steve!

At the dinner, he became re-acquainted with her parents and younger sister Nancy and very young brother Larry whom, in their hiking-back-in-the- woods days, he called her kid brother "ol' Dan'l". Even at that young age, Larry was a guy's guy. With a pat on the back, they settled down to eat.

During the dinner Rosann's mother asked Steve questions about his mother and step-father.

"Aren't they living in a new house?" she asked.

"Well, yes. A house that Harold LeMert himself built." Steve wondered if she were probing his well-being to find out if Stephen was financially worthy of her daughter. He surmised a split in her parents' interest. Between the lines, he read that they wanted Rosann to settle somewhere nearby, and Steve was a favorable prospect in this regard. But was Steve financially capable of providing for her? No. And was Steve a decent fellow? Yes and no. Rosann most likely shared her feelings with her parents, considering her closeness to them. And they had liked Stephen. In high school, right after Rosann began driving, they would sometimes go for a ride, maybe just along the river, not just a river but along *the* River, a favorite, the Hucklebery River.

One weekend, her parents allowed her to drive him and her sister down to the Ozarks to visit their grandmother. It worked out to be a very pleasant trip. The feelings she likely shared with them was that Steve had his grumpy times, which was fictional and his I'm-a-tough-guy attitude, which likewise was fictional.

But now suddenly, immediately after dinner, Mr. Hammer asked him, "Do you want to smoke a cigarette?" The Hammers were very strict Baptist, the kind that did not smoke or drink. Steve had only smoked a few times, along with Rosann, but was not addicted. All eyes focused on Steve. He was expected to light up. He was clearly a smoker. One of those. He reached down in his pocket and came up with nothing in his hand. They all stared at him.

"No, that's alright."

A few months later, when Steve was back at his studies in Columbia and Rosann was back flying, mainly to St. Louis, Dallas, Phoenix and Los Angeles, Steve received a letter from Rosann asking him if he would like to come and visit her in Santa Monica at the end of his semester. If he could get himself out there, she would handle all their other expenses, including his flight back home. Wow! Her offer was impossible to reject. He had never been to California, had never seen an ocean, and hadn't had a real vacation in years. That springtime's end of 1953 was the time ROTC students on course to get their commissions in June of 1954 were obligated to attend their cadet training camp, Steve's at Connelly Air Force Base in Waco, Texas. He had two weeks before time to report to the base. He talked with his NROTC buddies who likewise had to serve their basic training, but their duty station was San Francisco, California, to begin just a few days after the close of the semester.

The timing couldn't have been better. Bill, Don and Steve arranged to deliver a new car, originating in Detroit, from a dealer in nearby Illinois to a dealer in San Francisco free of charge, except for the price of gas which the young men/drivers agreed to share. What a deal! Two thousand miles at the price of about ten dollars each. There were supposed to be only two travelers but the young men hedged a bit. Steve being the last minute third party became the persona non grata. He told them this was okay, that he would sit on the protective covering in the back and pretend he was not there. Of course he would do his share of the driving. They would cover the seats well with protective material and deliver the vehicle in perfect condition.

Steve accepted Rosann's invitation and the day after the semester ended, the young cadets-to-be drove westward. All went according to plan, except when they came out of Colorado Rockies and into Utah, the fully rested Steve was driving and Bill and Don, having driven all night and having kept each other awake while Steve slept were now resting. All was fine for a few hours and then the tires started squealing around the hairpin curves, Bill grumbled,

"Take your foot off the gas pedal on these curves!"

"My foot is not on the gas pedal on these curves."

Another squeal. "Yes, it is!" Bill sneered, pointing out the window to the steep canyon off the side of the road.

"It isn't!" Steve retorted.

"Yes, can't you tell. Hear that squeal! You are pressing down on the gas. Going too fast. Get your foot off the gas!"

"How can I take my foot off the gas pedal if it is not on the gas pedal? You don't see that the road here is in a steep decline. It doesn't look like it, but it is—in steep decline," he insisted. "Downhill makes us go faster. My foot is on the brake where it should be."

Bill seemed to scoff at him. Steve was not going to argue further. *Time to bail out,* he concluded.

While Steve was a passenger, he had navigated mentally with the road maps. He had noticed that he was actually going out of his way to go straight across Utah west to San Francisco. His direction to Los Angeles was much more southerly. With a few more grumpy retorts from Bill, he decided he would leave his companions to fend for themselves, that he would let himself out near Salt Lake City at a highway intersection, where he could hitchhike a ride more directly to his destination.

He explained his intention to Bill and Don, and coming out of the mountains, there it was, a perfect taking-off point for Los Angeles.

"This is it, guys, I'm pulling over. It's been great. You guys have a good rest-of-the-trip, and I'll see you back at Mizzou in September."

He pulled over, grabbed his suitcase out of the trunk, waved to the guys, and off he walked as if he knew the place like he knew home.

It was a relief to be away from the vehicle and his otherwise close buddies and to have his own destiny in his hands. Now to hitchhike. He had never done it before, but it seemed simple enough. He found a convenient spot for a car to pull over, stuck his hand in the air, and in minutes, a sedan pulled over to offer him a ride. When he made it to the car, he was amazed to discover that there were three cheerful young ladies, all in the front seat, with the back seat fully available.

"Hi!" he smiled.

"Hop in!" said the smiling driver.

"Thanks." Steve figured since that was the main highway to Los Angeles, it was clear that the girls—for so they looked—were headed in his direction. At different times, as if Steve were some sort of amazing entity, each of the three girls swung her head back and forward to get a look at him, and what luck! They were all pretty! The car sped off.

"Where you headed?" asked the driver.

"Los Angeles."

"Oh, sorry, we're not going there. We live near here. We thought you were going somewhere close."

"Oh, that's all right. You can just drop me if you're taking this road to where you're going. I'll just continue on my way when you turn off."

The girl directly in front of him next to the door turned, stared at him with big brown eyes and said—like out of the blue—"You sure are cute." The girls giggled.

Steve wondered if he had heard her correctly. He blushed, looking around out the window. It was like he pictured the West. Cattle country, he thought. And the girls are probably Mormons, one man and multiple wives. The thought intrigued him. Should he stay here? He wondered about what that would be like. But only briefly. His thoughts were being silly! But he couldn't afford one wife, let alone three. Besides, he was anxious to see Rosann.

About twenty minutes later, they arrived at the young ladies' turning off point, so he thanked them. Alongside the highway he resumed his hitchhiking stance. Gosh, that was an experience! he thought. What might that have been like? he fantasied. Can't wait to tell the guys back home. Very soon another car came, pulled over and offered him a ride. This time the occupier, the driver, was a guy. They exchanged greetings. Steve threw his suitcase in the back, took the passenger seat in the front and off they sped.

"I'm reporting to my duty port," said the driver. "I'm in the navy."

"Oh really? I'll be a cadet in the Air Force this summer at Waco, Texas. Right now, I'm going to see my girlfriend in Santa Monica."

"Great. Say, I've been driving all night. Would you like to take over the driving while I get a little shuteye?"

"Sure," said Steve, thinking, that's fair enough in exchange for a free ride.

"Stay on this road. It'll take us all the way to San Francisco."

Oh no, thought Steve. *How did we ... ? I'm going to San Francisco after all. Oh well, I'll get a bus from there.* He then realized the fellow was on the wrong road and, Steve figured as he took over the wheel, he would wind up correcting their highway to suit the navy guy's destination. The bus fare thought brought to mind his finances. How was his money situation? He wondered. He counted his cash in his head. He had a whole sixty-seven dollars in his pocket. Plenty for the bus fare. So the young man pulled over. They exchanged seats. Steve drove the car on while the navy cadet leaned his chair back and fell instantly asleep.

Steve drove them the full distance across the better part of Utah and all the way across California right into San Francisco while the fellow slept the entire way. As it happened, luck was with Steve. He spotted a Greyhound Bus Terminal. He pulled over, awakened the sleepy fellow, grabbed his suitcase and bid the chap goodbye. He was just in time to catch a bus going right to Los Angeles and getting there right through Santa Monica. By evening, Rosann was saying hello to Stephen.

Come in. They hugged and Rosann began showing him around her and her two girlfriends' apartment. He could see out the back windows that they were practically right on the beach. Wow. The whole Pacific Ocean out there! Stephen couldn't believe his eyes. Sand, blue, more blue and sky! Soon her apartment-mates showed up, Mayvus and Diana. They were introduced, both attractive young women. Stephen changed into a sport shirt and shorts, and Rosann and he set out on a walk over the sand along the water's edge of the beach. Stephen had never seen anything like it. All that sand and the broad, broad blue ocean.! What a change from the Middle West.

In Addition to Steve's discovering the wonders of the Pacific beach, he and Rosann, lounging about "the beach house," spoke of old times at Ferguson and Columbia, trips to the Admiral on the river and to see *Show Boat* and the rides at night along the moonlit river.

For several days, they walked all around the beach. They ate at little snack bars, all on or close to the beach.

"I have a surprise for you tomorrow evening," said Rosann. "We're going to eat at the Fox and Hounds Restaurant. On one of my flights, I met the owner of this famous restaurant, and he invited me and a friend to come for a free dinner—at the Fox and Hounds!"

"Sounds nice."

"Oh it is. A very nice place, a restaurant that gets all kinds of famous people."

And so it was. There was one hitch. Rosann cautioned him to assume a new identity that was to become her brother Larry for the next several days. She had reserved a seat on an American flight back to Lambert Field, St. Louis, as her brother ol' Dan'l, Larry, a free flight for a relative, one of the airline's perks for its employees.

Fair enough, Stephen thought, for a free flight home! So now he was ol' Dan'l. It was strange, of course, to start being introduced to people, mainly those with some connection with American Airlines, as "brother Larry." The restaurant meal went well. Then the next night, Rosann and her sister flight stewardesses went out with three young men, two associated with the Airlines. So all evening, Stephen had to act like a brother and watch a fellow he didn't like very much from the start flirt with his girlfriend. It wasn't easy. But how else would he get home? It came off without a hitch.

The next two days, they played along the water's edge and slowly, gingerly made their way out into the surf. These were Steve's first times ever in the ocean. He was enthralled. He tested the water a little farther out several times, got surfed off his feet, came up dripping and laughing. And they spent some of the time under an umbrella, lying on the beach, basking now and again in the sun.

"Have you read *As a Man Thinketh*? It's a wonderful book."

The suggestion, Stephen later surmised, suggested Rosann's more serious, sometimes philosophical state of mind. It set the tone for the rest of the visit.

And once, just after Stephen confronted a mighty Pacific wave swishing in, she commented, "There's a lesson here. If you go out and force yourself against a wave, it will likely knock you back and off your feet. But if you take the wave with a gentle, giving approach, being with the wave, you can stay upright and shortly continue out. This is the way to live life."

"Interesting," replied Stephen. "I'll have to try that."

Later, he told her how true it was, that is, giving in a little to stay afloat.

"In life it is true, too," Rosann confirmed. "We often must give in to pressure to steady our course." This was contrary to Stephen's macho aura in which he had tried to represent his he-man self. He nodded acknowledgement at the time. He could not see himself in another light.

Later they lay down in her bed together and became moderately amorous. He spent he knew not how long right up against her, very close and with a slight rhythm. She did not resist him. With Rosann's girlfriends around somewhere, it seemed too awkward a situation to pursue to the ultimate moment. He soon moved off. "Goodnight, dear." He went to the couch to sleep.

The next day, Stephen as Larry Hammer was introduced to various Airline employees, and just before he boarded the plane, Rosann whispered to him, "I won't get pregnant, will I?"

"Good gosh no!" *Their feelings had never been consummated. She knows better than that,* he thought to himself. *I know she's naïve but could she really be this ignorant of the facts of life?*

The goodbye moment was here. They hugged and kissed, and looked longingly into each other's eyes. Soon he was aboard and gone. He flew out of Los Angeles Airport and headed back to St. Louis, wondering what all this astonishing visit meant to them. How did this dramatic visit fit into their lives? Into the grand scheme of things? She was very pretty and very sweet. But he had never thought of her as ever belonging to him. He had much to think about in anticipation of Air Force training in Waco, graduation in Columbia, a commission in the Air Force, a duty location—God knows where!—and Law School. How, at this time, could he think seriously about a future with Rosann? He sensed that this had been their last shot at something in life together. He felt that she was more than ready for marriage, that she would soon meet someone, probably someone wealthy (!), on a flight and she would soon be married. She would have a child before Stephen would even graduate from law school. Coming right down to it, he may never see her again.

It was sad. In a few years, Mansini and Mercer's song would mesmerize the country and Steve in particular, not solely because of the wonderful melody but also because the words were so apt to the special closeness of the two, Rosann and Stephen, at that particular time in their lives. What were they going off to in their lives? And how especially lovely were those Johnny Mercer lines:

> *Moon River, wider than a mile, I'm crossing you in style some day. ...*
> *Two drifters, off to see the world, there's such a lot of world to see.*

> *We're after the same rainbow's end, waitin' round the bend,*
> *my huckleberry friend, Moon River, and me.*

Steve was essentially right. They came to be about as far apart as they could get. Yes, he would see her again, but not for about a half century. She will have married a wealthy man from Phoenix, Arizona. They would have two children, a boy and a girl. In 1997, Rosann and Stephen would learn of their divorces, that she was staying at her old family home without her parents, who were living in retirement in Florida, that she was in sole possession of the old family estate, that her brother and sister would be after her to sell so they could all three divvy up the proceeds.

But the old estate that she was determined to hold on to, her "Tara," and "the value is on the land, Scarlet. Never forget that!" She told him too that her brother, at one time long ago, was bitter toward her because when she had once, many years before, brought her little daughter to the farm to visit her mother and father, Larry was still living at home and had a dog that he was very fond of. The dog went wild and bit the face of Rosann's little girl. The little girl had to be rushed to the emergency room of the hospital. Rosann insisted the dog be put to sleep at once. Despite Larry's bitter objection, her father complied. Rosann said that her brother eventually forgave her and she him, and the incident faded into the past. Wounds do heal."

Further, Stephen learned that Rosann's divorce had been a bitter one. In the settlement, she wound up with a ranch near Santa Barbara, California, but with very little cash. Further, after her parents moved to Florida, the family home had caught on fire. It had been promptly put out, but the insurance company was reneging on a complete renovation of the house. Rosann was spending a great deal of time making trips to St. Louis and therewith to Washington University Law Library, trying to move her case against the insurance company forward. A side note here is, her ex-husband in Phoenix was suffering from cancer.

From here, this is what we know. A year or so after her meeting with Stephen, both then in their late sixties, Rosann went missing. She never made the flight she had a reserved a seat on. It was announced in the *Post-Dispatch* that her now grown son was offering a 10,000 dollar reward for information leading to the whereabouts of his mother. After a year or more, with the aid of DNA, the police in a Gulf state identified a body tied to a weight in the Gulf of Mexico as that of Rosann Hammer Stiegel. Forensics determined that she had died from two bullet wounds in the chest.

Now the question: Who is the murderer?

Epiglimselogue Twenty-seven

"And you know nothing more about her murder?" Rupert asked.

"No, nothing. The police told me this one, like so many others, is in a file gathering dust, what they call 'cold cases'. But if nothing else has been discovered, what would set the police onto the case? Still, we hear of cases that years later have been solved."

"Shot twice in the chest, how horrible!" exclaimed Sally.

"What about cousin Phil Hambrick, the professional detective? Have you had him look into the case?" asked Ben, folding his arms.

James replied. "No. But for an update, when Steve was in the police library in Clayton, County Police headquarters, he explained to the Librarian what Rosann had told him about various persons in her life before her disappearance. Looking back, she mentioned no one relevant.

"And do you know who are the prime suspects?" asked the librarian.

"The County Police never told me. Would Rosann's stories to Stephen have a clue? Rosann had told him about a neighbor, a small farmer named Ed, who offered to and looked after her estate when she was away in California."

A complete stranger (presumably someone involved in criminal justice) on the other side of the library called out, "Ed didn't do it!"

The librarian and Steve, stunned, turned and looked.

"It wasn't Ed, the small farmer," said the stranger.

"How do you … ?" said Steve, confounded.

"It was someone with a lot of money to spend, someone who had great hatred of her. To have her bound and taken in the back of probably a van all the way to the Gulf, probably alive, so she could suffer greatly, and then bound to a weight of some kind and taken by boat three miles out into the ocean. That would take a lot of money. Find a person filled with hate for her, a person with a great amount of money."

"You have a valid point," Steve said.

"And for a clue," the stranger concluded, "have the weight she was tied to examined. What kind of material and where did it come from?"

"Well?" said Rupert. "Did Steve check into this? Or the police?"

"Steve? No. And the police?" James replied. "The St. Louis County police term it 'a cold file.'"

"Send it to that T.V. program, *Unsolved Mysteries*," suggested Lisa.

"Good idea," said James.

"It is disgusting that a woman as sweet as Rosann who grew to womanhood, had borne and raised two children to adulthood should have to have her life ended in this horrible manner!" said Sally. "It is hard to believe that we live in a world where there are such horrible people who commit murders."

"True," said James, "absolutely true."

"And that a case like this can go unsolved, without the murderer being brought to justice," added Rupert.

Glimpses Twenty-eight

GIL MOORE AND THE "I CAN'T HEAR YOU!" METAMORPHOSIS

This is about people Steve has known who have or have had extraordinary lives. One is Thomas Gilbert Moore, a high school and college teacher. He taught English and Drama for years and years on both (all!) levels, at Ferguson High School and Washington University in St. Louis. His expertise was teaching the student how to think, and in the late 1940s, Steve was one of those fortunate ones. From the time he was Steve's teacher and mentor in high school up until the time Steve reached adulthood and became a teacher himself, they came to be friends and colleagues.

It begins. When Steve closes his eyes and is transported back, he finds himself in the large school gym-auditorium. Suddenly he hears a familiar voice, Mr. Moore shouting—from way back, back against the wall.

"I can't hear you! I can't hear you!"

Were the cast members merely squeaking or mumbling their lines? Indeed. It was time to get serious, to speak out. Speak out or—get the hell off the stage! Mr. Moore meant business.

"Come on, guys, out with it!" said Jim Poor in a punctuated whisper.

Jim was Gil's chosen lead in Kaufman and Hart's play, *The Man Who Came to Dinner* with Jim's role that of Mr. Whiteside, a gentleman of fictional fame. Also, Jim Poor was their elected class president. Steve remembers well because he was Jim's campaign manager who helped steer him to victory in the school election, not that he needed steering. As stated here, as well as being campus leader, Jim Poor had the major role in the high school plays. And here too he took the role of leader, to help Steve and the others "get onto serious stage," the reality that was theirs to create.

Gil Moore's background included banging away on a honky-tonk piano in an old saloon down town, St. Louis. When Steve and his peers witnessed Gil's playing and singing, it would be on a rare occasion when a piano would happen to be in their class room (by hook or crook), and you could see Gil's eyes light up. It wouldn't take much for Gil to succumb to the cheering and suddenly flop down and start banging and singing away:

Clang, clang! "I'm the sheik of Araby!"

"Attaway, Gil!" they'd shout. "Go, go!"

"Your love belongs to me!"

"Yeh, yet. Tell 'm, Gil."

"At night when you're asleep,

Into your tent I'll creep!" and Gil would practically bump off the end of the bench with rhythm.

Isn't it funny how some sounds, like sights, never leave us? There it is again, back in the hall, Gil Moore in resounding, ever-reminding voice:

"I can't hear you!"

What this really meant to Steve would take years and the acquaintance of two more remarkable persons Karen and John, coming up shortly, for him to fully realize.

Two of Mr. Moore's classes and many years later, Steve graduated. He went to college, matriculated, and came back (before returning to the University for advanced degrees) to be hired on as an English and History teacher at this, his previous High School, which made him one of Gil Moore's colleagues and an admiring understudy. In college, Steve had not taken a single methods (how-to-teach) course and had to be hired on as a "provisional teacher." The understanding was that he would need to successfully complete three to six hours of methods course work each semester until the requirement was fulfilled to continue to be employed. He did so begrudgingly. He didn't want to bother with methods classes.

Because who needed methods? Steve had Gil Moore as his methods-master, a man who could teach students how to speak and therewith how to think! And now, looking back, after his many college hours of methods, not a single methods course was ever to match that level of achievement. Gil Moore, by example, was an outstanding methods teacher by his way of teaching as well as his content teaching.

A professor at Oxford once replied when a student asked him, "Sir, when will we learn how to teach?" The professor answered. "You will learn how to teach by being well-taught." By way of Gil Moore, his teacher, mentor and friend, Steve felt that he had been well-taught. In his mind's eye, Steve remembers well *Oedipus Rex, Antigone, The Iliad, The Odyssey, Richard III, Hamlet, Merchant of Venice,* and on and on, brilliantly taught by Gil Moore. When the student can re-live learning moments because of unique dramatization through speech in the classroom, that is a remarkable pedagogy. Moore had the uncanny ability to speak out and see lines well ahead, perhaps a whole page ahead, hardly looking at the script. Undoubtedly, he had large chunks of manuscript completely memorized, not just one character's lines but all the characters' lines, their expressions, intonations, and movements.

Of course, he had his students reading parts—and, of course, these had to be projected with clarity and vitality. But it was greater entertainment when he, the master performer, enacted the entire scene, or the entire act, or even the entire play in front of them, right there in the classroom. It was the ultimate demonstration, a virtual metamorphosis of a person into a colossus.

Even today, years and years later, Steve can see Gil Moore—depending on the role he was portraying—gliding, strutting, marching, or slinking across in front of them, reciting lines in mood, dialect and character, making literature live and breathe, from *Hamlet* to *Macbeth* to *Richard III*. So often, he presented dramatic lines, leaving his book on the desk, walking over to raise or lower a window or a shade from one end of the room to the other without missing a beat. Did they have students nodding off as you often see today? That would be impossible in Gil Moore's classroom, where they could hear and understand every word! No one had to be told to pay attention. It would be nearly impossible not to.

His classroom was more than a theater and a stage. With motion, gesture, projection, elocution and intonation, it came to be a part of his listeners-viewers. And this was true not only for Steve, but for everyone who sat in his classroom, for all who would genuinely experience Gil Moore's teaching. Years after they graduated, running into one another and reminding each other of Moore's classroom would bring smiles to their faces and old classroom stories into their conversations.

One day in the faculty room, Steve, now as Gil's fellow teacher, made an amazing discovery. He talked away to Gil—talked, talked, talked incessantly. Suddenly, Gil Moore broke into the middle of Steve's spiel and said,

"Move around to my right side, where I can hear you."

Good God, Steve suddenly realized. Gil is virtually deaf in his left ear. And Steve soon learned, his right ear was not all that receptive. Steve had to make his words super-clear. Steve learned that Gil Moore had always had problems with hearing, but very few knew it. What did this mean? Steve eventually realized that Gil Moore had turned his loss—what we one day will call disability, an inadequate term, as we shall see—into a plus. And drama, speaking with projection, elocution, and clarity would become his remarkable strengths and, subsequently, the strengths of those around him. An inability becomes an awareness; awareness becomes a keen stimulus which enhances subsequent, sometimes alternate, strength.

Many years later, Steve became acquainted with John Foppe who was born without arms. He read John's book *What's Your Excuse?* and listened to several of John's motivational lectures. Steve learned that all of us, every human being, has a disability of some kind. We all like to think we are perfect or at least perfectly normal.

"Nothing wrong with me!" we tell ourselves. Of course we are aware of the obvious disabilities (blindness, deafness, armlessness, leglessness), but let's not forget speech impediments, like stuttering (note here the highly acclaimed motion picture "The King's Speech," the wartime king who had to speak to millions in their dire, life-or-death circumstances) or personality quirks like shyness, muscle twitching, or some other handicap, shortcoming, defect or such, which we have to learn to deal with, and the question becomes, can we learn to work around it, or rather through it, and thereby supplement it or, even in some more marvelous way, to overcome it? The best way is, as John shows us so amazingly with his own talent, to make the defect into a miracle-like strength. Watch John with his toes pick up and manipulate all kinds of objects. John can do with his legs, feet and toes what most of us need our arms, hands and fingers to do.

Now we can apply this to shortcomings of hearing and speaking, in short, communicating. What abilities could be closer to our very being—these basics of communication so important to all human beings—than hearing and speaking?

In the real English tradition, we see that equally important to hearing is speaking correctly. Class and status have depended upon it. It was and in many places still is imperative that the speaker does his/her part in bringing about proper understanding.

What about hearing impairment? Many of us with a weakness of this sort soon recognize that if the person we are trying to understand would speak out clearly—not necessarily shout—how less often we would have to say, "What? "How's that?" "Say that again?" In many cases, it is to the speaker's advantage not only, not just to have to repeat the words but more importantly to enhance the speaker's pride in knowing that every word spoken one time is perfectly understood. Ask persons in audiences, at plays, movies, speeches, etc. questions that call to mind what's been said. How often, even when they grasped the idea, they really didn't hear all of what was said? Again, it is not necessarily loudness, although increased volume sometimes can help.

When Steve complained once about not hearing, a friend said, "You must realize that YOU are the one with the hearing problem, not them."

Steve told himself, *yes, that is right. It is my fault that my hearing is not perfect. Hey, is that fair? I've done my therapy. I've spent upwards of $6,000 on hearing devices. I'm up to .75% of normal hearing.* True, but how much less would the problem be for so many (forty percent of males over sixty and ten percent of females over sixty and who knows how many of the general population?), if the speaker spoke clearly. Or in this age of electronic, technological miracles, if we had devices, in addition to ourselves, that would make every syllable we utter perfectly clear to listeners. Nevertheless, as she said, this is his fault, not theirs.

Wait! Listen to John Foppe, resident of Breese, Illinois, motivational speaker, who was born without arms. Was this disparaging? Setting the little boy John on the kitchen counter one day, his mother noticed how well the little guy could pick things up with his toes. Later, she told the rest of the family not to help John. "Let him do things for himself." John became remarkably capable of doing things for himself. Indeed, he managed his own life. He became a motivational speaker, speaking throughout the world to diverse audiences. It is a great experience to watch the members of his audience look amazed when they see John turn pages, pick up his coffee cup and drink, manage his computer, and so many other things we couldn't begin to do with our toes, feet and legs. He is quite competent at driving with his feet, and he does this with no special handicap devices. As John says, "struggle creates muscle."

And what about the example of Gil Moore? His defective hearing contributed significantly to making him one of the most outstanding speakers, drama coaches, speech therapists, English teachers, elocutionists that we could hope for. The lesson is clear: When a person has a defective ability of some kind, that person knows the importance of lacking the ability better than those without the defect. The person with the defect might then have the motivation and therewith the opportunity to enhance another ability, converting this other ability into an exceptional talent. Ah, a caterpillar into a butterfly!

Gil's message and John's bring out resoundingly this: we must not go around feeling sorry for ourselves because we think we can't do something because of conditions outside our control. Weaknesses are matched by strengths. Look how ennobling it is to work with our strengths and to make them truly outstanding.

All things come out in the end. But what kind of an end?

Gil Moore continued to teach for many more years. When Steve went to England on a Fulbright Hays Teacher Exchange and Grant program, Gil, his wife Helen and his daughter Mary went on an European tour and, along the way, visited Steve. All together, they batted around London, Oxford, Reading, and Windsor and Dover Castles, the play houses of Piccadilly and Trafalgar Squares. A few years after they returned to Ferguson, Missouri, Gil retired from teaching. His daughter Mary married, and his wife Helen grew ill but eventually recovered. Steve always asked for Gil to be his substitute when he was away on a teacher's program.

Then a year or so passed, and Steve lost track of Gil. Word was that he was traveling. That made sense. Gil would never rest "unburnished, un-used." One afternoon, the teachers were all in a faculty meeting. Suddenly, their principal solemnly stood. All was quiet.

"I've just received some sad news," he said. "One of our most respected and admired former teachers has passed away." The teachers looked around the room and at each other.

"I've just been informed by his wife Helen," our principal continued, "that Gil Moore has passed away."

Complete silence. No. It can't be. It was what we so often feel when we receive such a word; it never occurred to them that Gil could ever pass away.

Indeed. There was general disbelief. "What happened?" everyone seemed to ask at once.

"Gil was climbing up a pyramid in Egypt and had a heart attack."

And there in the meeting, the most amazing thing happened. At once everyone, almost simultaneously, shouted in exuberance:

"Okay, Gil!"

"What a way to go!"

"Hooray for Gil!"

"You did it! What else but a dramatic ending! You did it, Gil!"

Indeed you did it, ol' friend. We'll never forget you!

A few years later when Steve acquired his doctorate, he applied for a teaching position at Florissant Valley College. The interview committee numbered about half-a-dozen professional teachers. It happened that one of the committee members, when he was a student, had had a class under Gil Moore. When they discovered this common experience—they shared this common passion—this interviewer and Steve dominated the conversation with their raised voices and obvious enthusiasm, talking about the teaching of Gil Moore. Although there were more than a dozen qualified candidates for the one position, when the interview was over, Steve knew that he would be the one hired.

"I can hear you, Gil!"

This brings to mind one of the most dramatically extraordinary occurrences in history, the battle of Agincourt. Shakespeare captured it well in his King Henry V's speech to his troops. They are at a disadvantage in almost every way one can imagine: logistics, weaponry, numbers—ten to one—positioning, etc. when Shakespeare emulates Henry's speech:

> if to live, the fewer men the greater share of honor. ... he that sheds his blood with me this day shall be my brother ... [and those Englishmen back at home] shall think themselves accursed that they were not here and hold their manhoods cheap whilst any speaks that fought with us upon St. Crispin's Day.

The lesson of growing strong over weaknesses brings to mind another, a later colleague of Steve's. This teacher, at Florissant Valley College was Dr. Karen Kalinevich. She and Steve taught for many years together as friends and colleagues. Karen was known for her one-woman, in costume, stage performance of Emily Dickenson, a remarkable performance.

A few years ago, Karen retired and returned to her original home in Delaware. Always concerned about the improvement of human culture and the environment, she took over the old family farm, bought out her siblings and, in an agreement with the State, turned the farm acreage into growing trees to help counter the East Coast pollution problem. She herself, unlike so many retirees, could not turn idle. Further, like so many of them, she could not remove herself altogether from teaching and performing, so she availed herself of several cultural programs of widespread interest on the East Coast.

In addition to coaching drama, she auditions for parts in plays and keeps up with other auditions, rehearsals and performances in the area.

Karen calls from time to time to keep Steve up on the news of her career and of the plays and other cultural events in the East. For the last several years, she has been aghast at how often those who conduct auditions, including directors and their appointees, miss the point.

"Most of them do not know that unless they select or hire actors that, on stage, can make every word they speak perfectly audible to the audience, the play is doomed from the start. The play closes after a short time—always for the same reason: the lines simply do not go over with the audiences. The plays that do go over have chosen actors and actresses who project their voices beautifully, Karen insists. How many plays actually make it? The larger number of plays simply belly up after only one or two performances. These are predictable. Simply notice the quality of the speech of the selectees. The actors mumble their parts. Karen insists, "It is not shouting that carries the part; rather, it is projection with clarity. Getting down to the nitty-gritty, these play directors, pathetically, do not understand what projecting the voice means!" Karen can predict with better than ninety percent accuracy which plays will make it and which will fail—by the directors' selections of the key performers in the auditions.

Here is a recent article from the *St. Louis Post-Dispatch* by nationally known theater critic Judith Newmark, who comments on a St. Louis performance of Shakespeare's *Coriolanus*:

> [All] the scenes of battle are infused with drama, thanks to Shaun Sheley's fight choreography. But what are these ancient warriors fighting over? That's anybody's guess. *Coriolanus* is an unfamiliar play ... people see *Romeo and Juliet* or *Hamlet* ... with some idea of the story; if you want that kind of recognition for *Coriolanus*, you better confine your audience to Shakespeare scholars. Without that background, you

must depend on the actors, who [in this performance] prove unreliable. ... Lewis is outstanding, not only because his nuanced performance shows us Mencius as a man of feeling ... but simply because you can understand every word he says. This is much more a distinction than it ought to be. Because many of the actors in this big cast seem to make only halfhearted efforts at diction ... (Newmark)

The point is clear. With Shakespeare, the reason many people do not catch on to motivations, psychological conflicts, cross-purposes is that the audience cannot properly hear the actors. From the point of listening, is there a standard, a sameness, for everyone? Is everyone's hearing exactly the same? Of course not. In their position, length, ability to vibrate, are our little hairs in the inner ear exactly the same? No way! No two bodies are exactly the same. Why wouldn't the delicate instrument of human hearing be the same? If we speak differently as well as hear differently, does this not increase the problem of audio perception? So if we can speak with clear, proper diction, would this not greatly enhance communication which is what we all depend upon for our physical, mental and psychological needs: Again, it is not loudness or shouting, although loudness might help, but not loudness without clarity of speech. How much better we could understand and how much better we could think, if we could genuinely communicate. We must consider diction, elocution, distinctiveness, projection.

"Yes, Gil, I hear you!"
"I hear you, John!"
"I hear you, Karen!"
"I hear you all!"

Epiglimselogue Twenty-eight

"This sounds like a biased argument: Steve doesn't like it because his hearing is not as good as the hearing of others," said Rupert.

"Steve admitted that, that the hearing problem was his alone and not that of the speaker," said Lisa.

"Well," said James. "When you see the stats on numbers of people who do not have perfect hearing, the problem is staggering. Men have the greatest problem, especially those over the age of sixty, and among women, it's as high as twenty percent. There is a large percentage of people in the general population whose hearing is far from perfect."

"Then why can't those people get hearing aids to help them join those who have good hearing?"

"In England, every schoolchild is expected to learn to speak clearly, to enunciate properly, in short to strive to be heard," responded James. "England is a nation whose powerful inheritance is the Shakespearean stage. Schoolchildren drill on pronunciation and elocution. They practice, do enunciation exercises."

"I understand," said Sally, "that Steve had another title for this Glimpses."

"You know," said James, "Steve's original name for this glimpse was 'Hearing and Other Philosophical Positions.' He thought what could be learned from this was important."

"Why did he change it?" asked Rupert.

"To be consistent with the other chapter titles—getting the name of the featured person in there from the start."

"What about this word 'metamorphosis'?" asked Lisa.

"The idea of converting weaknesses into strengths to most people seems like something out of never-never land," replied James, "in other words, a completely impossible act, something entirely out of mythology. It is a classical Greek word, but look what John Foppe did. He converted himself into practically another specie! What fundamental changes we could make in ourselves, if only we would become aware. Would that we could all be so ingenious and determined!"

Glimpses Twenty-nine

STEVE—TOWARDS LIFE'S WORK VIS-À-VIS THE LOST GENERATION

When he was born, what did he suppose it was all about? Steve was the third son. The Harry Fulbrights were nicely settled into their two-story brick suburban house in Normandy, St. Louis County, from which Harry could reach his law office in Wellston by his Model T Ford in about twenty-two minutes. Both Harry and Gladys had taken to smoking and drinking beer in modest proportions. Yet they were not disinterested in good health. Harry's father had been an exceptional farmer, an exemplar for the State of Missouri Department of Agriculture. When Steve was born, Harry looked at the new baby and said, "Look at that boy's hands! Aren't those the hands of a farmer? Gladys, this boy is going to be a farmer!" Was this more so than the hands (and looks?) of his two older brothers at their birth? His mother had told him in his youth numerous times what his father had said, but apparently he never said anything of this kind about his brothers. Yet Steve never gave farming a moment's thought. The hands of a farmer—large and tough?

In any case, here was a healthy baby boy. It is interesting that Harry thought of the farm, a farm like his father's, a place of health and nutrition. There he and his dad planted their crops, cultivated them and watched them grow. Harry was not all that satisfied with what people bought at the market and ate as substantive, nutritious food. Harry told Gladys and others what he felt was the real truth of the matter. "We feed our livestock the best food—mainly soy beans," he said. "Animals grow healthy and strong on soy." In later years it would be discovered that soymilk was a worthy health drink for humans.

Gladys added her two cents when Steve was born. Down home in Russellville, Arkansas, she and Dot walked the cow to and from the pasture every day. Milk was vitally important for growing bodies. In St. Louis during the depression, she insisted that the milk always be delivered no matter her ability to pay the weekly bill. "My boys' growing bodies need milk."

When Steve came along in 1932, she had heard of Dr. Ketterington's study on the wholesomeness of buttermilk. If ordinary whole milk straight from the cow was good for growing boys, what about the rich thickness of buttermilk? Therefore, in the early days of Steve's life, rather than store-bought regular milk, Steve was fed buttermilk; the lady who helped his mother with the new baby was given these instructions. Buttermilk is best for little ones, for their bones, for their growing bodies. The older boys were too far along to appreciate such science, so they didn't take to it, but Steve was a baby, too young to know any difference, and he took to buttermilk very nicely.

And his mother learned how to concoct this brew herself. She put a third of a cup of cultured buttermilk in a quart bottle and filled it up the rest of the way with condensed (Carnation) milk from cans, shook it well, and then left it in a warm room overnight. The next morning, Lo! The result was rich, thick buttermilk throughout. This became the practice, and soon the nursery maid took to calling baby James Stephen "buttermilk Jim." Today we have buttermilk in the way of Kefir, a health drink.

Like most very young boys growing up, soon, ages four on, Steve looked around for his image. Since his father was deceased, he was alert to words about his father. He heard very little of what his father thought. Everyone told him that his father was "a fine man." His mother had told him his father liked to write stories, and she read one to him, a story, a copy of which in later years Steve could never find in any of the old family belongings.

It was about an old guy named Jud, a local farmer, who one evening had had too much to drink at the local town bar. He was on his way home, decided to take a short cut through a field and wound up staggering into an abandoned well hole in the ground. His fall was broken by a root, a slim one only big enough to hold his weight but for a a few minutes.

The old guy knew of several deep abandoned well holes in the area, and such accidents had happened before and resulted in deaths, either from the fall or from the isolation. So there he found himself suspended in the hole's narrow space some eight to ten feet from the top with no way to know from the blackness around him how far it was to the bottom, a ghastly abyss in which one could imagine harsh, jagged rocks and deep water down below with no way to escape, with little possibility of anyone being around to help for maybe days, weeks, even months. He felt around, but there were no other roots, jutted rocks or any way to gain the leverage to climb up and out. Every movement he made caused a creak in the root he stood on. Fear gripped Ol' Jud. And were he to shout his lungs out, he knew he was a long way from any road or path that could bring help and it was late, too late for casual walkers. "Oh, why did I hang around that bar and have those last few drinks?"

Was this to be Jud's end? He could hear people gossiping days on end, "Wonder what ever happened to ol' Jud!" like he was dead and gone forever. And here he was, about to be gone forever. What could he do? He started praying. "Dear, God, please, please, get me out of here. Save me, dear God! Save me and I promise I will … " and he made promises to God that he would hereafter change his low and despicable ways: give up drinking, become a better husband and father, a better citizen of his community, a better church member, a kinder and more giving person.

"Oh, good Lord ... !" The root holding his weight began to split. His voice grew louder. He raised his voice to high heaven. "I promise never to ... !" and on he raved his sincerity. Not only did he repeat his promises, but also he added more good deeds to his assurances, good deeds he had never in his wildest imagination thought of performing. Yes, good deeds he would perform, and he even enumerated them to make sure he never omitted one of them. He would make it to church every single Sunday, and with the best of the congregation, he would sing hymns loudly and pray loudly..

Moments seemed like hours. "Yes, Lord, I promise!" Time dragged on. "Oh God, what was that?"

Suddenly the root snapped entirely. His booted feet had nothing to support them. But, Instead of falling a great distance, down, down, and into God-knows-what as is true with most abandoned wells in this dry country, it turned out he slipped only a foot or so and came resting solidly on the bottom.

"Well, of all the ... !" He stretched and grabbed, found a few holding spots and, in minutes, climbed out of the hole. Laughing at himself, he hiked on home. The next morning, everything returned to normal, and ol' Jud forthwith forgot all his soul-salvation promises.

Harry wrote the briefs for his law firm. He was very much into writing. This story of Jud was much in keeping with Steve's mother's and father's view of the shallowness of their contemporaries' religious beliefs, and the story with its surprise ending matched the spirit of popular contemporary writers like O Henry and Earnest Hemingway whose works followed such experimenters and their success as classical short story writers Chekhov and Maupassant. In the early twentieth century the short story, especially with an ironic ending, was much in vogue. With pride, his mother told Steve that his father often wrote stories.

The mementos and possessions of Harry which included his

writings were stored for years in the basement's small club-like room. The manuscript, the flag that draped his coffin, and other effects were stored there for years, where the young boy Steve could go and be with them, always in solitude. But sometime during or after the family moved away, these were all lost. *Is this what a life comes down to? What a human life comes down to—all lost.* One item, however, kept in his mother's jewel box did survive the many years. Harry's gold watch, which was not of much value in dollars, but which somehow was hung on to and eventually passed on down to Steve, that all-important token of time.

His mother and brothers and those close to the family said, too, that Steve should become a lawyer like his dad. Having no knowledge of what a lawyer's life would be like, Steve kept the idea in mind, but never thought seriously about becoming one. Did they say that Steve would make a lawyer because around home he liked to argue? Was their judgment of him influenced by knowledge of kinsmen who went into jurisprudence and politics? Perhaps it became a little of both of these. For his own part, he liked learning, school, writing, teaching, culture, music, acting—quite an array of interests. His favorite subjects in School were history, literature, sports, and music.

In his early years growing up, Steve followed somewhat in the footsteps of his older brothers. When they talked about school, he envied them. But in a few years he realized his distinctiveness, and emotionally and philosophically he became his own person. In high school, for the most part, he had outstanding teachers, teachers like Gil Moore, Eileen Smith, Regina Jerzewick, and Bentley Bolin. He made B's with occasional A's; he went out for football, basketball and track, each in season, playing in interschool competition; he sang in the school chorus, acted in plays, especially the senior play, *The Man Who Came to Dinner.* He liked girls, dated when he could, that is when he could double with someone with a car (oh, how he wished he had a car of his own!) or when they could walk to a nearby destination and when he had a little money—at best, little is all he ever had.

At the University of Missouri, he early on entered campus politics. He made friends with his dorm monitor Harry Briggs, who was a second-year law student. Harry brought Steve along in campus politics. Steve was, in turn, president of each of three men's dormitories three different semesters, and became a representative to the University of Missouri Student Government Association. His junior year, he was one of a group of students selected and given expenses to attend the National Student Conference at Indiana University. Later he was elected by the University of Missouri student body to the vice presidency of the Student Government Association, gaining the largest number of student votes any candidate had ever attained in the history of the student government, some nearly 2,000 votes from the student body which was overwhelmingly Independents. Most of the other candidates were sorority and fraternity members, a fact which, more than his political and administrative expertise or his character, accounts for Steve's popularity and success.

At the University of Missouri too, he had his first confrontation with racism. Although the Garrisons of his family were from Arkansas, he knew of none of them to be racists. His family had operated grist mills through several generations. They were certainly never slave owners. In fact their background was quite diverse. Going back in time, his great-great grandfather Allen Garrison, an Indian scout, had married a full-blooded Cherokee Indian, one Francis Polly Poole, and settled into quiet farm, family, and community life. Some of their off-springs had dark hair, dark skin, brown eyes. This describes Steve's maternal grandmother, his mother and his oldest brother Neely. He and his middle brother took after the German-Fulbright side of the family with their fair skin, blond hair and blue eyes. Ah, diverse background and genetic inheritance, typical Americana. Again eclecticism wins out!

Further, at the University Steve's active interest in campus-wide affairs began with his third dormitory Defoe Hall. There were four men's dorms, and Steve became the student president of three of the dorms during different semesters. As president of the third and oldest dorm, following the vote of his fellow residents, he arranged a Christmas dance at one of the prominent local hotels. He paid the owners several hundred dollars deposit to assure the ballroom rental. A few days later the hotel notified Steve that they had learned there was a black student in his dorm and that the others could come but the hotel could not allow this black student admittance to the hall. This outraged Steve and his board members. He went to the hotel and demanded the deposit back, assuring the management that they had no intention of patronizing such a place! "He has a right to come as well as any of us!" Steve thundered at them. The dorm's deposit was returned. The St. Louis papers picked up the incident and published the story. The University Dean of Students was proud of the dorm's students' prompt action.

This action and his experience in campus politics won him membership in the national leadership fraternity Omicron Delta Kappa and changed his opinion of the whole voting process. He was appointed by the Dean of Student's Office to be the Chairman of the Campus Leadership course, a one-hour per week campus course for which Steve was given the responsibility of setting up a schedule, selecting university professors to come by invitation and lecture students on leadership responsibilities and techniques. During these two semesters, Steve developed an idealistic view of representative government—learning, following, applying what ought to be rather than what is! Steve was settled into the intention of attending law school and carrying out a career in public service.

Then came the student caucuses in the spring before his senior year. In total naiveté, Steve went to the evening caucuses at Harry Briggs's fraternity house Delta Upsilon, expecting to join with old friends who worked with him in the previous years' elections and expecting a totally open and democratic process. Much to his shock, he found himself ignored. Even shunned. In addition to receiving no credit for prior services to the party and the student body, he was not given even a courtesy nomination, which he was prepared to refuse. Nor any word of appreciation. How could this be, after his success at pulling the independents' vote the year before to bring about their party's success, serving the council conscientiously, chairing the campus leadership course, representing the student body on other university campuses? As far as he was aware, he had performed his duties well ethically. Now he was completely ignored. Had he been a failure? The Dean of Student's opinion was quite the opposite, nothing but high praise. Now, what was happening? Were these fraternity delegates whispering something else behind his back?

After the major decisions were made and candidates had been chosen, Steve learned that there had been a plot from the beginning to isolate him in favor of Sigma Chi member Syd Radley, younger brother of a second-year law student and son of a former candidate for governor of the State of Missouri. In his innocence, Steve had made no plans to run for student body president himself, had flattered himself into thinking that his modesty would set well with his friends, and didn't find out until it was all over that the session was rigged to isolate him from the delegates of the caucus because he was regarded as the main threat to one Syd Radley's candidacy.

If he wanted to think well of himself and his chances, he would have realized that the manipulators wanted to make sure that his name was not even put into the pot because this could draw votes away from their previously decided upon candidate and render the caucus out of their control. A worthy, truly public-minded democrat concerned about the ultimate good would have himself courageously taken the bull by the horns, fought for the nomination. In addition to being soured on politics, Steve had law school yet to consider.

This is, however, what Steve did do. Steve and a few others, mainly Independents, realized what had happened after the fact, broke with the party and put up their own candidate, Steve's old high school friend, Jerry Reeves, and as it turned out, Reeves won the election the next year. So, in the long run, the Radley strategy backfired on them.

With Steve from then on, it was live and learn. In addition to turning sour on politics, later in life, he made decisions based on this unpleasant but realistic experience. He favored genuine democracy, but that earlier campus caucus's secret plotting and manipulating contradicted his ideals. Now he knew better than ever that he wanted to be a writer, to delve into the world of the mind and imagination, to explore ideas, but public life as he had thus far experienced it, with its biases, injustices, prejudices turned him against politics, not all politics, only the worst kind of politics. This is not to take sides with Steve against politics. Not at all. In short, had Steve a tougher hide in him, he might have used the experience to nobly and heroically fight to improve the system.

So in what direction was Steve headed? The warm-up to decision time was upon him. The times were telling. The GI Bill had been carried and continued. Veterans were selecting colleges to begin or to return to for an inexpensive advanced degree, perhaps the one chance or last chance they would have for such achievement, a solid foundation for a profession. With the large number of returning veterans, Steve, even as a senior, found himself one of the youngest in his classes. For a while he identified himself with the J-School students, who, for the most part, wanted to be news reporters, feature-writers and media commentators.

The war was well over, but problems were brewing in the East, and the Russians were not about to lift the iron curtain. It was an Earnest Hemingway era. Like then, values were not the same as they were before and during the war. So here was another lost generation. The vets had seen death and destruction that others had not. The GI bill had given a chance to millions of young people who would never have had a chance otherwise. The ones he knew or met at the University of Missouri were mostly journalism students who were into emulating the surface of the lost generation, namely the Earnest-Hemingway kind, especially his partying and heavy drinking. Steve had recently read *Farewell to Arms* and *The Sun Also Rises*. Even without their conversation, you could see it in their faces and watch it in their actions—live it up and write it down! That was the way of it.

Steve was invited to a journalism students' night of rowdy socializing and boozing. The very moment he entered the tavern annex, reserved for such blasts, Steve felt he was rubbing elbows with

Sherwood Anderson, T.S. Eliot, Gertrude Stein and Ezra Pound (one day, Steve would have lunches with Omar Pound at the Princeton University annex and learn how much Ezra was not appreciated by Omar and his mother Dorothy—nee Shakespeare). And when? Right after a Bull fight? Or was it right after a Mizzou football game? There was something exhilarating about it. He was on the brink of his writing career. He was rubbing elbows with elite writers.

After a few hours of wild conversation, literary allusions, emphatic assertions and excessive laughter, one journalism student, who, like several of the students from his literature classes, had been drinking whiskey, he extensively straight from the bottle throughout the evening found he had not quite finished his bottle and handed it, or rather jabbed it at, Steve, shouting to get above the noise,

"Kill that!"

"You bet!" Steve accepted it in the true spirit of the rowdy gathering, like it was an everyday stash. He was Earnest Hemingway, a guy's guy.

He put it straight to his lips, swallowed the remaining lot, and turned instantly away. It burned and choked him as he had never experienced before. Embarrassed and panicking, he dashed to the men's room and threw up. When he washed his mouth out and regained his composure, he reconsidered. That guy's guy with the whiskey bottle was not Ezra Pound, this was not Paris, and Steve definitely was not Mr. Machismo Earnest Hemingway.

Sure, other things fit. He loved adventure and excitement. He was physical, competitive, adventure-loving. He loved excitement.

He'd love to go to Paris and Madrid, to hobnob with artists and writers and go to bullfights, attend the salons, but the "I can drink more than you!" adage did not appeal to him. It seemed self-defeating. So much for the live-it-up part, but that didn't mean he couldn't write it down.

And then there was, if you want to truly appreciate life, you must regularly come face-to-face with death. War? Bull fights? Or just ordinary life? What really constitutes that kind of awareness, fear, and anxiety? He left the party early, went back to the dorm, went to bed, and instantly to sleep.

Epiglimpselogue Twenty-nine

"So Steve couldn't handle the liquor," said Ben.

"Steve was a wimp!" Rupert said, grinning.

"Did Hemingway continue to be Steve's idol throughout these latter college days?" asked Sally.

"Yes, but he admired Faulkner, Welty, Arthur Miller, and Steinbeck, and others, as well. And Europeans, too, like Maugham, Maupassant, Chekhov, Dostoyevsky, and Cervantes."

"Hemingway would consider Steve a wimp, don't you agree?" Rupert wanted to confirm his point.

"Steve would soon have his European tour and his brush with death," responded Mr. Narrator. This is coming up. Then the question is, what is Steve's point? Would he have something important to say, to feel, to pass on to future generations? Of course we are all going to die."

Sally waved him off. "Well, of course, we are. But don't we ignore it? Don't we make ourselves comatose on the subject? Don't we fail to look death in the eye and, thereby, don't we fail to really live? Isn't this where Hemingway is coming from?"

"I think so," said Ben. "Facing death frequently, often minute by minute, as in war or in a bull fight, makes the hero more alive."

"Like Emily as she visits the graveyard says in Thornton Wilder's *Our Town: Life,* do we ever appreciate it every, every minute?" paraphrased Sally.

"But Steve doesn't have to face death every minute to appreciate life!" James said emphatically.

"Yeah, but it would improve most of us," stated Rupert.

"Yes," nods Sally, "or send us off to despair and perhaps an early self-demise!"

"Are we having fun yet?" grimaced Ben.

Glimpses Thirty

LIFE'S SURVIVAL BOOT CAMP, ABERRATING BY HUMAN CONTROL

A number of accidental factors played a role in teaching Steve what comprised a healthy, survival lifestyle. Yes, lack of funds being one—perhaps at the top of the list. In those undergraduate days, other than for the bare necessities of room and board and books, there was virtually no money available for anything like luxurious living or entertainment and fun. A season ticket for Mizzou football games was it.

After an evening of studying, many undergraduates would take off for The Shack, the college trysting place, for a few drinks to relax with. Steve was not often at liberty to partake, and when he was, he could only afford one or two soft drinks or one beer, which he would have to nurse along for an hour or two. Many who frequented the place were true guzzlers and would stagger back to the dorm perhaps after midnight. The Shack was an appropriate place for swilling because the establishment was precisely that, a shack, an ordinary plain, square, wooden structure with small windows, all one cheap, blue-green color inside and out, and the décor inside was dark and dingy with tables that had hardly a smooth surface anywhere on them because, over the years, these were carved upon with initials, names, often embarrassing words and expressions. Generations of students had come and gone, knowing this place. It was, after all, a hoot. Most people laughed whenever the words "The Shack" were uttered.

Realizing that he would soon be out of college and on his own, that is as a second lieutenant in the United States Air Force earning a salary, he could start thinking of himself as an eligible bachelor. Being nearly two years since Rosann Hammer had graduated and gone off to stewardess planes for American Airlines, another young lady from Stephens College named Nancy Vogt, a real darling, lasted as his girlfriend for a year and a half but alas, this didn't work out either. Regarding time, Steve was getting closer to that economic self-sufficient state when he could start looking around for a mate in earnest.

The summer before, the Waco, Texas, boot camp for young officers to-be challenged him as a young man of the military. He passed the eye test to be a pilot, his only physical question mark, and for that year, he seriously thought about being a fighter plane pilot or observer crewmember. He had never flown in an airplane in his life. Now here he was. In the cockpit strapping himself into the seat behind the pilot-instructor, and off they sped down the runway. As the pilot explained his instruments, Steve looked out and down and all around, and he suddenly felt a misplaced stomach sensation. With only seconds having passed, there they were, thousands of feet up with what looked like all of the state of Texas spread out beneath his feet.

This miracle conveyor was a fighter t-80 trainer and, in what seemed like a few more seconds, the instructor blurted, "The controls are yours!"

"Huh!" Had he missed something, Steve wondered.

"Don't do anything rash," the instructor said. "Take ahold of the control stick in front of you. What you're going to do is very lightly push the control stick forward and then bring it back again to its original position. This will make us do a dip. Okay, ready. Now."

Steve moved the stick—it was so easy—forward, and the jet started down toward all those deep down ghastly yellow and brown fields. "My God!" Then he moved the stick back, and the jet leveled quickly and even started to climb, up, up, up--out of the universe! "I, I, I ..."

"That's it," said the instructor, "I've got the controls again."

"Wow! " Steve gasped. "My stomach flipped."

"Well, you see, you do these maneuvers gently until you get the hang of it." Now Steve thought, my God, I can tell my friends that my first time ever in the sky, I flew the plane, a jet! He was elated—now that he wasn't in control.

When they landed, he felt actually having the controls was one of the most exhilarating experiences of his life. And yet, no one could be happier to be on good ol' terra firma than he. Was he really pilot material?

On another day, Steve was taken up in a transport trainer and allowed to take the controls briefly. It was a heavy creature. Compared to the jet fighter, this was a large semi-truck lumbering about in the Texas skies. He went into a bank, looking out over the vast expanse of the miles and miles of Texas landscape, from thousands of feet up.

"Pull it up! Your nose is dropping! Pull your nose up, we're losing altitude."

He pulled back and sure enough, the nose of the big craft rose. It was fascinating. He had made it happen. Hence, Steve was sure that one day he would be a pilot or crewman of something, flitting about in the sky. It was exciting. To think, the only times he was ever in airplanes in his entire life, he actually flew them. Both of them! Both a transport and a jet fighter!

When his graduation day ceremony came in Columbia, he first received his A.B. degree, and immediately afterwards, he received his commission into the United States Air Force. He could now wear his second lieutenant bars with dignity. Right away, he slithered into the crowd, avoiding being saluted by a college ROTC sergeant instructor because Steve did not have a five dollar bill to give him.

The well-known tradition was the first airman to salute you (you the newly made officer), you must give him a five-dollar bill. And regarding more important matters, would Steve be able to fly?

In September, he reported to Connelly Air Force Base, San Antonio, deep down in Texas, right across from Mexico. He had never been even close to being out of the country in his life. Once there, he received all kinds of instructions and then was given one last thorough physical examination. He was in perfect health, but there was one problem: he did not pass the eye test to enter pilot training. They had him read the chart several times. They looked at him scornfully. It seemed these examiners were saying, "With your eyes, how in the hell did you ever get this far?"

Steve shrugged as if to say, *Damned if I know*. And then wanted to say, *"It was all that damned studying for finals!"* He never thought he was cut out to be a fighter pilot or fighter crewman to begin with, but the testers, those "nice guys" of the summer before, at Waco, had passed him on to here.

"I passed even my equilibrium positioning test?" Steve offered, as if to say, *"Hell, I did my part! You can't blame me."* He assured the testers.

"Apparently," came the Examiner's scornful reply.

"Jeez," was added by the examiner's assistant, for good measure.

"Well," said the Captain, after Steve was passed on to personnel, "you made it into the Air Force; now you have a choice to make. Here is a list of fields and duty stations. Decide what you want to do and where you want to go. You've got overnight to think about it. Your choosing does not mean that is what you will get, but it may be a factor. Headquarters will see your preferences, will look at the needs of the Air Force and will decide your case."

There on the pad were all kinds of career fields in the Air Force, which included cartography, supply, air traffic control, etc., but the field that caught Steve's attention right away was Air Intelligence. And for this AF Intelligence School, Laury Field, Denver, Colorado, was the location. Laury Field was near the home of his aunt, uncle and cousins, where he had spent a whole glorious summer when he was fourteen. And near the scenic Rocky Mountains where his Uncle Charley drove them thousands of feet high every weekend. Wow!

What was Air Intelligence anyway? The Air Intelligence field included pilot briefing (locations of potential enemy positions), pilot debriefing after aerial combats (simulated in peace times), language instruction, escape and evasion information and survival techniques. The Cold War was at its peak, so Steve figured he would learn all about Russia, the land that produced writers that Steve had read and admired: Tolstoy, Dostoyevsky, Chekov, Zozulya. Fabulous! Just the thing. He signed up for Air Intelligence. And for preferred areas, he would see Europe. No second thought was needed. He signed on.

"Well, Lieutenant Fulbright, if you think you're going to get your first choice, you'll be disappointed."

"I gave the same answer to all three choices. See, Intelligence, Intelligence, Intelligence, and Europe, Europe, Europe."

"Well, lieutenant. You can try that, but the Air Force gives no guarantees."

Later, when he saw his friend from Mizzou, one Silvio Viglino, second generation Italian, Silvio said for school and location he made the same three choices, especially for his choice of location because he wanted to go to Italy.

Steve thought, "Oh no, that makes it unlikely I will get my choices. There'll be too many like us."

Apparently, there weren't. Both Silvio and Steve got their choices of school and duty station. They were both going to Lowry Field, Denver, for their Air Intelligence schooling, and they were both going to Europe, Silvio to Italy and Steve to England. That evening, he and Silvio celebrated at the Officers' Club.

"What'er'yer havin'?" Silvio asked Steve. When Steve didn't answer, Silvio turned to the bartender. "I'll have a Chianti." He turned to Steve again. "You too?"

"No way. A St. Louie mild brew will do. Falstaff."

"Ugh!" said Silvio. "No taste. A sissy beer!"

When the drinks came and Silvio swilled his at once, he motioned to the bartender to set him up again. "Hey Stevio, you know what I hear about those English gals? Well, how about when we get to Europe, me to Italy and you to England, I come and visit you, and you set me up with a few hot ones. Silvio searched his thoughts. The word is out, England is ripe with chickios. We'll be in touch and I'll arrange a flight there, and we'll have a la fiesta, with muchos chickios."

Steve laughed. This was the mad-lover Silvio that Steve knew about so well from Mizzou co-eds. "Watch out for that Italian lover!" they'd say to each other.

Steve replied, "I haven't heard that about English gals. I was too busy with Chaucer and Shakespeare."

Silvio grimaced.

Steve said, "So, give me time in England to meet a few."

"Meet hell. I hear they're all over the place. You'll see."

"Hmmm. We'll see."

"That's my buddy, good ol' Stevio!" Silvio patted Steve on the back, buddy-like.

To attend Intelligence School, Silvio had an old Studebaker and invited Steve to ride with him up to Denver. The next day, their orders were cut, and in a short time, they were on their way, driving over the deserts, plains, and through the mountains. At one point, Silvio grew tired of driving and asked Steve to take the wheel.

While driving, Steve heard loud gun shots. Bang, bang, bang!

"What's that?" He looked over, and there was Silvio firing a pistol out the window of the moving car.

"Getting a little target practice in," he said, as if it were the ordinary thing to do while driving around in the country. "Yeh," said Steve, trying to sound nonchalant. "What if the police object?"

"What police. Nobody lives out here. It's barren." Bang, bang, bang! Still Steve was hoping for a close to this chapter.

When they reached Denver, at the first opportunity, Steve introduced Silvio to his two cousins, who were likewise in their twenties, but a year or two older, Shirley and Joan. When they left, Joan whispered to Steve, "This Silvio thinks he's God's gift to the world of women!"

"It didn't take you long to pick that up!" Steve said, laughing. "Good ol' Subtle Silvio!"

Three months at Lowry Intelligence school, then came departure time. Silvio and Steve had different flights to Europe, and as it turned out, Steve never heard from nor saw Silvio again, but Silvio always remained a vivid picture in Steve's memory. "Silvio must have fallen for some Italian chickios," Steve told himself.

Epiglimselogue Thirty

"Really," said Lisa, "Steve's first time ever flying in an airplane, he flew in a jet and actually took over control of it?"

"That's right," said James. "Not too many can claim that distinction. Keep in mind it was minimal controls. The Air Force was trying to get more young men to become pilots. It worked, I believe."

"So," said Rupert, "when the young American soldiers got to England, did they find what Silvio's informers said they would find, some hot Patooties?"

"American soldiers did seem to have some fascination about them that attracted English girls. Many English brides were brought to America in those years. Consensus was that many of the English men were dull and slow on the uptake. The aura of Americans may have had to do with the American Hollywood films."

"And Steve was on his way into the Air Intelligence field?" said Sally.

"Yes, and soon on his way to England, specifically RAF Station Manston, in Kent where he had never been before," replied James. "This would change his whole life, his whole perspective, as we shall see."

Glympses Thirty-one

SURVIVAL OF THE FITTEST

England bound, Steve flew to Westover, Massachusetts, there to Ayr, Scotland, and then by rail on to RAF Station Manston, just north of Dover, which was to be his duty station for the next three years. He was assigned to the 406th Fighter Wing Intelligence Section, the 513th Fighter Squadron, to a Quonset hut near the airdrome, which was comprised of one long room with twenty or more file cabinets containing mostly classified documents, a half a dozen desks and several teletype machines. The personnel operating the Section were comprised of the head of the Intelligence Section Major Halavachek to whom Steve reported, top Sergeant Howden, Master Sergeant Quinlin, and Airman Second Class Hopkins. Steve knew the Airmen were reliable sources of practical information that he would need right away.

The Master Sergeant Quinlin, elderly compared to the other airmen, had served in World War II and was approaching retirement age. A few years back he had married a young English woman who already had had a child . He was a great story teller and held strong opinions. One opinion that stayed with Steve forever was appropriate to their times and situations. He was always saying, "What the Air Force needs when a crisis comes are men who do not panic, who can stay cool and get the job done."

Steve was appointed the Squadron (and Wing) Escape and Evasion Officer, which meant that when a program of such a nature came "through the pipeline" usually involving traveling to somewhere on the Continent and usually requiring numerous days, maybe a week or two, away from the home base, that meant that someone from their Wing had to go and bring back knowledge and info to disseminate to the pilots and crewmen. The pilots balked at the prospect. Virtually no one wanted to go, especially the pilots because they needed to get their flight time in for flight pay.

When Lieutenant Fulbright arrived, he immediately became one of the most popular men on the base. He would automatically be given every survival and evasion assignment sent down to these units "in the field." He didn't have flight pay eligibility, so TDYs were his cup of tea, extra pay! So by his being there, everybody won. Steve got to travel extensively, see more and more places, come to know more and more people, and receive extra pay.

Of course, some of these programs were downright ghastly affairs. One of his trips took him to a less populated area in Bavaria, Germany. He flew to Wiesbaden and took a train from there to a location in the foothills of the northern Alps. There, he was going to have to live off the land with little or no help from the Air Force and certainly not from the local population. They were the simulated enemy, not really the enemy of course; the war had been over for a decade and a half, but the population knew how to cooperate with the military, and the war was quite alive in the minds of the overwhelming majority. The idea was to run the trainees through as realistic and rugged an experience as possible—the trainees were to learn to get by on their own in an unfriendly, even hostile, environment. Some of these programs, sometimes referred to as "exercises," resulted in serious injuries and even death.. A short time after Steve's active duty, there was a US Senate investigation, and the Escape and Evasion-Survival programs were discontinued or sharply modified.

But during Steve's service period, the reforms were only talked about but not initiated into action. The President of the United

States was Dwight Eisenhower, a West Point educated military man, formerly in charge of the NATO forces in Europe, a stalwart against the advancement of the Soviet forces beyond what now they already occupied in Eastern Europe, which was quite beyond the original Russian national boundaries before World War II, and there seemed no end to the Communists' aspirations. With the whole of Western Europe at stake, the Allies meant serious business and preparedness was essential to making the point. Simulation had to be realistic and therefore dangerous if the point were to be made effective. Eisenhower's administration and the military were in charge. Many of the young men in the armed forces had little or no wartime experience. This had to be rectified.

To start the would-be evader-survivors on their way, a jump-out of a down-plane was simulated by hauling the trainees in the back of a truck out to the remote spot, then pushing them out one at a time at ten-minute intervals, some distance apart, and leaving them on their own from there with a minimal survival packet hidden in their jump suits. Of course straggling trainees would be hunted down. For this purpose, the Air Force had contracts with agile, well-trained men from different parts of Europe, men who were looking to gain US citizenship for their services rendered. The idea was to make the whole simulation as real as possible so the trainees would gain the utmost knowledge and experience in how-to get away and keep away from an enemy determined to catch them and to punish them. After the drop, they had to make their way to a certain location pin-pointed on a make-shift map. They had twelve days to achieve this.

Of course, the supposed US pilots would be hunted down and, if caught, thrown into one of the many long-abandoned prison cells where POWs were kept during the World War.

"Ous!" So out Steve jumped from the slowing-down, covered back of the truck which then would quickly speed off and squeal around some corner and out of sight. If he dared look for any of his buddies, who were in line for the pushing behind Steve, he might be spotted right off the bat and hauled in to prison. Tom, Allen and

Pete were his mates. If he could hook up with them, they could help one another, sharing their maneuvering and survival skills.

The first action for Steve to take was to run like hell and to find a place to hide. Across a meadow, he spotted a clump of trees about a football field distance away. He could seclude himself there and take stock of the countryside, take a look at his map, gain his "orientation" as they would say at Intelligence School, and then decide the direction to the destination.

When secure behind the trees, he studied his map, took his bearings from the setting sun. He calculated that his mates would be up the road dropped at two kilometer intervals. He noted that the edge of the woods meandered somewhat with the winding road. As soon as it was dark, he would head that way. This was in a north-westerly direction, roughly in the direction of his destination. Anxious to get going while there was still a little daylight, he moved cautiously just inside the shadows of the trees.

When it was totally dark, he figured he had moved one or two kilometers. If his mates were hiding or moving slowly and very cautiously, he could now catch up with them. He looked about. Seeing no one, he picked up the pace. When he saw no one for twenty minutes of such movement, he began to think he would never find any of his mates. Then he saw a suspicious movement in some bushes up ahead.

"Tom?" he whispered. "Allen?"

"No. It's Pete."

To Steve, this was both pleasing and disappointing. It was good to find somebody. But Tom and Allen were the older and more mature of the three. Pete was not the sharpest mate, by far.

"Have you seen Tom and Allen?"

"I've seen no one except a couple of Krauts."

"The important thing is, did they see you?"

"Probably not. They sounded like they had been boozing it up."

"Well, let's get moving. We have about seventy miles to travel. And we have to travel mainly at night."

"Which way?"

"See that bright star overhead? That way." He pointed, "West-northwest. Follow me."

"What if you're wrong?"

"If we travel too far east, the Russians will grab us, make Communist monkey-propaganda out of us, then beat us mercilessly and send us to Siberia. Or maybe, if lucky, just shoot us for spies. If we travel too far north, we'll fall into the Baltic Sea. Have you your rations, water, halizone tablets?"

"Whatever they gave us."

"Let's keep very, very quiet. So let's get going."

They walked all night. When light began to show in the East, Pete was having trouble keeping up. "Can we rest awhile?'

"As a matter of fact, we have to find a place to hide ourselves during daylight, and that's when we can sleep, one at a time."

"This isn't much fun, is it?" Pete whined.

"It's no Boy Scout jamboree, that's for sure."

"I can't go any further. Can we rest right here?"

"Are you kidding? The Special Forces are out to nab us. They are experts. We have to find a really secure place."

"How about over there behind that barn?"

"Too obvious. Let's get over that next hill, away from the road, and see if that'll work."

"Up there. I don't think I can make it."

"Come on. You can do it."

Steve and Pete went on like this for four days, Steve directing and scolding and Pete whining. Steve had the silent, internal shoving of his big brothers and the street games of his youth to keep him going.

When they were a little more than a two-day's trek from their destination, Pete was devastated. He had thrown up twice and tried again and again to call the whole thing off. Even though they had fought down a few edible plants along the way, their survival rations were nearly out. Steve had to slow down to almost a crawl. Even when he could hardly go any slower, again and again, he had to wait for Pete to catch up.

"Listen, be very quiet," said Steve. "Dogs are barking ... back, down there. Special Forces—the enemy! I knew we would hear them sooner or later."

Steve looked at Pete. He was certain that Pete was crying. Good God, a fully grown man crying! He thought to himself, *What would my brothers do about this guy? I can't believe it!* "How would it look if I carried you?" he said, his hands and arms akimbo. Suddenly a stench caught them unaware.

"Ugh!" Pete was first to catch it. "What's that smell? I'm going to be sick again. That smells like dead fish."

"Whew. Smells like dead fish alright. It's over there in some kind of garbage dump. Stay here. I'm going to check it out."

"Are you crazy? That's sickening."

A quick look and Steve motioned for Pete to join him. "Hey, we're in luck. Look, the town's garbage dump. Fish guts."

Steve found a crinkled empty bag and a piece of rope. He scooped some of the foul-smelling fish guts into the bag and shredding the rope, he tied one end of it around the top of the bag. Then he displayed it to Pete, showing the bag as if he had just won the lottery.

Pete grimaced. "I don't care what you say, I'm not eating any of that muck!"

"Aw, why not?." Steve laughed.

"So what are you going to do with that garbage? Smear the Special Forces guys with it? Bargain them for it? I don't think it'll work."

"You'll see," Steve winked. With the rope, he secured the bag to his belt at his waist side and took off down the slope. "Come on. Down the slope."

"That's a river. Are we going swimming?"

"Hell no. It's just a rill." Looking at his map and around at the lay of the land, he calculated, "We need to cross it." From the barking, it was obvious that the dogs were getting closer. "Hurry!"

When they reached the stream, Steve said, "Wait here."

He took the bag from his side, opened the end and began streaming the contents little by little along the bank, downstream fifty yards or so. He threw the bag and remaining contents in a bush and returned to Pete. "Okay, let's cross." At the deepest point, the water came up to their thighs.

When they reached the other side and went upstream about fifty yards, Steve said, "Good, over there." He turned and they took off across a field toward some hills. "Don't talk until we get to those hills. Come on. Faster!"

Once over several hills, they found a clump of high bushes and weed, hid and rested. No longer were there any barking dogs in earshot.

"I get it," said Pete. "The smell of the fish guts was to throw the dogs off our scent. Where did you learn that trick—Air Force Escape and Evasion School?"

"No. In Logic class at the University. It's called 'the red herring fallacy.'"

"Oh."

It was daylight, time to sleep. Again they took turns sleeping. When evening arrived, Pete asked, "If I pick up my pace a little, can we make it to our destination by morning?"

"Yes. We have only a half-dozen kilos to go. We're close. But we have to be especially cautious."

"Okay. I'm starved and tired of this bullshit. Let's get going."

So, with a careful look around, off they went. When they reached a road into town, with just a few kilometers to go, Steve said, "We've got a whole 'nother day and night. Let's not be seen. We have to get away from this road."

Pete spoke as if he hit upon a revelation. "There's a barn over there, let's make it for the barn and maybe we can hide out there."

"Nah. Too risky at this point."

"I'm going." He grabbed Steve's arm and pulled him into the open field. They broke into a run, trying to reach the back side of the barn.

Suddenly, they were being chased by several men of Special Forces. In less than five minutes, they were sitting on the ground, surrounded by the smirking pursuers. Shortly, they were handcuffed and shoved into the back of a pickup truck.

When they arrived at their destination on a sleazy side of town, Steve individually was tossed into a grimy, bug-infested jail that probably had not been used since the days of Nazi Germany, perhaps last used as the holding tank for unfortunate Jews . There he sat for hours without having been given any water or food. Steve felt that his body was drying out, that he could not last much longer without water. "Hey, you guys, people have to have water you know or they'll die!"

There was no response. It seemed there was no one anywhere near who would know he was there, or who could hear him. This was scary. "I don't think the program wants its evadees to die!" he shouted. Still no response. Steve was transported back to his literature class.

"'Is there anybody there?" said the traveler, knocking on the moonlit door.'

Steve tried to find a comfortable position on the floor, but there was none. Still, he lay down and dozed out of complete exhaustion for how long he did not know. When he awoke, again, and even more severely he felt he was drying out.

"Hey, is there anybody out there! I need water!" And he thought, 'but no one descended to the traveler, no head from the leaf-fringed sill leaned over and looked into his grey eyes.'

No response.

"I'm dying, for God sake!" he shouted, violently rattling the jail bars.

He heard footsteps. A sinister-looking man came with a bucket of water. "Open sie mouse." When Steve opened his mouth, the man threw the water at his face. He was able to swallow a little of it, but most splattered all over him. Still, it had a cooling effect. The man disappeared.

Soon, he was hauled individually before a Captain and here interrogated. When the interrogation was concluded, the Commandant came in and addressed Steve.

"Well, you didn't do badly. All you blokes were caught, you know."

"No one made it?"

He laughed. "Of course not. But you and your mate were second to last to get caught, if that interests you. You are free to return to your base. Your train leaves in two hours."

Steve assumed Pete was being sent back to his base as well. He never saw good ol' Pete again.

The second day, back at his home base Manston, Steve was asked to brief the pilots on Escape, Evasion and Survival. He did so in the crowded Operations hall. He got carried away, became dramatic. He raved on and on about what to do and what not to do. He closed with, "I learned the vital importance of maintaining obscurity and the vital importance of water to the human body. You can live for many days without food, but only a few days without water."

When he finished, the pilots and other officers applauded—something they rarely ever did at a briefing.

Ceremonially, the squadron commander took charge and after a few moments of silence, remarked, "Damn college punks!"

The pilots all laughed..

Epiglimpselogue Thirty-One

"Poor Pete," said Lisa. "I wonder if he ever had a clue what was going on."

"Steve liked the chap and always wondered what became of him. Pete was stationed somewhere else in Britain. They never saw each other again."

"So they actually applauded Steve when he finished the briefing? How brief was it?" asked Ben.

"About twice as long as the usual briefing, but remember, they liked Steve from the start because he was committed to doing all the Survival, Escape and Evasion TDYs for them, leaving them to get their flying time for flight pay!"

"That bit about the Red Herring was a gasser," said Rupert.

"Well, you never know when something you learn may be a lifesaver," said James.

"Was this when Steve became a survival kook?" asked Rupert.

"It helped. Steve always said his grandmother Garrison and his big brothers had a lot to do with his survival motivation."

Rupert jumped up, "Did that really happen? The Commandant and Squadron commander and all?"

"Yes. Just so. And they had all kinds of treks to go on. One was simulated being passed through the underground. That was a dilly!"

"I know that poem," said Sally. "The Listeners" by Walter de la Mare.

"Some of the later lines would one day become particularly apt," said James, "which gives us additional understanding of surviving. In a little more than ten years, his two brothers will be deceased, thus all four males of his original family will have died, his grandfather Garrison, his father Harry Wilkes, his oldest brother William Neely, his middle brother David Stanley—all died in their early forties."

"I know the lines," said Sally. "'though every word he spake

*Fell echoing through the shadowiness of the still house
From the one man left awake.*"

"That's how he felt," replied James.

Glimpses Thirty-two

SURVIVAL OF ANOTHER KIND

To clarify, as Squadron Intelligence officer, Lt. Steve was responsible for all the latest information and techniques that would assist pilots were they forced to go down in an unfriendly environment. Of course, survival on the one hand and escape and evasion on the other are related, but the various schools that sprung up here and there across Europe and North Africa usually focused on just one or the other, that is just on survival or just on escape and evasion. For two years, Steve went to all the schools that sent for squadron and wing Intelligence Officers. As said above, this is what made him popular with the pilots. They had enough TDYs (temporary tour of duty for pay) without it. Being unrated, Steve looked forward to TDYs—interesting places and new experiences.

Survival schools existed wherever a wretched environment could be borrowed or rented by the government. These were generally short in duration, three to five days. One day would be devoted to theory presented in the classroom, then the remaining days meant being dumped out in the middle of nowhere. Escape and evasion was usually five to ten days mainly because of logistics.

His Survival Schools emphasized ways of getting nutrition and water, again water the primary need. So some kind of water carrier along with halizone tablets, plus some kind of food rations, the kind you can carry with you or on you for days without it spoiling, were necessities. One time, when the soldiers like Steve were put out in the woods, each twosome was given a drugged rabbit. They were shown how to lop its head off, skin it, cut it up and then place it in a minuscule makeshift tent to be smoked; that would make it into long-lasting jerky. Steve told his mate to go ahead with the preparation, cutting the head off—that rabbit was his least-desired sustenance. Steve built the fire, made the small smoke tent, and so felt that he did his part, but ending the little furry creature's life in such a brutal manner was not part of Steve's repertoire for survival techniques. There were plenty of farm boys in the Service, so he figured he would let them handle that part, but for himself he would get his nutrition from vegetation.

"But, Steve, if you're out in the wilderness alone, you're going to have to catch game, skin it, the works, to survive," commanded their survival instructors.

"Well, you live like you want. I intend to live on roots and berries, maybe some fish. I just have a different palate from most. But I can teach the pilots. They're a bunch of carnivores. They'll have no trouble with it." And Steve wanted to add that *they were not likely to be as squeamish as he about taking a little furry creature's life,* but Steve felt he had said enough.

Then there was the time the downed pilots—Steve and his counterparts from other Air Force Wings—in this phase, were passed through the "underground." Now that was neat! Again he found himself in Germany, being dumped in a farmer's field and told to run, look for the sign, make contact and, above all, follow instructions. The sign was a German beer bottle top, the kind made to serve as a stopper on the bottle and placed in a location where one was not likely to be unless deliberately placed. All evaders were expected to travel alone to avoid detection.

When Steve crossed a country road bridge over nothing more than a rill, he looked over the railing and below, on a narrow ledge, just within reaching distance, and there it was! A beer bottle stopper-cap doo-hickey. Because he expected the contact symbol to be difficult to find, he couldn't believe his eyes. This was too simple. Nevertheless, the cap was there. He waited until there were no pedestrians around; then he bent over, reached down and snatched the object. He slipped it into his pocket, walked on across the bridge, and hid in the first clump of trees. He hadn't waited very long when a middle-aged German farmer-looking type came along over the bridge, looked casually down precisely at where Steve had snatched up the cap, waved his arm and then spoke barely above a whisper something like (which Steve took by gesture and phonetics), "Ach, Meine comrada, ich bin hier." The man walked on.

Steve waited until the man walked on across the bridge and came near to his clump of trees. "Comrada?"

"Vo ist ... ? Ya. Komen mit mier."

"Ja-vol." Steve followed the man a few paces behind, as he had been earlier instructed, but ready to bolt at the slightest hint something was not right. "Arouse no attention!" he'd been told. Shortly, the man turned down a dirt road, and then off the road and onto a narrow path through a wooded area. Steve dutifully followed.

When they reached the edge of the woods, the farmer moved slowly, allowing Steve to catch up with him. He stopped abruptly and swung around. "Gut! Wier gehen nach hause," He pointed across an unplanted field, and together they headed in that direction. Soon the farm smells saturated the air—cows, pigs, horses, the lot. It was to a barn Steve was led, taken into, and told to mount a ladder to the loft. He did so and found two of his evasion comrades sitting on piles of hay, looking relaxed and not being the least inquisitive. Then before Steve and the two could get acquainted, two more comraden were added to the loft. Shortly there was added one more, and their numbers were complete. After they were settled and after all acquaintances were considered complete and the light had turned to dark outside, they were taken one at a time, surreptitiously, into the farm house. The floor of the dining area was wooden. They quickly learned, each in turn, the floor was, in part, a false floor. A piece of the floor was lifted and lo, this revealed a ladder going down. Below was a secret cellar meant for hiding in during earlier, more dangerous times.

In this cellar, they were kept until long after dark. After hours, "How long will we be here?" was on everybody's mind. There was no talking, no noise allowed. Everyone was dozing or musing on his own thoughts. When the hour was about nine, suddenly the trap door above sprung open, the ladder was extended, and someone called down in common English, "Dinner time!"

"Huh? Do we get dinner?"

"Yaval. Komen zee up, bitte."

No one could believe it! They were ushered into a farmhouse dining room, asked to be seated, and were about to be passed bowls and platters of deliciously prepared food. All the windows were covered with blankets, quilts, and tarps. Nothing could be visible from outside.

"If you are asked to return to the cellar, do so quickly and as quietly as possible," they were instructed.

But there was no need. After dinner, the Americans were taken back to the barn hayloft. There, they slept on bales of hay, and in the pre-dawn morning they were delivered a batch of used clothing to wear so they could pass in public for local farm-hands. After they had tried on, accepted or rejected, and passed around clothing, they were given a small amount of deutschmarks and taken to a bus terminal to begin a local travel to several towns. So they wouldn't give themselves away by their speech, they mingled speechlessly on the waiting platform with eight or ten locals residents awaiting a train.

Later, one of his fellow evaders remarked to Steve, "What an odd appearance we must make: a batch of young males in poorly fitted clothes—phony dress, foreigners no doubt—guys who very likely know each other, but stand aloof in silence. I can just hear the locals sniggering."

"Yeh, I can hear them saying, 'Who do they think they're fooling?'"

At a completely out of the way station, they were corralled and pushed and hoisted into the back of a truck. And thus they were passed through the underground, debriefed and sent back to their units.

In a few days Steve was asked by his commander to tell the squadron about his experiences. Hence Steve's life for two-and-a-half years was dominated by travel in foreign countries, by simulated cloak and dagger activities and by basic survival programs. His talks with pilots were supplemented by occasional appointments to interrogation teams. These were designed for a team to try and discover certain secret information from the poor targeted airman to see who could prevail in the hokey cat-and-mouse game. Often, his team included a mammoth Notre Dame tackle type who towered over the captive shouting questions and orders at the smallest, meekest fellows in the armed services of the country which participated.

All the while, it was presumed that sooner or later, the cold war would turn into a hot war, that all hell would break loose, that the U.S. soldiers would be in a life-death struggle with Russians and other Communists who saw Americans as nothing more than capitalist flunkies that were standing in the way of the workers' paradise.

So what was the effect of all this "be ready when" or "watch out for" on the young lieutenant Steve Fulbright? Was it the instilment of imminent doom, inevitable tragedy? But if there were in mind abundant situations of danger, what was the point of living with it day in and day out? Like the time he was on his way to another war game, when he and a dozen other airmen were flying over the Alps in a C-119, and the others decided to give the pilot trim-tab problems by shifting themselves in unison from one side or end of the fuselage to the other. He put on a phony smile and pretended to be too lethargic to make sudden moves.

"Come on, Steve, shift your ass!"

"Sure. Sure." But he couldn't bring himself to really do it. He thought to himself, *Don't you guys know you could screw up this plane and crash us into the Alps? In fact, that very thing had happened a few weeks before when an American Air Force transport, pilot and crew and passengers, had gone down in the Alps and all had been killed. Flying around and playing wargames were dangerous enough without teenage tricks. Were the airmen playing around? Probably not, but it was enough of a risk without goofery.*

About a year later, one of his good friends, one Lt. Mackey, went down in his fighter jet into the North Sea, and that was the end of him. He was a nice guy too; they had had many a beer together with jokes at the Officer's Club. *These things happen*, thought Steve. *Yep. Call me a coward. And here daily we confront the Cold War. What is going to happen? I think I'll get out of the Air Force*, thought Steve. *I'll become a teacher like Gil Moore and risk myself at the chalk board. Marry. Have children. And live to pamper my grandchildren.*

When he told this to an Air Force mate, the latter said, "What? Get out of the Air Force! Are you kidding. They have the best retirement system in the world. In twenty years, you can retire for the rest of your life with a steady income. And then do what you want."

"I'm going to live this life so I can retire when I'm fifty?"

"Sure. Where else could you do that? Besides, you're not a pilot. You're in Intelligence."

"I've thought of that, but in the Korean War the first line intelligence officers had the shortest life spans of any of the servicemen." So the argument ended for Lieutenant Steve Fulbright.

Getting out was not immediate. The up-side was the social life in England that ensued. Steve and his two Air Force pals Gordon Beales and Sydney Smith rented a house just up from a North Sea cliff, a two-story house with three upstairs bedrooms, a downstairs living room, dining room and kitchen, complete with a part-time cleaning lady and a part-time gardener—all easily affordable by three lieutenants with steady salaries. Hardly barracks living! When they weren't driving around the seaside towns, strolling along the cliff looking out over the sea, they were frequenting the nearby St. Mildred's Dance Hall. They preferred it to the downtown Margate Dance Hall because St. Mildred's was a little higher class; the Margate attracted airmen; St. Mildred's attracted officers.

"Hey, St. Mildred's is the place for me," said Syd Smith.

"Why so?" asked Gordon Beales

"Because it includes a finer set of people, ones we can socialize with."

"Don't tell me you've become one of these la-dee-dah English people hyping up into class consciousness."

"Well, do you want to hob-nod with a bunch of riff-raff?" Syd had that I'm- better-than-that look on his face. "Well, if you don't mind the scruffs ..."

"You're even sounding like a snooty bloke."

Syd turned to Steve. "What do you say, Steve. We've agreed to go together to check out a dance hall, but now the question is which dance hall? There's St. Mildred's two blocks over, and there's Margate's Dance Hall five or six blocks in the opposite direction. What a choice! Which shall we check out?"

Steve's brow knitted. "Well, I've been having conversations with my RAF counterpart, Flight Leftenant [sic—pronunciation] Bilford and he cautioned me about English women. He said, and I quote, 'Common English women are quite common indeed!' with the unmistakable emphasis on *common*."

"There you are, Gordon! That makes St. Mildred's the clear choice. The common, loose English women would undoubtedly frequent Margate."

"Settled!" they said in unison, and they prepared to "sight-see" at their nearby boon just after dinner.

So it was. Just after dark, they pulled up in the parking lot in front of the four pillars marking St. Mildred's Hotel dancehall. Popular band music wafted through the entranceway. A couple of steps down paired them with a smiling gentleman in a dark suit and tie. He stood just behind the ticket box. They bought their admittance and faced the gentleman.

"Welcome. I'm Fred." He smiled holding out his hand for a shake. Each in turn shook his hand and entered the door he now held open for them. The band music was pleasant and inviting as was the small, dimly lit, smoke-filled hall with a small dance floor circled by a dozen tables with two to four chairs to each. Just to the right was an active bar: two bartenders attended several men who, from their dress, one could judge were Americans. Further down the bar was an adjoining room with more tables. Gordon, Syd and Steve each in turn ordered a lager and together found an empty table bordering the dance floor. Several couples were dancing smoothly to the music.

"I'm going to like this place," said Steve when they were comfortably seated.

"I'm not sure," said Syd. "I was told the only place you can get a breath of fresh air here is in the W C."

"Hey Syd and Steve, fancy meeting you guys in this place." It was Mike Sanford from the base, another lieutenant, this one with a law degree, working in the judge advocate's office.

Syd laughed, turning to Gordon and Steve. "This is the very guy who told me where to get a breath of fresh air." Then turning to Mike, Syd said, "So what are you doing here, you old sot?"

"Oh, I'm not really that. I come to St. Mildred's now and again to regain perspective. You've got to know all kinds, you see."

"Who are those women over there at the bar, the sexy-dressed ones you were talking to?"

"Oh, I wasn't talking with them. I was ease dropping on their conversation."

"Oh," said Syd, "and what did you learn?"

"They're waiting for guys like you to come in to wrap their charms around," Mike replied, smirking.

"Well," said Syd. "No point in wasting time." With that, he sauntered over to the bar, a little like a good ol' American cowboy, and proceeded to butt into the young ladies' chat. He introduced himself. In a minute, he danced off with one nicely, illustrating his mastery of the swing-trot.

"What do you know about that!" Steve was fascinated.

Turning to Steve, Mike winked. "Your turn, ol' chap."

"Huh?" he gulped. "But I don't know that step."

"Doesn't matter. Note the rhythm and pick it up as you go."

In a short while, all three newcomers were dancing; Mike retook his position, leaning at the bar, and ordered himself another drink. Mike, from New Orleans, with a law degree from LSU, somehow seemed outside of all this what some considered as andy-pandy nonsense. When Steve had been selected as assistant defense council to stand with an airman charged in gross neglect of duty, after the trial was over and Steve had lost, Steve asked Mike what he thought of the case. "After all," Steve asserted, "when we stood before the court and pleaded, shouldn't the airman be given another chance. Yes, the airman was on duty guarding a jet aircraft, and hadn't the Officer of the Day walked up and snatched the rifle right out of the hands of the snoozing airman, but hadn't the airman earlier that evening told his sergeant that he was sleepy? Shouldn't this have given the sergeant reason to make some arrangement—brought coffee, relieved him of duty, etc.—to accommodate the poor fellow? Of course, the prosecution contended that this comment by the airman, even if stated, did not constitute proof of the airman's somnolence. Whoa! We of the defense say that the issue was not, was the airman actually sleepy, but that the airman had actually made a statement that his sergeant could then have acted upon."

Mike smiled. "The penalty of 'dishonorable discharge' was devised for cases like this!" Nothing else then needed to be said. Thus, Steve gained a lesson in jurisprudence and in the world of the military life and death situations, had gained respect for the unbending law.

The young lieutenants with their new lady acquaintances danced on. A few more trips of this sort to St. Mildred's, and Steve, Gordon and Syd had greatly expanded their social life. The activities included dancing at St. Mildred's, an invitation to a nearby restaurant for dinner, a run out to the Officer's Club for a drink and tete-e-tete, and a nightcap back at their House (on Gresham).

Steve's RAF friend often cautioned "Be on the lookout, ol' chap. Some of these women down from Birmingham, London, and other places are looking for an American husband."

"Well," Steve would say, "what's wrong with that?"

"Nothing, if your eyes are open. What is she really like? Is she just looking for a Yank husband, a ride to America? A softer life than she would otherwise have here. Remember what I said about common English women. And what does she sound like?" Steve thought about this: *A Pygmalion context. An Englishman's way of speaking classifies him!*

"Yes, indeed. I met one who is an English instructress down in Margate. She instructs mainly Italians and Germans who have come over to learn to communicate with Americans in businesses such as hotels and restaurants. Quite intelligent she is. Frankly, I may not be good enough for her. I don't think we met each other's standards although I quite like and respect her. I think her mother likes me better than she does. But thank you, ol' chap. I quite appreciate your caution. The point is, here we are, hundreds of young American men, mostly unmarried and at the right age for mating up."

"But looking at the economics of it, many of the young English women hear stories about how well-off the Americans are, and how much better off are the English ladies that marry Yanks and move to America to establish a home and start a family."

"Which reminds me. I've had some of the 'bloke-gals' tell me that there are only three things wrong with the Yanks: 'they're over-paid, over-sexed, and over -here.'"

"Yes, I've heard that, but don't let it fool you. Too many of them are pleased by all three so-called complaints. How to judge? I suggest that you pay close attention to the way the woman speaks. That can be a dead give-away."

Ha! Thought Steve, *back to Pygmalion and I am Professor Higgins. Thank you, Mr. Shaw.*

Very early in this quest for fun, pleasure, and perhaps a mate, Steve met a young lady named Gloria Goaler. She appeared to be quite well-to-do. Well, that would be a switch, he thought. Her family is better off than mine by far. Her father was an owner of a shipping company. Steve and Gloria went out together on several occasions. The problem was that Steve was never quite sure of her age. It remained a mystery until the end of their relationship. It seemed she kept her family quite away from him. Eventually, he concluded that she was too young; In fact, on occasion she seemed like a thirteen-year-old. Steve was never a cradle robber. Yuk.

He soon found another lady. Maureen was twenty. She was not book clever, but she was socially clever. She was affectionate; he had to be very careful he did not unintentionally get her in the family way. They dated regularly for about six months. Fortunately, she had a regular job in a London department store and was limited in her trips to Ramsgate-Margate. She hinted often of marriage. This was likely out of the question because, as he saw it then, Steve still had at least graduate school, if not law school, ahead of him. If he thought about marriage, it would have to be, still, somewhat in the future. Was she the one for a long-term commitment? He was uncertain.

Then, at dear ol' St. Mildred's he met someone else, Joan Millar. She was a model in London for a fashionable dressmaker named Nettie Vogues. Her occupation, too, kept her from frequent trips to Margate, so as their relationship grew more intimate, Steve began making frequent trips to London. There, they attended plays and the American London Officer's Club to dance. This relationship lasted several months, and now it was getting close to the end of his European tour of duty. Soon it was time to leave England, and the couple made plans to marry; Steve would return to the USA, start graduate school, start a teaching job, and settle in a place to live. And so it eventually came to be. Steve sent for Terry (Joan's modeling name); they were married at St. Steven's Episcopal Church in Ferguson, Missouri, and they lived at various times in Columbia and St. Louis County. They raised four children.

Steve won a Woodrow Wilson Fellowship (thanks to the first president of UMSL, one Professor James Bugg), earned his doctorate and moved from high school teaching to college teaching. He taught at all the St. Louis Community Colleges, including Meramec, Florissant Valley and Forest Park, at University of Missouri St. Louis, Fontbonne College, and Maryville University. He taught on the Fulbright Grant and Exchange program in England. He and Terry had two of their four children at the time, with one on the way. This was a son who would have dual citizenship status until age eighteen.

On a major event for the Exchange Teachers, he and his wife were presented at Lancaster Gate to her royal majesty Queen Elizabeth, the queen mother. Recognizing the fact that his wife was originally from England, Queen Elizabeth said graciously, "Oh, sealing Anglo-American relations. How splendid."

Later, back in America, Steve won graduate National Endowment for the Humanities awards/programs during different years, one at Carnegie-Mellon University in Pennsylvania; one at Princeton University; one at Reed College, Oregon; one at the University of California—Davis; one at Boise State University (Utah); one at Duke University, North Carolina, and as evidenced hereby, Steve was devoted to an academic career.

Epiglimselogue Thirty-Two

"Another kind of survival, indeed," said Rupert. "So Steve left the U. S. Air Force behind him."

"And the Cold War," added James.

"Oh yeah," said Ben. "Cold War Stuff. For years, the whole world was holding its breath over the horrible dangers of nuclear war."

"Yes," replied James. "Survival concerns take many forms. The concern of dashing and fighting back and forth over the continent of Europe, and over the whole world for that matter, had many in, psychologically speaking, Doomsday clutches for years."

"I believe," said Sally, "that human beings suffer paranoia by nature. In Darwinian terms, we rely on our suspicions to keep us aware of external dangers, some real and some imaginary."

Rupert scowled. "But surely not to the point of obsession, mental derangement?"

"In some, yes," replied James. "Where do you think these mad-killers, these mass murderers, come from, if not from our own sickness? With the accessibility of assault weapons, isn't this why it has become a dire national concern?"

"In some, definitely," said Rupert

"Here is relevance to Hardy," said James. "From our fellow humans we do not expect violence, especially against each other, a friend or acquaintance. Ironic. Look at the study by Martha Stout entitled *The Psychopath Next Door*. Who would suspect our next door neighbor whom we say "Hi" to every day and chat with occasionally, of being a psychopath, a dangerous person?"

"Amazing," said Sally. "Are we up to the present?"

"In a way," replied James.

The Fulbright family reunion, Springfield, Missouri, 2010.
Can you name them? No? We need all their stories!

Epilogue [sic!]

"So we're coming to an end, are we?" says Charlene.

Right off the bat Rupert jumps in, "So what's this book all about?"

"I can tell you," says Ben.

"Me too," says Lisa.

Ben and Lisa look at each other, smilingly. "You go ahead, Ben," says Lisa.

"Well," responds Ben, "This is about examining life, especially through its narratives, its stories if you wish, to tell them, which here you have. Are we not on the brink of learning from scientists, our human, genetic basis for narrative-telling, and above all, these must be written down so they can be told and re-told again and again, and passed on to future generations. For dire enlightenment. And it is perhaps true that what we have the genetic basis for anyway, but further it's saying, we must get on with it—to be fully alive, to complete our gifts to others, indeed, to enhance our survival. Your turn, Lisa."

"We're always needing purpose," says Lisa with a steady knit brow. "Maybe more so down the road toward the end of life. Our purpose is to narrate our experiences, our story, our *storIES*. The purpose is ongoing—to pass these on, and for all, in finding purpose, to benefit from them."

"Right. So what do we gather from these, as Rupert enquires?" asks Ben "from the more biographical aspects?"

"Yes," says Rupert. "So, now biographically, we've followed

Steve (and others) from pre-birth, and after, with Steve to a stint with the U.S. Air Force, and after."

"What do all of you, Sally, Lisa, Ben, Rupert and Charlene, think? Is there a point being made?" asks James.

"Yes, what is important here?" reiterates Rupert.

"What is important here is," says Sally, "we gain from the stories we tell."

"True," says James. "In our narratives we strip away our self-imposed barriers, our reluctance to share ourselves with others—our guilt, our shyness, our modesty, our lethargy, our arrogance, our deleteriousness, our lethargy, our fears of facing life head on, our aging, our forgetfulness—whatever it is that prevents us from sharing this our more human side with others."

"And in addition to rampant story-telling," says Rupert, "is there something more to emphasize here?"

"I think so," responds Sally, "and it has something to do with surviving."

"True, Sally!" says the exalted James. "Maybe everything to do with survival. Surviving is a complex phenomenon. Physically and psychologically, narratives with a strong element of reality—through strengths, weaknesses, foci, and negligence—can certainly help. Don't you think? I should mention that Professor Steve begins his classes with: 'Read, read, read; write, write, write. And I add, listen, listen, listen and, of course, think, think, think!"

"About this genetic question," says Rupert, "Is there any real science to this assertion?"

James replies, "There are many who surmise that story-telling is genetic with the human species, but how many of these speculators are real scientists experimenting with the biological human brain, the real substance?"

And James then adds, "These well-intentioned souls, like Baschal Baute and his ilk that harken back to Wordsworth and co., appear swathed in Wordsworth and company's *Cult of Childhood*. Of course, what child wouldn't love story-time—the gathering around, the family-like intimacy, the suspense—but proof of a genetic link? We'll have to wait for that one."

"And don't forget, there's Professor George Lakoff and that Lexington crowd," chimes in Sally, "and his *Metaphors We Live By*. How our brains are keyed into thinking by metaphors. And are not stories expanded metaphors?"

"Interesting, Sally," replied Charlene. "And the stories themselves with symbolic movement: from the past, life in the country and small town, Harry and Gladys, to the city of a modernist and swinging generation, Steve from the dark closet out into the daylight of reality, into the bright sky, first time ever in a plane and flying the jet himself; and looking back again, from six year olds, he and from down the street Deloris, from walking Ravenwood and riding out to Lambert, watching the planes land and take off, to Rosann in high school, and Rosann herself off to fly as a stewardess for American Airlines, and then Steve and Nancy in college, soon with Nancy off to Hawaii and Steve, an Air Force Intelligence officer, off to England 3,000 miles away; Steve's quest eventually coming down to an English Dance Hall, and back, to the U.S., to marriage that produced four children, and then on to, intellectually, university graduate schools, lectures, books, discussions; philosophizing, learning, and teaching." Charlene drew in a deep breath.

Eyes roving, James surveys all his guests and says, "Before we depart, before you wrestle with telling your own stories, grappling, perhaps with illness and the age factor, allow me to refer you to Alfred Lord Tennyson's remarkable poem "Ulysses." No doubt, many of you know, that is, in part, what makes it so relevant here.

"In a great act of imagination," James continues, "the poet moves into the mind of the aging leader-adventurer Ulysses. Is it all over? At my age (or whatever your condition), am I, as a thinking and vital human being, finished, washed-up? Ha! Far from it!"

> *[As I look back, I have] ... enjoyed greatly, have suffered*
> *Greatly, with those that loved me, and alone ...*
> *Always roaming with a hungry heart,*
> *Much have I known ... I am a part of all that I have met ...*
> *This gray spirit yearning in desire to follow knowledge*
> *Like a sinking star beyond the bounds of human thought ...*

"And these following lines strike at our core:"

> *Old age hath yet its honor and its toil ...*
> *Some work of noble worth may yet be done ...*

"And then we move on with the masterful poet and therewith conclude our session tonight with Tennyson's vivid imagery:"

> *Lights begin to twinkle from the rocks, the long day wanes,*
> *The slow moon climbs. The deep moans round with many voices,*
> *Come, my friends, tis not too late to seek a newer world ...*
> *[We have been] made weak by time and fate but strong in will*
> *To strive, to seek, to find, and not to yield.*

As if magically, the book club members all rise and shake hands and hug each other.

"Voila!" says Steve. "Good night, fellow and sister book-club members, and dear readers, until our next session—at one of your homes—when you tell your stories. We look forward to this. Good luck and good writing. See you then!"

Rupert pauses at the door, "I've noticed that we've used the word *story* and the word *narrative* rather interchangeably. Is this right?"

"Never mind. We'll draw distinctions next time, or maybe in the next several times!"

"Surely." Rupert winks and retreats out the door.

Charlene pauses at the door, spins around and asks, "But, James, or should I say Steve, what about reality?"

"Don't puzzle with that now. Just prepare to tell us your story."

The last guest there, Charlene shrugs, turns and swirls out the door.

ACKNOWLEDGEMENTS

I wish to acknowledge and express my appreciation to friends, colleagues, and kinfolk, those who contributed directly (and albeit in diverse ways) to the completion of this manuscript: Shamin Ansari, Deborah Burns, John and Christine Fulbright-Foppe, James(II), Krista, Brooke and Erika Fulbright, Suzann Fulbright, Karen and Dan Hightower, Minnette Jessup, Trevin Jones, Karen Kalinevitch, Gail Lay, Tera and Kenneth LeCroy, Hal and Annie LeMert, Janise Lindeman, Dick and Louise Roden, Craig Shumate, Sara Seymour, Larry Sokol, and Rebecca Winter.

Moon River, c. 1961 by Johnny Mercer and Henry Mancini with appreciation to The Johnny Mercer Foundation for permission.